Islamic Education and Indoctrination

Islamic schools, especially *madrasahs*, have been viewed as sites of indoctrination for Muslim students and militants. Some educators and parents in the United States have also regarded introductory courses on Islam in some public schools as indoctrinatory. But what do we mean by "indoctrination"? And is Islamic education indoctrinatory?

This book critically discusses the concept of indoctrination in the context of Islamic education. It explains that indoctrination occurs when a person holds to a type of beliefs known as *control beliefs* that result in ideological totalism. Using Indonesia as an illustrative case study, the book expounds on the conditions for an indoctrinatory tradition to exist and thrive. Examples include the Islamic school co-founded by Abu Bakar Ba'asyir and the militant organisation Jemaah Islamiyah. The book further proposes ways to counter and avoid indoctrination through formal, non-formal, and informal education. It argues for the creation and promotion of *educative traditions* that are underpinned by religious pluralism, strong rationality, and strong autonomy. Examples of such educative Muslim traditions in Indonesia will be highlighted.

Combining philosophical inquiry with empirical research, this book is a timely contribution to the study of contemporary and often controversial issues in Islamic education.

Charlene Tan is an associate professor at the National Institute of Education, Nanyang Technological University, Singapore. She has held visiting appointments at the Syarif Hidayatullah State Islamic University, Jakarta; the Oxford Centre for Islamic Studies; and the Prince Alwaleed Bin Talal Centre of Islamic Studies, University of Cambridge.

Routledge Research in Education

For a full list of titles in this series please visit www.routledge.com

Islamic Education and Indoctrination

The Case in Indonesia

Charlene Tan

Routledge
Taylor & Francis Group
New York   London

First published 2011
by Routledge
711 Third Avenue, New York, NY 10017

Simultaneously published in the UK
by Routledge
2 Park Square, Milton Park, Abingdon, Oxon OX14 4RN

Routledge is an imprint of the Taylor & Francis Group, an informa business

© 2011 Taylor & Francis

The right of Charlene Tan to be identified as author of this work has been asserted by her in accordance with sections 77 and 78 of the Copyright, Designs and Patents Act 1988.

Typeset in Sabon by IBT Global.
Printed and bound in the United States of America on acid-free paper by IBT Global.

Library of Congress Cataloging-in-Publication Data

Tan, Charlene.
  Islamic education and indoctrination : the case in Indonesia / by Charlene Tan.
    p. cm. — (Routledge research in education ; v. 58)
  Includes bibliographical references and index.
    1. Islamic education—Indonesia   2. Education—Religious aspects—Islam
  3. Brainwashing—Indonesia   4. Religious pluralism—Islam   5. Education and state—Indonesia   6. Indonesia—Religious life and customs   7. Indonesia—Social conditions   I. Title.
    LC910.I5T355 2011
    371.077—dc22
    2010045457

ISBN13: 978-0-415-87976-7 (hbk)
ISBN13: 978-0-203-81776-6 (ebk)

To my parents and Win

Contents

Figures

Tables

Preface

"Peng Peng," an elderly woman called out to a little girl.

"Nyonya!" responded the little girl.

"Suda makan?" asked Nonya smilingly as she clutched Peng Peng's tiny fingers.

"Suda, bye bye!" replied Peng Peng chirpily as she ran to the playground.

It was another regular day for Peng Peng, a five-year old Chinese girl living in a cramped government flat in Singapore in the 1970s. While the neighbourhood was predominantly Chinese, Peng Peng's next door neighbours were Malays. She grew up mingling with her "Nyonya" (aunt), "Inchek" (uncle), "Kakak" (sister), and "Abang" (brother).

Peng Peng's family and Nyonya's family were close. Their neighbourliness extended beyond the usual daily greetings ("suda makan" means "Have you eaten?"). Peng Peng looked forward to chatting with Nyonya and eating the Malay cookies baked by her. Peng Peng often wondered why her mother did not share the Chinese food she had cooked with Nyonya. It was only many years later that Peng Peng learnt that it was because Nyonya was a Muslim who couldn't eat the food prepared by Peng Peng's family members who were non-Muslims. But Peng Peng's mother knew that, of course. That was why she made special efforts to buy raw eggs or cookies that came with a "halal" stamp as gifts for Nyonya. Whenever Peng Peng's brother caught fish from the river, Peng Peng's mother would also set aside some for Nyonya's family. Nyonya's family members didn't have a telephone, so Nyonya's son Abang would come over to Peng Peng's flat every now and then to make calls.

Peng Peng's family were Taoists—followers of a traditional Chinese religion that worshipped a pantheon of deities. Peng Peng would excitedly assist her parents in performing the periodical Taoist rituals along the narrow corridor, where the choking smoke of joss sticks and flying pieces of burnt incense paper would drift into Nyonya's flat. But no matter. These inconveniences were gladly accepted by Nyonya and her family as Chinese customs to be respected. To Nyonya, Peng Peng and her family were not "infidels guilty of the sin of polytheism"; they were simply her neighbours.

And to Peng Peng, Nyonya was not just a Muslim who happened to live next door; she was *her* Nyonya.

Fast forward a few decades, and Peng Peng now lives in a very different world. She still has a few Muslim neighbours, friends, and colleagues, but the relationship is no longer like the old days. Though cordial, the interactions are sometimes blended with self-consciousness, uneasiness, and even suspicion. She looks back at her childhood and marvels at the love and concern between her family and Nyonya's—a closeness that transcended religion, ethnicity, and language. The 9/11 attack has not helped the situation. News that some Singaporean Muslims have been arrested for attempting violent activities in Singapore has further heightened the tensions between Muslims and non-Muslims in Singapore. In a post-9/11 era, it is common to hear people say that Muslims have been indoctrinated in Islamic schools to become "terrorists". Some educators and parents in the United States have also regarded introductory courses on Islam in some public schools as indoctrinatory. But what is indoctrination? And is Islamic education indoctrinatory? I am Peng Peng, and this book is my endeavour to answer these questions.

RESEARCH FOCUS

In explaining my research focus and methods, I find it helpful to refer to the philosopher I.A. Snook's distinction on disagreements regarding values, concept, and facts.[1] A debate on *values* focuses on whether a concept is neutral, positive, or negative. For example, is "liberal" a good word? I thought so until I went to Indonesia and used that word to compliment an Indonesian Muslim academic. Looking visibly offended, he gently corrected me: "I am open, not liberal". The second disagreement is on the meaning of a *concept*. Even if the Indonesian Muslim academic and I agree that "liberal" is a derogatory word, we may still disagree on its precise meaning: what makes "liberal" so derogatory? Complicating the disagreement is the question of *facts*. Let's say we agree that "liberal" is derogatory because of criteria x, y, and z. We could still disagree over its application: in a given situation, we could quibble over whether a particular action or person qualifies as "liberal" based on our criteria.

I am only interested in the first two questions in my study on indoctrination. For the first question on values, I shall treat indoctrination as a pejorative term, although I am aware that that was not the case from the start—a point I shall return to in the introductory chapter. The second question is more tricky and challenging: given that indoctrination is pejorative, what makes it so, especially in the context of Islamic education? This second question will be my chief occupation for the rest of the book. I shall set aside the third question as this is an empirical question that is beyond the scope of this book. Even when consensus is reached on the value and concept of indoctrination, there will always be disagreements on whether particular cases of alleged indoctrination are really so. But it is important to note that the practical difficulty in identifying all instances of indoctrination in reality does not mean that we do not or cannot have a clear concept of indoctrination.[2]

I shall critically examine the concept of indoctrination in the context of Islamic education by highlighting the central role of *control beliefs* in shaping Muslim traditions. Arguing that an indoctrinatory tradition is one that aims to implant control beliefs that result in ideological totalism, I expound on the conditions for such a tradition to exist and thrive. Through examples such as the Islamic school co-founded by Abu Bakar Ba'asyir and the militant organisation Jemaah Islamiyah, I explain how indoctrinatory Muslim traditions exist and flourish through formal, non-formal, and informal education. I further propose approaches to counter and avoid indoctrination, with a particular focus on the creation and promotion of educative Muslim traditions that foster religious pluralism, strong rationality, and strong autonomy.

Given the rich varieties, forms, and orientations of Islamic education for over 1.5 billion Muslims in the world (that's one quarter of the world's population), it is difficult and risky to make any generalisations about Islamic education. At the same time, it is necessary to concretise our discussion by situating it in a real and specific context. I have therefore chosen to focus on Indonesia as an illustrative case study. Why Indonesia? First, Indonesia is the largest Muslim country in the world with 203 million Muslims in 2009, accounting for 80 percent of all Muslims in Southeast Asia.[3] Second, Indonesia is the country of origin for Jemaah Islamiyah, a trans-national Muslim militant group that has been accused of indoctrinating its members through its activities and affiliated Islamic schools. At the same time (and paradoxically), Indonesia is known for its tolerant and inclusive form of Islam and progressive Islamic scholars who challenge the indoctrinatory endeavours of the Muslim militants. Hence Indonesia offers an intriguing and important case study on indoctrinatory and educative Muslim traditions, as well as the ideological contestations among Muslims. Finally, the choice of an Asian country emphasises the fact that the bulk of the world's 1.57 billion Muslims are located in Asia (62 percent).[4] Commenting on this point, Brian Grim who is the senior researcher of the Pew Forum project maintains: "If the goal is to create better understanding between the United States and the Muslim world, our focus should be on South and Southeast Asia, not the Middle East".[5]

RESEARCH METHODS

My research methods combine philosophical inquiry with empirical research. My basic training is in philosophy, and both my Master's (1994–1996) and doctoral research (2000–2003) focus on indoctrination. I became involved in an empirical study of *madrasah* education in Singapore when I was appointed the Principal Investigator of an ongoing university-funded research project in 2007. In 2009, I was granted a sabbatical from my university to concentrate on my research in Islamic education. I spent the large part of 2009 as a visiting research associate at the Oxford Centre for Islamic Studies, and a visiting scholar at the Prince Alwaleed Bin Talal Centre of Islamic Studies, University of Cambridge. This was followed by another period of leave from my university where I was a visiting fellow at the Syarif Hidayatullah State Islamic University, Jakarta, in 2010. My association with the above-mentioned educational institutions provided me with valuable access to research materials on Islamic education, and opportunities to visit Islamic schools in Britain, Indonesia, and Singapore.

The specific research data on Indonesia were obtained from literature review, document analysis, and fieldwork conducted in May 2010 with 12 Islamic schools in Indonesia. The 12 schools have been carefully selected to represent different types (Pesantren, Madrasah and Sekolah Islam) and orientations (Nahdlatul Ulama, Muhammadiyah, Persis and others) of Islamic schools in Indonesia. I obtained the school's official documents (brochures, manuals, student handbooks, magazines, PowerPoint slides, CDs, etc), toured and took photos of the school compound, and conducted interviews with the school's directors, staff and other key personnel. (I conducted interviews with all but one school due to a clash in schedules.) The interviews were recorded, translated into English, and coded for analysis. Additional research materials were obtained from the schools' websites, interactions with some of the schools' alumni and parents of children in these schools, as well as discussions with the lecturers, students, and graduates of an Islamic university. Unless otherwise indicated, all interviews were conducted in confidentiality and the names of interviewees have been withheld by mutual agreement.

A quick note on language: non-English words will be italicised only in the first instance when they are mentioned. While I support using inclusive language, I have avoided using the expression "he or she", as I find it cumbersome. I have instead opted to refer to "he" on some occasions, and "she" on other occasions, with the pronouns representing both genders in all instances, unless otherwise stated.

OUTLINE OF THE BOOK

Our discussion begins with the problem of indoctrination in the Islamic context. The introductory chapter also sets the stage by defining the key terms used in this book such as "Islam", "Islamic education", and "terrorism".

The next two chapters establish our theoretical framework on indoctrination and Islamic education. I explain in Chapter 1 that an indoctrinated person is one who holds to core beliefs (what I call "control beliefs") that result in ideological totalism. I elaborate on the characteristics of control beliefs and illustrate their functions using the example of *jihad*. Chapter 2 extends our exploration of indoctrination by focusing on an indoctrinatory tradition. I elucidate the conditions required to create, sustain, and strengthen an indoctrinatory tradition, and the impact of such a tradition on the development of one's rationality and autonomy.

Chapters 3 and 4 apply our theoretical framework of an indoctrinatory tradition to two case studies. Chapter 3 spotlights on an indoctrinatory tradition in formal education through the example of Pondok Pesantren Islam Al Mukmin. Chapter 4 examines how an indoctrinatory tradition exists and thrives in non-formal and informal education through the example of the militant Muslim organisation Jemaah Islamiyah.

Chapter 5 shifts our attention from indoctrination to education. I propose that indoctrination can be countered and avoided primarily through the creation and promotion of an educative tradition. I argue that an educative tradition is one that is anti-totalistic and is underpinned by the control beliefs of religious pluralism, strong rationality, and strong autonomy.

The next two chapters survey and analyse the Islamic schools in Indonesia. In Chapter 6, I maintain that most Islamic schools in Indonesia are not rooted in indoctrinatory traditions. On the contrary, they are open to gaining knowledge through studying non-religious subjects, and encouraging rationality and autonomy through student-centred pedagogies and student activities. However, I critique the Islamic schools in Chapter 7 by contending that most of them do not sufficiently emphasise the students' development of strong rationality, strong autonomy, and religious pluralism.

Underscoring the need to move beyond indoctrination to creating and promoting educative traditions, Chapter 8 focuses on how educative traditions can exist and thrive in a society. I explain how the control beliefs of religious pluralism, strong rationality, and strong autonomy can be fostered through formal, non-formal, and informal education. This book concludes with a discussion of the international significance and implications arising from our study on Islamic education and indoctrination.

ACKNOWLEDGMENTS

Researching and writing this book have been a most rewarding experience. I am indebted to the following people who have accompanied me in this invigorating and memorable journey, graciously and generously helping and supporting me along the way.

First, I am grateful to my institution, the National Institute of Education, for granting me various types of leave so that I could concentrate on researching and writing this book from 2009 to 2010. In particular, I thank Associate Professor Lee Ong Kim, Head of the Policy and Leadership Studies Academic Group, for his kind support and constant encouragement.

My visiting appointments with three Islamic institutions opened doors for me to access valuable research materials and conduct fieldwork in

Britain and Indonesia. I express my appreciation to Professor Yasir Suleiman and staff of the Prince Alwaleed Bin Talal Centre of Islamic Studies, University of Cambridge; Professor Farhan A. Nizami, Dr Basil Mustafa, Professor Mohammad Talib, Professor Francis Robinson, Dr Mohammad Akram Nadwi and Dr Naim Mohammed Mohktar of the Oxford Centre for Islamic Studies; and Professor Azyumardi Azra and staff of the Graduate School of the Syarif Hidayatullah State Islamic University, Jakarta.

I am grateful to my research assistant Ms Diwi Binti Abbas for her hard work and cheerfulness, and Ms Haula Noor for contacting and facilitating my visits to the Islamic schools. I also appreciate and remember fondly the warm reception, kindness and friendship from my Indonesian friends: Professor Azyumardi Azra, Dr Yusuf Rahman, Dr Jajat Burhanudin, Dr Fuad, Ms Huala Noor and her family, Ms Heny Maryamah, and the directors, staff members, and students of all the Islamic schools I have visited.

Special thanks go to individuals who have sacrificed their time to read and provide critical comments on various sections of my drafts: Professor Chong Kim Chong, Dr Ida Glaser, and especially Mr Wong Yew Leong. Many thanks to Mr Benjamin Tan for his careful proofreading and Mr Ngamino for his translation work. I also acknowledge the wonderful editorial assistance from Mr Max Novick, Ms Jennifer Morrow, Ms Eleanor Chan, and Ms Rachel D'Annucci Henriquez. All the persons mentioned are not in any way responsible for any mistakes found in this book, which are wholly mine.

Finally, my gratitude goes to my parents for, among other things, showing me how to love my neighbours; and my loving husband Lim Pin for being my valley of Achor. This book is dedicated to these three most important persons in my life. Ebenezer.

Charlene Hwee Phio Tan
Singapore
October 2010

Introduction

"Especially when it is Islam, faith is the forbidden f-word in education."
—Head teacher of an Islamic school in Britain[1]

One can sense the palpable frustration of the head teacher in the above quote. And his feelings are understandable. Just look at the following recent headlines:

Afghanistan: Would-be Suicide Bomber Speaks of Indoctrination
Alleged Terrorist Group Steers Young Men to Fight
'Islamic Indoctrination' Taken to Supreme Court
Islam in America's Public Schools: Education or Indoctrination

These headlines no longer surprise many of us who are plugged into the daily news.[2] The first one tells the gripping story of an Islamic school teacher from Afghanistan's southern Helmand Province who was recruited by Pakistani militants to become a suicide bomber. The second article documents how Lashkar-e-Taiba indoctrinates young Muslims to become deadly terrorists in the 2008 Mumbai attack. The third article reports on a public-interest legal group accusing a California public school of allowing its students to be indoctrinated through its three-week intensive course on Islam.[3] The last headline sounds the alarm of a perceived insidious attempt by Muslims to indoctrinate students in American public schools. It is claimed that students in one school learned during an "Islamic Awareness" presentation that "there is one God, his name is Allah", while another school set up an "Islamic religion station" to offer its students verses from the Qur'an, prayer items, and a compass pointed towards Mecca.

Besides newspaper articles, research papers and books have also proliferated, linking indoctrination to Islam, Muslims, and Islamic schools. William J. Bennetta who is the president of The Textbook League publishes an analytical piece contending that students in an American public school have been subjected to "gross, prolonged indoctrination in Islam" through a textbook on Islamic history.[4] Robert Spencer, in a chapter entitled "Education or indoctrination? The Islamic ideological straitjacket in American Universities" claims that anti-Western professors have turned Middle Eastern Studies departments in American universities into "propaganda mills" that spread "Islamic supermacism in their own backyards".[5] Other publications advocate the thesis that Islamic schools are indoctrinating young Muslims into a cult of armed jihad (struggle) so that they may later be recruited as suicide bombers in Muslim militant organisations.[6] For example madrasahs have been described as "incubators for violent extremism" and "jihad factories", "indoctrinating them [Muslim students] with a hatred for the West" and "an ideology of intolerance, violence, and hate".[7]

This association of indoctrination with Islamic schools is reinforced by television footage showing "Spartan classrooms in which children rocked back and forth reciting passages from the Koran [Qur'an]".[8] Potential suicide bombers, including children, are believed to have been indoctrinated through Islamic schools to embrace an ideology of hatred and martyrdom.[9] Further affirming this image of indoctrinated Muslim terrorists is a report that 80 percent of all suicide attacks since 1968 occurred *after* the 9/11 attack, with the majority of these attacks (31 of the 35) being carried out by Muslim groups in the name of jihad.[10] It is indeed a worrying phenomenon if the allegations of "Islamic indoctrination" are true.

But are they?

Before we can answer that question, there is a more fundamental question staring at us: what do we mean by indoctrination?

WHAT IS INDOCTRINATION?

What do we mean when we say that someone has been indoctrinated? We could start by examining the etymology of "indoctrination". The word "indoctrination" is derived from the Latin words "docere", meaning "to teach", and "doctrina", meaning "whatever is taught". So indoctrination literally means the imparting of what is taught.[11] Now that is not a very helpful start, as it has effectively told us *nothing* new about indoctrination. But not really, on second thought. It has drawn our attention to an important fact that indoctrination, in its original form, carries no derogatory meaning. It started out innocuously to refer simply to instruction. The word "doctrina" (where we get the English word "doctrines") was not associated with religion until the Middle Ages where it became identified with the teachings of the Roman Catholic Church.[12] As late as 1900, indoctrination was not widely used pejoratively, as evidenced in its entry in the *Oxford English Dictionary* in that year.[13]

But indoctrination somehow morphed into a big bad wolf from the start of the twentieth century. That was largely due to the influence of Progressivist educationists in the United States who vilified all forms of authoritarian education, including religious education.[14] Aggravating this negative perception was the American opposition to Nazi Germany and Communist China—two countries infamous for their brainwashing techniques during and after the World War II. European history has also left many people in the Anglophone world feeling wary of religious education, especially the type that relies on a confessional approach to implant religious beliefs in the adherents.[15] Subsequently, indoctrination has been seen as the handmaiden of totalitarian regimes and their coercive educational methods; conversely "education" has been upheld as "the humane and rational process of instruction", which democratic states are presumed to practise.[16] Notwithstanding the general view of indoctrination as a derogatory concept, scholars could not agree on the definition of and criteria for indoctrination. Is indoctrination about certain objectionable intention, content, method, and/or outcome? Despite being subjected to intense scrutiny and scholarly debates especially in the 1970s and 1980s, no consensus has been reached and indoctrination today remains a contested term.[17]

So we've come full circle and returned to where we started. One possible way out of the impasse is to throw away the word "indoctrination" and substitute it with another word, such as "brainwashing", "programming", or "conditioning". But this will not work, as it begs the question of what these other words mean as well. Besides, it's unlikely for the word "indoctrination" to disappear from our daily vocabulary. It has been used, to a good effect, to castigate "Muslim terrorists", cult group members, and practically anyone you do not agree with. Just respond to your proselytising neighbour or a persistent salesman with "Don't try to indoctrinate me!" Interestingly, the charge of indoctrination has also been levied against public schools in Britain and even teacher education, science education, and secular education—domains that are traditionally thought to be free from indoctrination.[18]

So indoctrination is here to stay. And given the current climate of religious resurgence, inter-religious conflicts, and religion-motivated terrorism, indoctrination will continue to be featured prominently in the mass media and everyday discourse. Therefore we have an intellectual and moral duty to critically examine and understand the term. Only then can we apply the term—justifiably and consistently—to describe Muslims and Islamic education.

DEFINITIONS OF KEY TERMS

Before we begin our study of the concept of indoctrination and its relationship with Islamic education, we need to ensure that we're using the same word to mean the same thing. This helps us to establish accuracy and consistency, and avoid possible confusion and misunderstanding.

Islam

The first key term is "Islam". It is instructive, at the outset, to distinguish two levels of Islam, as noted by Syed Farid Alatas:

[A] distinction could be made between Islam at the abstract level (*din*) and concrete translations of this in the sense of different kinds of social groupings such as *tariqah* (ways of life), *ahl* (people, relations) and so on. The variations among Muslims can be captured by such terms. From the point of view of Islam, it would not be erroneous to speak of a backward *tariqah* or *ahl*.[19]

Accordingly, I will focus on Islam at the concrete level, that is, how Islam is translated into practice through different kinds of social groupings. In adopting this approach, I follow another Muslim scholar, Bassam Tibi, in highlighting the *cultural* aspect of Islam. Tibi explains that "Islam is conceptualised as a cultural system that is always in flux, and is therefore placed in a historical and social context".[20] Islam as a cultural system encompasses complex networks of cognitive and behavioural dispositions that are political, religious, moral, epistemological, and aesthetic in nature.[21]

That I have chosen not to discuss Islam as a faith or a divine phenomenon does not mean that I deny the status of Islam as such (of course it is), or that I think that a theological study of Islam is unimportant (surely it is). Furthermore, my approach does not imply that I subscribe to the proposition that there are many "Islams". I agree that there is one Islam in the sense that it is a religion comprising shared foundational doctrines held by Muslims, premised on the belief that the Qur'an and the *Sunnah* (exemplary behaviour of the Prophet Muhammad) are the revealed texts from God to human beings.[22] However, we need to guard against essentialising and homogenising Islam by affirming the presence of diverse articulations of Islam found among Muslims and their communities. In a post-9/11 world, it is particularly important to transcend the simplistic labels of Muslims as "extremist" or "moderate" by acknowledging the plurality of representations found within the Islamic landscape. Such multiplicity is the natural outcome of the interplay of complex historical, geographical, religious, political, social, and cultural factors.

Islamic Education

I define "Islamic education" as any form of teaching and learning that is based on the principles and values of Islam. It follows from our interpretation of Islam as a cultural system that there are diverse approaches to religious teaching and learning for the different social groupings among Muslims. It is in alignment with this understanding that the leading Indonesian Muslim scholar Azyumardi Azra avers that "there is a plural Indonesian Islam, resulted from different interpretations of Islam that in the end gave rise to different schools of thought (*madhhab* and *aliran*) and tradition".[23] The word "education" reminds us that the focus is not only on schooling or *formal* education. Education also includes *non-formal* education that refers to any organised educational activity outside the school system, and *informal* education that takes place through our daily experiences and interactions with our environments.[24] These three types of education are helpful for us to gain a broad and complete picture of how Islamic instruction and inculcation take place for Muslims both inside and outside the school compound. But I should add that the three types of education are not always clearly demarcated and that overlaps do occur in reality. For example, a sizeable number of Muslim children in Indonesia attend *pesantrens*, which are Islamic boarding schools. But such an arrangement is officially regarded as non-formal education (not formal education), as the pesantren is a private institution not under the state jurisdiction.[25]

It follows from my definition of "Islamic education" that an "Islamic school" is any educational institution that emphasises the transmission of Islamic knowledge, and inculcation of Islamic values and ethos. Instead of teaching Islam as a discrete subject, such a school seeks to develop "along the lines of Qur'anic scriptures, with a strong nurturing of an Islamic ethos, which permeates the school curricula both formal and hidden".[26] It should be noted that in using "Islamic school" rather than "Muslim school", I am not implying that the school has achieved its goal of living up to the standards of Islam. I make this point because some writers have argued for the distinction between "Islamic school" and "Muslim school". For example, Susan L. Douglass and Munir A. Shaikh have posited that it is more accurate to describe "Islamic schools" as "Muslim schools" to indicate "the goal of living up to the standards of Islam, rather than implying its achievement".[27]

While I agree with their reasoning about differentiating a goal from its actualisation, I prefer to retain the term "Islamic school", as it is already widely used in official and popular discourses as a generic term to refer to schools that emphasise Islamic instruction and nurture.[28] In using this term, there is no evidence to suggest that the writers and their readers assume that these schools have succeeded in meeting the standards of Islam. Furthermore, some writers have used "Islamic school" and "Muslim school" interchangeably. For instance, although Azyumardi Azra, Dina Afrianty, and Robert W. Hefner entitled their article "Muslim schools", they use the term "Islamic schools" on some occasions in the text.[29] I also wish to avoid using the term "Muslim school" because some readers may confuse that with a "secular" or public school attended by Muslims, rather than a school that centres on Islamic knowledge and values.

Muslim

Some readers may wonder why there is a need to define a term as obvious as "Muslim". I thought so too until I attended an international conference in 2008 where a keynote speaker who is a Muslim professor proclaimed on stage that Osama bin Laden "is not a Muslim at all". The former Indonesian president Abdurrahman Wahid has also been criticised as "not a real Muslim" based on the charge that he is a Communist and a friend of

Christians and Zionists.[30] I have also come across Muslims who object to people (mostly non-Muslims) calling the terrorists "Muslims" (or Muslims "terrorists"; I shall discuss that later). But it is highly problematic and questionable for anyone (especially non-Muslims such as myself) to decide who is or is not a "Muslim". I adopt Ronald Luken-Bull's approach in accepting the self-identification of Muslims: a person who professes to be a Muslim will be treated as such, namely, as a person who wants to be known as a Muslim and partakes in activities he has identified as Islamic.[31] So I will refer to convicted mastermind of the Bali bombing, Iman Samudra as a "Muslim" and militant organisation Jemaah Islamiyah as a "Muslim" movement. However, by describing individuals, groups, or community as "Muslim", I am not thereby asserting that they are "true", "real", or "good" Muslims. I am simply acknowledging and respecting their public profession of faith.

Muslim Tradition

Another related concept that is central to our study is "Muslim tradition". A tradition, according to Talal Asad, is a discourse that seeks to instruct a community of believers on the correct form and purpose of a given practice.[32] A discourse is a social process of constructing shared meanings through textual transmission and human interaction.[33] In other words, a discourse is (re) constructed through the dynamic interplay of the text (textual transmission) and context (formal, non-formal, and informal education). That "tradition" and "transmission" are etymologically related is pointed out by Seyyed Hossein Nasr who notes that tradition "contains within the scope of its meaning the idea of the transmission of knowledge, practice, techniques, laws, forms, and many other elements of both an oral and written nature".[34] It follows that a Muslim tradition is a social process of constructing and transmitting shared meaning, through both the text and the context, that seeks to instruct a community of Muslims on the correct form and purpose of a given practice.[35] I shall use the term "Muslim tradition" rather than "Islamic tradition" to emphasise the active role of Muslims in creating, shaping, and influencing their own religious traditions.

While Islam in general can be viewed as a discursive tradition, I agree with Muhammad Qasim Zaman that facets of Islam such as the *shari'ah* (Islamic law) and institutionalised Sufism can be viewed as traditions in their own right.[36] Other traditions I would like to add to the list and which I shall discuss later are jihad and Islamic education. Besides recognising different types of traditions within Islam, we also need to acknowledge the variety of traditions *within the same type*. For instance, the discursive landscape of the shari'ah contains a variety of shari'ah traditions, each with their own discourse, history, trajectory and community. The same applies to other facets of Islam such as the jihad traditions and the traditions of Islamic education.

What then are the salient features of a Muslim tradition? First, a tradition presupposes the existence of a *community of believers*. A religious tradition encompasses not just religious beliefs but social and cultural values and practices essential for the identity formation of its members. That explains why many Muslim immigrants favour faith-based schools for their function in transmitting and preserving not only religious knowledge but indigenous cultural and linguistic heritage.[37] An adherence to a tradition entails that members share a common set of core beliefs that define and are defined by that tradition. The core beliefs include concepts such as "rationality", "critical thinking", "evidence", and "autonomy" that are understood and acquired within the context of a specific tradition. I should clarify that I am not arguing that these concepts are subjective, relative, or incommensurable across traditions. My point here is that a satisfactory understanding of rationality, autonomy, and their cognates must take into consideration the vital role of a "convictional community" to objectivise and legitimise the public structure of beliefs and give it internal coherence.[38] (A fuller treatment of these concepts will be given in subsequent chapters.)

Second, while a community with an effective programme of enculturation and socialisation is likely to nurture members who are bonded by a set of common beliefs, not every member of a tradition holds the same beliefs or holds them to the same degree of commitment. In other words, different members are influenced by and committed to the tradition to varying extent; community leaders, for example, are more likely to identify themselves closely with their tradition compared to young children and confused teenagers. It should also be noted that members of a community often subscribe to more than one tradition. For example, an Indonesian Muslim teenager may subscribe to a particular Sufi tradition (due to his family upbringing), a particular shari'ah tradition (due to the teachings received from his mosque), and a particular tradition of Islamic education (due to the type of Islamic school he attends). Also, there may be different communities within the same tradition, such as the Muslim communities who live in different parts of the world but are united by a common jihad tradition.

Third, a tradition is not static and unchanging. It constitutes elements of an ongoing interaction between the present and the past. Asad avers that a discourse "relates conceptually to *a past* (when the practice was instituted, and from which the knowledge of its point and proper performance has been transmitted) and *a future* (how the point of that practice can best be secured in the short or long term, or why it should be modified or abandoned), through *a present* (how it is linked to other practices, institutions, and social conditions)".[39] A tradition is also constantly defined and redefined through external exchanges and conflicts; these changes are initiated and contributed by critics and enemies outside the tradition as well as fellow believers who have been involved in internal conflicts.[40] In the process of their encounters with the past and present as well as external and internal conflicts, specific beliefs belonging to the tradition are strengthened, weakened, added, or replaced, thereby challenging and modifying the fundamental agreements of the tradition through time. An example is the ideological struggle between competing jihad traditions on how jihad should be interpreted and practised by Muslims—an example I shall return to in subsequent chapters.

Terrorism and Militancy

The subject of Islamic education and indoctrination cannot be discussed without bringing in the issue of terrorism. "Terrorist" is a controversial concept that is notoriously difficult to define. One of the best definitions, in my view, is by Jessica Stern who defines "terrorists" as individuals or groups who carry out acts or threats of violence on noncombatants so as to exact revenge, intimidate, or influence an audience.[41] Muslim terrorists, in this context, are people who profess the Islamic faith and carry out acts or threats of violence on noncombatants for the sake of their religion.

The stigmatising connotation of the word "Terrorist" prompts some Muslim militants to object to this word. They prefer instead the term "Salafi jihadists" to underline a doctrinal understanding of and basis for jihad.[42] However, not all Muslims are against the use of the word "terrorist" to describe themselves or fellow militants. For example, Aly Ghufron bin Nurhasyim (better known as Mukhlas), a senior member of Jemaah Islamiyah, declares that Muslims are obliged to be terrorists:

> According to the sharia law Almighty God commands the faithful to become terrorists, as His decree (Al Anfal (8): 60) says: 'And *prepare to face them with whatever force you can*, and *horses tethered for war* (which are part of those preparations), so that you make the *enemies of God your enemies and others whom you do not know of*, yet God knows of, TREMBLE. Whatsoever you expend in God's path will surely be repaid sufficiently to you and you will not be wronged.[43]

Another Muslim Sulaiman I.W. Damanhuri argues in his book *Menabur Jihâd Menuai Teror: bom Bali, Marriot dan Kuningan dalam timbangan Syariat dan maslahat* [Sowing Jihad Reaping Terror: Bali bombing, Marriott and Kuningan based on Shari'a and Good Effect] that Muslims are called by God to incite terror in the hearts of evil and immoral people so that they will be afraid and cease from such behaviour.[44] This idea of Muslims terrorising non-Muslims through violent means was also mentioned by Kamaluddin, the brother of convicted Bali bomber Imam Samudra. Kamaluddin said in a recent interview that he supported his brother's action because Muslims are obligated to strike terror in the infidels.[45] Given the debatable and emotive nature of the term "terrorist", I shall refrain from using it in this study. Instead, I shall adopt a more neutral term "militant" to describe individuals such as Iman Samudra and organisations such as Jemaah Islamiyah. Militancy is defined as actual defensive and offensive violent group behaviour committed collectively against the state or other actors.[46] Accordingly, Muslim militants are people who carry out violent group behaviour against the state and individuals, including noncombatants, in the name of Islam.

On the topic of terrorism and militancy, I need to make two qualifications. First, while there are Muslims who engage in violent acts to realise their goal of establishing an Islamic state in a country or region, there are others who share the same goal but prefer peaceful means such as education and political election. Second, my interest in and focus on Muslim militants do not imply that only Muslims are capable or guilty of being militants or terrorists. On the contrary, people of all faiths and ideologies are capable of committing acts of violence on others. John Esposito and Dalia Mogahed cite the examples of Christian activists who attacked abortion clinics and gay bars, and Timothy McVeigh whose Christian cosmotheism led him to bomb the Alfred P. Murrah Federal Building in Oklahoma City.[47] Another recent example is that of members of a radical Christian militia known as "The Hutaree" that attempted to wage war against the U.S. government through killing and bombing.[48] Of course, I am not asserting that Christianity *qua* Christianity is directly responsible for these violent acts; rather it is a (mis)interpretation of Christianity by a segment of its followers that motivates them to turn to militancy. This illustrates, once again, the importance of differentiating a religion at the abstract level from its concrete translation into practice.

Islamism and Jihadism

I also need to mention briefly two other contested terms in the Islamic discourse: "Islamism" and "jihadism".[49] Jajat Burhanudin and Jamhari define Islamism broadly as "the belief that Islam is the perfect religion which offers teachings and the solutions for all aspects of human life"; Islamists are Muslims who "hold that their religion does not only regulate the relationship between God and human beings, but also that of mundane socio-political affairs".[50] John T. Sidel gives a more specific definition of "Islamist" by linking it to the Islamisation of the state: "the broad range of movements, organisations, and political parties mobilised in avowed defence of Islam as a body of beliefs and a community of believers, and in avowed promotion of the Islamisation of state and society".[51] Also focusing on the political nature of Islam is Daniel Pipes who regards "Islamists" as Muslims who actively seek to build a just society by regimenting people according to an Islamic orientation through political power.[52]

Based on the above definitions, it appears that Muslims such as Osama bin Laden and Muslim organisations such as Jemaah Islamiah would fit the description of "Islamist"—a badge that militant Muslims proudly wear. However, a Muslim colleague of mine told me that she objected to such a description, as these individuals and organisations are "bad" but "Islamist is a good word". Clearly, it is not just the meaning but the connotation of "Islamist" that is central here. The same controversy applies to the term "jihadism". In the current literature, many researchers use "jihadist" or "jihadi" to describe Muslims who profess to advance jihad through violent means, including engaging in militancy on noncombatants.[53] This is objected to by some Muslim scholars such as Syed Farid Alatas who counters that "using a term such as jihadism is insulting to a lofty idea in Islam. Jihad is an important concept in Islamic theology and is certainly not associated with aggression and violence towards non-Muslims".[54]

Again, it is interesting to note that not all Muslims think this way. Interviews with Muslim militants in Indonesia inform us that they are quick to identify themselves as "jihadists" (rather than "terrorists") for the same reason: "jihadist" is a good word that implies their struggle in the way of Allah.[55] Given that there is simply no consensus among Muslims themselves on what terms such as "jihad" and "Islamism" mean or should mean, I reiterate that the task of a researcher is to accept the self-identification of Muslims/Islamists/jihadists and seek to understand them. This debate on the Islamism and jihadism, not just between Muslims and non-Muslims, but among the Muslims themselves, remind us that there exist various and competing Muslim traditions, each with its own religious interpretations and articulations.

CONCLUSION

Readers may notice that I have left out the other key term, "indoctrination". As more space is needed to analyse this essentially contested concept, I will reserve a detailed discussion of indoctrination for the next few chapters. But I would like to make two points of clarification about indoctrination here. First, while indoctrination and militancy (and terrorism) are related, they are not used synonymously. Not all Muslim militants are victims of indoctrination, and not all indoctrinated Muslims will turn to militancy. Our study goes beyond the issues of militancy, terrorism, and security matters to the fundamental questions of indoctrination. These questions include: what is indoctrination, how does indoctrination occur, what are the conditions for an indoctrinatory tradition to exist and thrive, and how can we avoid and counter indoctrination. Second, that I have situated our discussion of indoctrination in the Islamic context does not imply that indoctrination is an "Islamic problem" or that only Muslims could be indoctrinated. I have chosen to focus on Muslims rather than, say, Christians, Confucians, or Hindus because of the current perception that a number of Muslim militants and students of Islamic schools are victims of indoctrination. While my focus is on Islamic education, my conclusions on indoctrination will apply to education in other religions as well.

Having acquainted ourselves with the problem of indoctrination and the definitions of key terms, let us proceed to unpack the meaning of indoctrination in the next chapter.

1 Struggling for Control
Indoctrination and Jihad

Five undergraduates were found murdered in the most horrifying way in New Mexico: flayed alive, mutilated and impaled. One girl named Ingrid Greisen escaped but it turned out that she was part of the gang that had carried out the killing. She had been kidnapped by her own father who wanted to protect her from the gang. The reason? She, as well as the rest of the gang, was a member of a cult group that brainwashed its members. The cult group leader who called himself "Grandfather" had indoctrinated them with the beliefs in Native American religion and instigated them to carry out the killing to reclaim the local Apache lands.

Ingrid's father told the investigators that she started to act strange when she joined the cult group. She kept repeating words such as "trespasser", "Grandfather" and "Ga'he"—jargons understood only by the cult group. When interviewed by the investigators, Ingrid robotically answered every question with only her name and social security number, leading the investigators to observe that she was behaving like "a prisoner of war". When Ingrid was later interrogated by a Native American John Blackwolf who was assisting in the investigations, she mindlessly regurgitated the information that "Grandfather" had implanted in her. John angrily told her that she has been lied to, manipulated and fed bits and pieces of a culture she did not understand.

The above scenario is scary. But thankfully it is only fiction. The story is taken from the episode "The Tribe" of the American television hit series *Criminal Minds*. But the scenario is not purely hypothetical; Ingrid's experience mirrors that of Patty Hearst who was kidnapped and brainwashed by the Symbionese Liberation Army in the 1970s. What is noteworthy about Ingrid's case is that her own beliefs have been hijacked and replaced by beliefs implanted in her by her indoctrinator. With the change of beliefs is her transformed worldview and personality. Her experience alerts us to the fact that indoctrination is essentially about the control of one's mind. To understand indoctrination, therefore, we need to explore what goes on in our cognitive landscape—in other words, we should take a closer look at "beliefs". Specifically, we need to understand the nature and functions of a special type of beliefs: *control beliefs*. This chapter begins by expounding the concept of control beliefs, followed by a discussion of how these beliefs play a determining role in indoctrination. The last section illustrates how control beliefs function through the example of jihad.

CONTROL BELIEFS

Control beliefs are the core beliefs we acquire in the natural process of enculturation, education, socialisation, and interactions with people and nature. While all human beings hold to control beliefs (unless the person is developmentally challenged), indoctrinated persons hold to their control beliefs *differently*. In other words, the way in which an indoctrinated person holds her control beliefs sets her apart from a person who is not indoctrinated. To understand this point, we need to understand more about the essence, types, and functions of beliefs in our cognitive landscape. Before I begin our analysis of control beliefs, I should point out that I have tried to make the discussion as accessible as possible for non-philosophers. Nevertheless, readers who find this section too technical or philosophical may wish to skip it for the time being and proceed to the next section on control beliefs and indoctrination.

Let us start with something very basic: what is a belief? A belief is essentially a statement a person holds as true. We can analyse beliefs in two ways. We can look at what beliefs are, or the way beliefs are held. The former focuses on the *actual* logical status of beliefs while the latter focuses on the *assigned* logical status of beliefs. I am interested in the latter. Let me explain what I mean with an example of a belief held by a religious person:

"God exists."

Adopting the first approach means looking at the epistemological aspects of this statement (epistemology is the theory of knowledge). For example, we can discuss whether this belief in God qualifies as "knowledge", whether it is "true", "justified", "non-inferential", and how it is related to other religious beliefs such as "God is omnipotent" or "God is speaking to me".[1]

This line of inquiry is important and deserves a lengthy treatment on its own. But it is not central to the purpose of this book, which is on the *ways* Muslims hold their religious beliefs and how these diverse ways affect their worldviews and practices, especially in the field of education. Often, the actual logical status of beliefs does not explain why a believer holds strongly to certain beliefs and reject the others. It is not uncommon for a person to cling to a belief that is not justified or true. That may explain why some women believe that having 20 pairs of shoes is not enough, or why a male colleague of mine believes that *Arsenal* is the best football team in the world. Therefore my focus, rather than being on the epistemic content of beliefs, is on the function of beliefs for the person who subscribes to them.

This requires, in our context of the example of "God exists", looking at what this belief means for a believer and how it affects her other beliefs (e.g. "God's justice means non-believers will go to hell") and behaviour (e.g. "I need to love my enemies because God's word tells me so").

Beliefs

My conception of beliefs is adapted from the writings of Thomas F. Green, Nicholas Wolterstorff, and Kathleen Taylor.[2] Let us begin with control beliefs.[3] A control belief, as the name implies, controls what goes into our belief systems and determines how we look at everything—ourselves, others, and the world. They inform and are informed by a person's thought process, logic, observation, and experience, thereby forming the basis of her "meta-view" through which she perceives, interprets, and constructs the world and its meaning.[4]

A control belief performs two main functions. First, a control belief performs an *adjudicative function* by determining the acceptability of other beliefs.[5] Regarded as a primitive or primary belief, such a belief is assumed to be true and not itself questioned by the person who holds it. A belief that is seen to be implied by a primitive belief will tend to be accepted while one that is seen to contradict a primitive belief will tend to be rejected. Beliefs that are accepted by control beliefs are regarded as derivative beliefs. Take for instance an occasion where I want to ascertain the number of children in a classroom. Upon entering the classroom and doing a headcount, I form this belief:

Belief A: There are 25 children in the room.

The truth of this belief is dependent on another belief that is assumed to be true by me:

Belief B: I can rely on my senses to make judgements about things.

Belief B serves as a primitive belief for me to accept belief A, which is a derivative belief.

But let us take another occasion where I start to distrust my senses (perhaps after watching the movie *The Matrix*). Now my belief B has been replaced by belief C:

Belief C: I *cannot* rely on my senses to make judgements about things.

With a change of the primitive belief, belief A is no longer accepted as true by me, although all other things remained unchanged: I have not lost my ability to count, I know what children look like, and I do see 25 children in the room.

A real-life example given by Wolterstorff is the case of physicist Ernest Mach.[6] Ernest Mach held to the belief that one should only construct or accept theories based on our senses. That primitive belief led him to reject all beliefs about non-sensory entities and consequently the atomic theory and the Newtonian theory of absolute space. The function of control beliefs as primitive beliefs also explains why some people firmly deny the existence of the supernatural such as ghosts and miracles; their control beliefs are likely to include a belief that only theories based on scientific evidence can be accepted.

Second, a control belief performs a *conditioning function*. This means that it provides the condition for one to accept other beliefs when one seeks to understand, weigh, and/or construct a *theory*.[7] A theory is basically a claim or assertion about something, such as the theory that "all the chairs in my office are brown" or "the Bali bombing is justified". But unlike a mere claim or assertion, a theory is supported by other statements—stated or implied—that function as evidence and presuppositions. Not all theories in the world are acceptable, of course, especially when we are presented with two contradictory theories explaining the same phenomenon. So it is up to a person confronted with a particular theory to make sense of it and judge whether it is acceptable.

But how does the person do that? Here I need to introduce two other types of beliefs: data beliefs and data-background beliefs. Our *data beliefs* provide the data when we want to make sense of a theory, while our *data-background beliefs* provide the condition of our accepting the data in a given occasion. The data-background beliefs are in turn dependent on our control beliefs that provide the condition for us to admit beliefs as data-background beliefs. The conditioning function of control beliefs leads us to reject theories that are inconsistent or do not comport well with our control beliefs. Conversely control beliefs direct us to accept and devise theories that are consistent and comport well with our control beliefs.

Let us take the case of my business partner telling me that the furniture company has mistakenly delivered pink chairs to our new office, instead of the black chairs we have ordered.[8] How did I make sense of and respond to that remark? Well, I dropped by the office and checked it out for myself. And true enough, my business partner was right—all the chairs in the office are pink. My thought process would look something like this:

Theory: All the chairs in the office are pink.

Data beliefs: This is a chair, this is the colour pink, etc.

Data-background beliefs: My senses are in a proper state for discovering its colour, the chair is lit in a proper way for me to discover its colour by observation, etc.

Control belief: One should accept theories that are based on our senses.

In the example above, my control belief provides the condition for me to accept the data-background belief about my senses. The latter in turn provides the data for me to weigh the theory. I conclude that the theory that all the chairs in my new office are pink is accepted because it is consistent with my control belief that theories that are based on our senses (in this case, my sight) are acceptable. We can see that the conditioning function of control beliefs is conceptually linked to their adjudicating function: control beliefs do not just determine the acceptability of other beliefs. They also provide the condition for these beliefs to function as data beliefs and data-background beliefs at that point in time.

We need to note two important points about the three types of beliefs. First, the different beliefs (control, data-background, and data) differ not in their essence but in their *function* relative to a person's understanding, weighing, and/or constructing a given theory on a given occasion.[9] They are not *foundational propositions* in the sense that their truth can be known non-inferentially and with certitude.[10] Examples of foundational propositions are self-evident beliefs such as simple arithmetic truths (e.g. "2 + 1 = 3") and logical truths (e.g. "No man is both married and unmarried").[11] Nothing has been said about the essence of these beliefs; as pointed out at the start of this section, our focus is on the *way* we hold beliefs, not what beliefs really are. Second, a belief may function as a control belief on one occasion but as a data belief on another occasion. Wolterstorff illustrates this point by noting that a person's religious beliefs will function as control beliefs when she is involved in hermeneutics (the principles of interpretation of sacred writings). However, the same religious beliefs will function as data beliefs if her aim is to weigh various theories about God and his relation to us and the world.[12]

Let me elaborate with an example of a Christian dispensationalist. A particular view of Dispensationalism holds that there are three dispensations or periods of time during which human beings are tested in respect of obedience to some specific revelation of the will of God.[13] Accordingly, each dispensation replaces the former dispensation, which means the third (and final) dispensation of Kingdom has replaced the earlier two dispensations of Law and of Grace. The belief that "the dispensation of Law has been replaced" functions as a control belief when the Christian dispensationalist is interested in formulating hermeneutical principles. An example of a principle of biblical interpretation accepted by her is:

Occasion A: Formulating hermeneutical principles

Theory A: The Law of Moses, which was given during the dispensation of Law, has been abrogated.

Control belief A: The dispensation of Law has been replaced.

However, the same belief functions as a data belief on another occasion when she is involved in weighing various theories about God and his relation to us and the world. An example of a theory accepted by her is:

Occasion B: Weighing various theories about God and his relation to us

Theory B: God has replaced the dispensations of Law and of Grace with that of Kindom.

Data belief B: The dispensation of Law has been replaced.

We can observe from the above that a belief functions as a primitive belief only when it functions as a control belief. This describes Occasion A where Control belief A is taken for granted and implies the truth of Theory A. But the same belief no longer functions as a control belief in Occasion B. Rather, it functions as Data belief B. (Also note that besides Data belief B, other data beliefs are needed for Theory B to be accepted, such as beliefs concerning God and other dispensations.) As a data belief, it is no longer taken for granted and *cannot* imply the truth of Theory B. When questioned about Data belief B by a non-dispensationalist, for example, the person will need to support it with a control belief (primitive belief) such as "One should only accept and reject any theory about God and his relation to us based on three dispensations."

Psychologically Strong Beliefs

Putting together what we have learnt about control beliefs, we can see that beliefs, when held as control beliefs, are primitive beliefs that determine the acceptability and functions of other beliefs as data and data-background beliefs. Control beliefs are able to perform these functions because they are held as *psychologically strong* or *central* beliefs.[14] Psychologically strong beliefs are those that are cherished and integral to a person's life and personal identity. They are usually embraced without question and most resistant to change. While all control beliefs are regarded as psychologically strong, they do not possess the same psychological strength. Some control beliefs are held more strongly than others in the sense that they are regarded as most important for the person and form the core of his existence and identity. A devout Buddhist, for instance, is likely to treasure his core religious beliefs on *karma* (doctrine of moral causation) and reincarnation more than his basic political conviction that parliamentary democracy is the best form of government.

To further understand the psychological strength of control beliefs, we need to see how beliefs are related to one another in a belief system. Beliefs are not acquired and do not function in isolation; rather they exist as clusters or webs of interlocked beliefs. When a person attempts to make sense of and assess a situation, clusters of beliefs are activated with the beliefs functioning variously as control beliefs, data beliefs or data-background beliefs.[15] The totality of the clusters of beliefs makes up a person's belief system. What then determines the psychological strength of control beliefs? There are two conditions: the quality and quantity of control beliefs.

First, the *quality* of control beliefs refers to the extent to which a control belief is embedded in a person's cognitive landscape. According to the research scientist Kathleen Taylor, our cognitive landscape is comprised of beliefs that are embodied in patterns of connectivity between neurons.[16] Psychologically strong beliefs are beliefs that are firmly entrenched in the cognitive landscape and intertwined in a web of connections with other beliefs. Control beliefs are embedded through intense stimuli and reinforced repeatedly by constantly being put to use on similar occasions. The more entrenched the control beliefs are, the more rooted and enmeshed they are with other beliefs in the cluster. The same principle applies to the cluster of beliefs. The more a cluster of beliefs is consistent and comports well with another cluster, the more embedded and stronger the beliefs in that cluster will be. Consequently these strongly embedded beliefs will be held in a psychologically intense manner by the person.

The embeddedness of control beliefs makes it extremely difficult for them to be dislodged; doing so will upset and transform the entire structure of beliefs. So embedded are control beliefs in our cognitive landscape that they lie safely below the threshold of our consciousness as "habitual" and "automatised" beliefs, taken for granted, and not subject to examination, doubt, and criticism.[17] However, this does not mean that control beliefs are immune or impervious to questioning and revision. When confronted by a new belief that is inconsistent with the existing cognitive landscape, weak control beliefs tend to change themselves in response to the new input as they are more subservient to reality; stronger control beliefs, on the other hand, are likely to resist and dominate by forming new control beliefs to explain away the new input.[18] This means that it will be extremely difficult but not impossible for psychologically strong control beliefs to be uprooted. Wolterstorff points out that our theory-devising and theory-weighing may induce a "painful process" of revising one's actual religious commitment by "sorting through his beliefs, and discarding some from a position where they can any longer function as control".[19]

The second condition that determines the psychological strength of a belief is the *quantity* of control beliefs. Having more control beliefs, especially if they are unrelated to or incompatible with one another, tends to weaken the strength of any control belief. This is because with more alternative paths for the flow of neutral activity from input stimulus to output response, each individual synapse is likely to be weaker.[20] On the other hand, the fewer the control beliefs, the more embedded they are in our cognitive landscape. The reason is that there are now fewer alternative paths for the flow of neutral activity from input stimulus to output response, thus making each individual synapse stronger.

For example, a person who holds to a control belief that her religion is compatible with science will permit this belief, together with its cluster of beliefs, to interact with and even shape her scientific commitment. An example of a scientist who takes this route is Denis Alexander, the director of the Faraday Institute for Science and Religion in Cambridge, who advocates the compatibility between the Christian theory of creation and scientific evolution. His contemporary is Francis Collins, head of the Human Genome Project, who wrote a book with a self-explanatory title, *The Language of God: A Scientist Presents Evidence for Belief.*[21] The reverse is also true. I once asked an undergraduate who majors in biology at Oxford University how she reconciles the theory of evolution with her Muslim faith. She replied that she simply keeps her religious convictions separate from her academic studies. A person who sees an incompatibility between her control beliefs is likely to consciously keep them apart and claim, for instance, that "matters of faith are beyond the reach of reason to appraise" or "science is one thing and religion is quite another".[22] Such responses are examples of new control beliefs being formed by our existing control beliefs to shield them from being challenged or revised.

So far, we have been focusing on the control beliefs of individuals. But that is not the complete picture. Our control beliefs are not formed or sustained in a vacuum but arise from within and are shaped by a particular tradition. In the context of a religious tradition, the control beliefs of a tradition shape that tradition by functioning as primitive beliefs, and providing the condition of one's understanding, weighing and/or constructing theories. Held as psychologically strong beliefs, control beliefs are like a cognitive roadmap that directs members of a religious tradition to order, regulate, assess, and respond consistently and coherently to the vast amount of varying experiences that impinge on them.[23] An example of how the control beliefs shape a religious tradition is the rejection of the Christian community, led by the Holy Office in Rome, of Galileo's defence of the Copernican theory in 1616. As noted by Wolterstorff, this rejection was due to a control belief held by the Christian community that the Holy Scriptures should be interpreted literally to assess, accept, and reject scientific theories.[24] This control belief has been rejected by most Christian scientists today, thereby demonstrating the dynamic nature of religious traditions in reconstructing their discourses over time.

CONTROL BELIEFS AND INDOCTRINATION

Let us now link the concept of control beliefs to the concept of indoctrination. An indoctrinated person is one who holds to his *control beliefs* in such a way that results in *ideological totalism*.[25] Let me elaborate on the term "ideological totalism" before relating it to control beliefs. I borrow the term "ideological totalism" from the psychologist Robert Jay Lifton who studied the indoctrination of prisoners of war in China after World War II. Lifton defines "ideological totalism" as "the coming together of immoderate ideology with equally immoderate individual character traits—an extremist meeting ground between people and ideas".[26] The term "ideology" is defined as a framework of beliefs that informs us about ourselves and our relationship with the world, and governs our individual and collective lives.[27] The framework of beliefs includes the values, customs, norms, and other elements that constitute the ideology.

A *totalistic ideology* refers to "immoderate" or extreme ideology that has a direct impact on a person's cognitive, affective, and behavioural development. Cognitively, a totalistic ideology severely limits one's intellectual horizon by constricting the person to a simplistic and binary "we versus you" worldview. Affectively, such an ideology incites an all-or-nothing emotional alignment through intense affection and loyalty for one's leaders and fellow members, and a corresponding hostility and hatred towards those outside the group. What follows in behaviour is a mobilisation of extremist thoughts and destructive emotions to protect one's ideology, advance its cause, and eradicate all obstacles and enemies at all costs. It should be noted that we can find ideologies that are totalistic not only in religious or political fields. Lifton rightly observes that a political movement or even a scientific organisation is equally susceptible to ideological totalism.[28]

Let us now apply what we have learnt about control beliefs to indoctrination. An indoctrinated person is one who holds to his control beliefs in three interconnected ways that are distinct from a non-indoctrinated person. First, an indoctrinated person holds to a very small number of control beliefs. The small number is ensured by removing all external stimuli that have the potential to be held as control beliefs by the victim. An artificial environment is imposed where the victim, usually isolated from her family and community, is exposed to only the beliefs privileged by the indoctrinator. The selected control beliefs are usually expressed in abstract and metaphysical terms such as "God", "truth", "freedom", and "progress". They are further represented neatly in a binary "for us or against us" worldview. Entrusted with an absolute authority, these simple and simplistic beliefs serve to guarantee that only a select number of beliefs are (and should be) privileged and implanted.

The second difference between an indoctrinated person and one who is not indoctrinated lies in the extent to which the control beliefs are embedded in his cognitive landscape. The control beliefs of an indoctrinated person are so deeply embedded and held in such a psychologically strong manner that they have colonised his entire cognitive landscape. They screen and censor new inputs that challenge or are inconsistent with the existing control beliefs by forming new beliefs to reject them, such as "this is from the devil" or "only unsaved/sinful/ignorant people think like that". Unsurprisingly, the person develops intense affinity and attachment for "Us" and a corresponding hostility and hatred towards "Them". By channeling all energy to themselves, these control beliefs shape the person's identity and control his entire life, making him interpret *everything* through the lens of the control beliefs.

The third difference is that the control beliefs of a non-indoctrinated person remain, to varying degrees, open to doubt and revision when subjected to contrary ideas and contradictory evidence. But this is not the case for an indoctrinated person: such a person's control beliefs stubbornly withstand the external challenge and even distort reality by filtering all incoming stimuli and re-interpreting new information in alignment with and support of his control beliefs.[29] This is possible because the control beliefs are fortified by a small but carefully implanted and deeply embedded cluster of intertwined beliefs. The result is that the person's total energy is mobilised to remove all obstacles, human and otherwise, to fulfil his higher calling to protect and propagate his ideology. I shall elaborate on a totalistic ideology in the next chapter. But it is helpful, in our remaining section, to illustrate what we have learnt about control beliefs and a totalistic ideology with an example of jihad.

CONTROL BELIEFS AT WORK: THE EXAMPLE OF JIHAD

Literally meaning "struggle" or "strive", jihad is generally defined as doing your best to uphold God's laws, propagating and establishing it.[30] This general meaning should not be equated with armed struggle or war. In Indonesia, a country known for its tolerant and inclusive form of Islam, many Muslims speak of jihad as giving their best for God. For example, I interviewed a director of a pesantren (Islamic boarding school), a mild-mannered elderly man, who passionately spoke about the jihad of his teachers:

> At that time, the spirit of jihad was very strong, as they [the teachers] themselves believed that the establishment of a pesantren is essential and considered necessary. . . . If you look at the teachers, they are committed and with high moral character. Their honorarium is minimal. They have the spirit of a fighter—*jihad fi sabilillah* [struggle for the sake of Allah], of course in the field of education, and they are sincere, with the current condition, the provisions provided for them are rather modest.[31]

However the term "jihad", especially "jihad fi sabilillah", is also used by many Muslim militants to refer to armed struggle or war against non-Muslims through violent activities. I shall use the arguments of Iman Samudra to illustrate how his control beliefs shape his beliefs and influence his actions. The views of Iman Samudra are taken from a book written by a Singaporean Muslim scholar Muhammad Haniff Hassan.[32] Iman Samudra, the field commander for the Bali bombing was convicted and sentenced to death by the Indonesian court on September 2003. The Bali bombing I, which took place on October 12, 2002, killed about 200 people and wounded about 300 in Bali, and was carried out by a group of Muslim militants as a professed act of jihad. To help us to link Iman Samudra's justification of the Bali bombing as an example of armed jihad to our discussion of control beliefs, I have presented his views based on the following belief schema:

Theory: The Bali bombing is justified.

Data beliefs: Data about the Bali bombing such as:

- what happened
- where it happened
- when it happened
- how it happened
- why it happened (a case of jihad fi sabilillah: fighting in the way of God)
- who were being attacked (Americans and their allies who are guilty of attacking Muslims in Afghanistan in 2001)
- who were the attackers (martyrs)

Data-background beliefs: Belief about jihad fi sabilillah: an Islamic act of retaliation against infidels who have transgressed the limit and contributed to the war against Muslims.

Control belief: The relationship that should exist between Muslims and non-Muslims is war.

For Iman Samudra, the Bali bombing qualifies as a case of jihad fi sabilillah (fighting in the way of God)—fighting the infidels who fight against Islam and the Muslims.[33] He argues that those who were attacked in Bali were Americans and their allies guilty of attacking the Muslim community. According to him, they were not tourists or innocent civilians but active contributors to the war against Muslims. That was because they had voted for their governments, which had initiated the war in Afghanistan, and paid taxes, which were used to employ the military personnel for the war. On the other hand, the attackers were seen as martyrs who were simply obeying the Islamic commandment to perform jihad fi sabilillah. These *data beliefs* are in turn conditioned by Iman Samudra's *data-background beliefs* on the meaning and application of jihad fi sabilillah. This concept, according to him, refers to a justified act of retaliation against the infidels who first attacked Muslims. He claims that his interpretation is supported by this verse from the Qur'an:[34]

> "And fight in God's cause against those who wage war against you, but do not commit aggression—for, verily, God does not love aggressors." (The Qur'an, 2:190)

Iman Samudra asserts that the Americans and allies are the aggressors and they have transgressed the limit by killing Muslim civilians in Afghanistan. Muslims are therefore justified in retaliating against them based on verses such as the following:

> "Thus, if anyone commits aggression against you, attack him just as he has attacked you". (The Qur'an, 2:194)

> "Hence, if you have to respond to an attack, respond only to the extent of the attack leveled against you." (The Qur'an, 16:126)

The choice of location (Sari Club and Paddy's Pub in Bali) is also justified, as these places are widely known to be popular venues for many Americans and their allies to congregate. Iman Samudra cites this verse in his support:

> "And slay them wherever you may come upon them". (The Qur'an, 2:191)

Underpinning Iman Samudra's data-background beliefs is his *control belief* about the relationship between Muslims and non-Muslims. He believes that the basis of relationship between Muslims and non-Muslims is war.[35] This view of an adversarial relationship between Muslims and non-Muslims is based on his interpretation of the sacred texts on the final stage of jihad and the conspiracy of non-Muslims against Muslims.

Iman Samudra argues that there were four historical and progressive stages of jihad as revealed in the Qur'an. The first stage was that of patience where Muslims put up with the physical torture from the ruling tribe of Quraisy who were non-Muslims. This was followed by the second stage where the permission to fight the non-Muslims who expelled the Muslims from their homeland was given. The third stage was the obligation to fight a limited war against non-Muslims and leave those who did not fight them alone. The final stage was the obligation to wage war against all non-believers and polytheists, based on verses in the Qur'an and *hadith* (sayings and practices of the Prophet Muhammad), such as the following:

> "[S]lay those who ascribe divinity to aught beside God whenever you may come upon them". (The Qur'an, 9:5)

> "I am commanded to fight against men till they declare that there is no deity except God and that Muhammad is His messenger, and they are constant in prayers and pay the alms." (Narrated by Al-Bukhari and Muslim)

> "And fight against them until there is no more oppression (*fitnah*) and all worship (*din*) is devoted to God alone." (The Qur'an, 8:39)

Iman Samudra maintains that the fourth (and final) stage has abrogated the earlier stages, which placed limits on the permissibility of jihad for Muslims. This means that armed jihad is the *only* kind of relationship that could exist between Muslims and non-Muslims. Muslims are obligated to wage war against all non-Muslims until the latter are converted to Islam and the Islamic law is completely instituted. He also cites other verses in the Qur'an that allegedly teach that all non-Muslims share a common hate towards Islam and are constantly conspiring against it:

> "[Your enemies] will not cease to fight against you till they have turned you away from your faith, if they can." (The Qur'an, 2:217)

> "For never will the Jews be pleased with thee, nor yet the Christians, unless thou follow their own creeds." (The Qur'an, 2:120)

We can also apply what we have learnt about the different functions of beliefs to the views of Iman Samudra. His belief on the relationship between Muslims and non-Muslims functions as a control belief when he weighs the theory on the justifiability of the Bali bombing.

Occasion A: Weighing the theory on the justifiability of the Bali bombing

Theory: The Bali bombing is justified.

Control belief: The relationship that should exist between Muslims and non-Muslims is war.

But the same belief functions as a theory to be weighed when his focus is on applying the principles of interpreting the Qur'an.

Occasion B: Applying the principles of interpreting the Qur'an

Theory: The relationship that should exist between Muslims and non-Muslims is war.

Control belief: One should rely primarily on *lafaz 'am* (words with general meaning) to interpret the verses on the relationship that should exist between Muslims and non-Muslims.

Our discussion of Iman Samudra's views shows that his views bear strong resemblance to a totalistic ideology. His control belief about the adversarial relationship between Muslims and non-Muslims severely limits his intellectual horizon by constricting him to a "binary perspective", which is a "either you are with us or against us" point of view. The affective aspect of a totalistic ideology—the incitement of an all-or-nothing emotional alignment—is also evident. Iman Samudra advocates feelings of intolerance, hostility, and hatred towards all non-Muslims without any reservation or exception. A logical conclusion of such an extreme ideology is that Muslims are obligated to bring into fruition the ideology by resorting to all means, including violent acts, against all unbelievers. We see such obligations being fulfilled by Iman Samudra through his polemical writings and personal involvement in the Bali bombing.

Iman Samudra is not alone in thinking and acting that way. Another Muslim who argued along the same line was Mohammad al-Faraj who was found guilty for his role in assassinating Egyptian President Anwar Sadat and was sentenced to death in 1982. Arguing that the Qur'an and the hadith were fundamentally about warfare, he asserted that jihad represented in fact the "sixth pillar of Islam"; consequently he called for war against non-Muslims and even Muslims who are perceived to have deviated from the "true meaning" of jihad.[36]

On the other hand, we should note that there are other Muslim scholars, groups, and communities who reject Iman Samudra's arguments and control beliefs (I shall discuss a different interpretation of jihad in Chapter 5).[37] The disagreements and debates among Muslims regarding jihad reveal contrasting control beliefs at work in the respective traditions. Recall that a jihad tradition is a discourse that seeks to instruct a community of Muslims on the correct form and purpose of jihad. A jihad tradition is a historically situated social process of constructing the shared meaning of jihad through the text (Qur'an, hadith, and writings by classical Muslim scholars) and context (formal, non-formal, and informal education from religious leaders, family members, and the community). Rather than one homogenised jihad tradition, there are different and competing jihad traditions across various Muslim communities, each with its own identity, history, trajectory, and struggles. It should therefore not surprise us that the concept of jihad today remains contested by Muslims (and non-Muslims) from various traditions.[38]

CONCLUDING REMARKS

We have seen how indoctrination is fundamentally about specific control beliefs that result in ideological totalism. Returning to the example of Ingrid in the television episode "The Tribe", is she indoctrinated or *brainwashed*? Lest we homogenise indoctrination, we need to remember that indoctrination comes in different shades and forms. In reality, indoctrination is likely to be manifested (and camouflaged) in myriad ways and even overlaps, at times, with socialisation and enculturation. In other words, there are varying shades of indoctrination, ranging from mild indoctrination on one end of the spectrum to intense indoctrination on the other end. But where does brainwashing fit in?

Like indoctrination, brainwashing exists in various degrees and shares intersecting points with indoctrination in some cases.[39] It is instructive to note that there is no consensus among scholars on the relationship between brainwashing and indoctrination. On the one hand, there are researchers who argue that brainwashing is distinct from indoctrination, on the basis that the former necessarily involves coercion. It is believed that brainwashing, unlike indoctrination, goes hand in hand with coercive strategies such as enforced isolation, interrogations, drugs, forced confessions, and self-criticisms, accompanied by emotional assault such as inducing anxiety, fear, and even mental breakdown.[40]

However, while I agree that brainwashing is usually coercive (due to its association with Chinese Communist brainwashing of prisoners of war), indoctrination may be coercive too. I concur with Robert S. Baron that we should distinguish two types of indoctrination: a voluntary form (for example, recruiting members to join a cult group) and a coercive form (for example, imprisoning prisoners of war).[41] Furthermore, it is not true that coercive strategies such as physical abuse are only used in brainwashing and not in indoctrination. As pointed out earlier, indoctrination may be achieved through methods such as physical stress and regimented daily activity schedule. In short, effective indoctrination requires a clever blend of cognitive, affective, and physical manipulative techniques that mutually reinforce one another.

Other writers argue that the difference between brainwashing and indoctrination is that the former only applies to adults whereas the latter is more appropriate for children. For example, Ben Spiecker argues that brainwashing involves more forceful techniques for the re-education of adults whereas indoctrination focuses more on hampering the development of a critical attitude in children.[42] However, I do not see why we should restrict the two terms to the age of the victims. Instead of being age-specific, which artificially confines the usage of both terms, it is better for us to define them in terms of intensity. Brainwashing is simply an extremely intense form of indoctrination on one end of the continuum. A brainwashed person is one whose control beliefs are so deeply embedded and held so strongly that the person becomes what Kathleen Taylor calls a "single-issue fanatic".[43] The case of Ingrid from "The Tribe" is a good example. Her own control beliefs have been totally replaced by the control beliefs implanted in her by her indoctrinator. She has been isolated from her own family by the indoctrinator to undergo intense indoctrination. Her parroting of the indoctrinator's views and participation in killing those outside the tribe offer further evidence of ideological totalism.

The example of Ingrid also reminds us that indoctrination does not occur in isolation. It requires a community of believers who share an indoctrinatory tradition. What are the conditions for an indoctrinatory tradition to exist and thrive? What are the common strategies to bring about ideological totalism? What is the impact of an indoctrinatory tradition on one's rationality and autonomy? The answers to these questions, supplemented by real-life examples of indoctrination, are given in the next chapter.

2 (De)constructing an Indoctrinatory Tradition

When I was living in Britain, one of my favourite television shows was *Big Brother*. It's a reality show where a group of contestants are forced to live together in a house. They compete to win the game by being the last contestant remaining in the house. Completely cut off from the rest of the world and monitored around the clock, the contestants are expected to abide by all the house rules. They also must complete the tasks assigned to them by "Big Brother"—an unseen person whose voice is broadcast over the PA system. It's a quirky, funny, and satirical show. Its motley crew of people from various social classes and backgrounds offers interesting insights on human behaviour and relationships. I recall a posh-speaking Oxford University graduate trying to downplay his status, a window fitter who styled himself as *X-Men*'s Wolverine, and an unemployed lady with a pink Mohican haircut who had a crush on a pretty female contestant in the show.

Entertainment aside, the character of "Big Brother" reminds us of George Orwell's *Nineteen Eighty-Four*. His book about a totalitarian society where everyone is under complete control and surveillance by the dictator is a classic case of an indoctrinatory environment. We have learnt in the previous chapter that indoctrination occurs when a person holds to control beliefs that result in ideological totalism. But indoctrination does not exist and flourish in isolation. It requires, as Orwell's book exemplifies, a conducive environment for a community of followers to submit to one or more leaders. It also requires corresponding strategies for control beliefs to be implanted and held in a psychologically intense manner in the victims.

This chapter begins by elucidating the conditions required to create, sustain, and promote an indoctrinatory tradition. The second section highlights the impact of an indoctrinatory tradition on a person's rationality and autonomy.

CONDITIONS FOR AN INDOCTRINATORY TRADITION

I have explained in the introductory chapter that a tradition is a discourse that seeks to instruct a community of believers on the correct form and purpose of a given practice. A discourse is a social process of constructing and transmitting shared meaning, through both the text and the context. Accordingly, an indoctrinatory tradition is a social process that aims to implant, through text and context, control beliefs in a community of believers that result in ideological totalism. It is important to note that an aim or *intention* to implant specific control beliefs must be present in an indoctrinatory tradition.[1] In other words, the inculcation of control beliefs is carried out in a deliberate, systematic and sustained manner.

An ideologically totalistic tradition is a closed tradition that endorses, prescribes, and permits one uniform monolithic ideology for its members. By insisting that it has the monopoly of the truth, it resists learning from other traditions, censors alternative worldviews, and is unwilling to adapt to changing times and places.[2] In the process, it undermines the social conditions for its members to critically reflect on their own tradition and judge between traditions.[3]

We can identify an indoctrinatory tradition based on the essential conditions or criteria needed to create, sustain, and propagate such a tradition. The conditions, which are adapted from Robert Jay Lifton, can be divided into three aspects: the key characteristics of the ideology, the justification for the ideology, and the strategies for indoctrination.[4] Given that indoctrination is not an all-or-nothing phenomenon but comes in various shades, an indoctrinatory tradition may manifest a combination of the above conditions in different ways and to varying extent. This means that the more clearly an environment expresses these conditions, the greater its resemblance to an indoctrinatory tradition.

Key Characteristics of the Ideology

The first aspect of an indoctrinatory tradition is its subscription to a totalistic ideology. I have already noted in the previous chapter that such an ideology is characterised by metaphysical concepts such as "God" or "Truth". These are *thought-terminating and ultimate terms* employed to entrench the control beliefs in the victim. Usually presented in a brief, highly reductive, definitive-sounding and polarising manner, these terms are "god terms" representing ultimate good, or "devil terms" representing ultimate evil. This stark and simplistic format makes the task of introducing and implanting the control beliefs easy by confining all human experiences and worldviews to a totalistic ideology and an all-or-nothing emotional alignment.[5]

Closely related to thought-terminating and ultimate terms is the *demand for purity* from the adherents. The indoctrinator implants control beliefs that divide the world and people into two neat categories: the pure and the impure, the absolutely good and the absolutely evil, or the ultimately moral and ultimately immoral. The first category encompasses all the ideas, feelings, and actions originating from the ideology, whereas the second category takes in everything else. Indoctrinated believers, as people who are supposedly pure, absolutely good and ultimately moral, are obligated to keep themselves separate and untainted by the Other. Describing this bipolar mindset as "oppositional dialectics", Farish A. Noor explains that it requires "the creation of a negative Other" and is usually "constructed along a strictly policed boundary line that demarcates the differences between the self ("us") and the other ("them")".[6] In their research on contemporary religious fundamentalists movements, Gabriel A. Almond, R. Scott Appleby, and Emmanuel Sivan also highlight an "enclave mentality" that builds a "wall of virtue" to separate themselves who are a community of virtuous insiders from the oppressive, morally defiled, and dangerous general society.[7]

Against a backdrop of thought-terminating and ultimate terms and demand for purity, the ideology exercises *milieu control* over the believers. This refers to a total control over a person, whether it is his inner life or his communication with the outside world. The purpose is for the control beliefs to permeate into all aspects of a person's life as beliefs that are firmly habitual, automised, and taken for granted. They are held as the "ultimate truth" that leads the person to a personal closure regarding the search for truth, reality, and happiness. By merging the self with the external world, one's personal identity and autonomy are intricately tied to the indoctrinated ideology. An absolute polarisation is aimed at where the control beliefs succeed in making the person see that only the taught ideology is real and the sole yardstick to everything else.

The indoctrinator also resorts to *mystical manipulation* where the victims acquire specific desired patterns of behaviour and emotions to carry out their "mystical imperative" as chosen agents of God or some other supernatural force. It has been noted that some militant Muslims believe that they belong to the "saved sect" (*firqa al-najiyya*) among Muslims who will be saved on judgement day.[8] Any contrary or doubtful thought or action is castigated as regressive and sinful, originating from a lower purpose or their own weaknesses. Their detractors including fellow Muslims who do not share their vision are regarded as "impure" Muslims who lack the proper religious understanding or "bad" or "immoral" traitors who are collaborating with non-Muslims.

An example of a totalistic ideology that manifests the above description is encapsulated in the concepts of *Dar Al-Islam* (land of Islam) and *Dar Al-Harb* (land of war). That these are thought-terminating and ultimate terms are spelt out by Islamic scholar Syed Qutb:

> In the world there is only one party of God; all others are parties of Satan and rebellion. . . . There is only one place on earth which can be called the home of Islam (Dar-ul-Islam), and it is that place where the Islamic state is established and the Shari'ah is the authority and God's limits are observed, and where all the Muslims administer the affairs of the state with mutual consultation. The rest of the world is the home of hostility (Dar-ul-Harb).[9]

The demand for purity logically follows from these ultimate terms, as argued by Syed Qutb: "A Muslim can have only two possible relations with

Dar-ul-Harb: peace with a contractual agreement, or war".[10] Under the milieu control of a binary worldview, Muslims are therefore obligated to accomplish a higher purpose of establishing an Islamic state through armed jihad against unbelievers.

Justification for the Ideology

The second aspect of ideological totalism is the attempt to justify the ideology to potential victims. The first condition is *sacred science* that combines an aura of sacredness for the ideology with logic and scientific explanation. In other words, the control beliefs are perceived to be grounded in deep knowledge and ultimate science, thereby making the ideology necessarily true, timeless, and universally applicable. Consequently, according to Lifton, reverence is demanded of all followers and any questioning is treated as unspiritual or unscientific.[11] For example, Quintan Wiktqrqwicz and Karl Kaltenthaler point out that some Muslim militant groups conscientiously refer to hadiths such as this verse to convince their followers that they alone are the "saved sect" (*firqa al-najiyya*) on judgement day: "And thus Ummah will divide into seventy-three sects all of which except one will go to Hell and they are those who are upon what I and my Companions are upon".[12]

The legitimacy of the indoctrinator's ideology is complemented by the condition of *doctrine over the person*. This means that all events and experiences are interpreted solely through the ideological lens of the group. The control beliefs function as gatekeepers to select, ignore, alter, rewrite, and rationalise all historical events and personal experiences to fit the ideology. Such a mindset is premised on the belief that the group's ideology is the ultimate truth and reality. A common strategy used by Muslim scholars who argue for armed jihad is to interpret the whole of human history based on an alleged international Zionist-Christian conspiracy led by the U.S. government against Muslims. Any course of action taken by members, especially those that appear to contradict the ideology, has to be justified by the ideology itself. An example is the case of Muslims killing fellow Muslims. For example, Mohammad al-Faraj who assassinated Egyptian President Anwar Sadat justified his action by maintaining that jihad is required not just against unbelievers but professed Muslims who have deviated from the dictates of shari'ah. That a religious justification is available explains why some Indonesian Muslim militants linked to Abu Bakar Ba'asyir are reportedly planning to assassinate their Muslim President Susilo Bambang Yudhoyono.[13]

A related condition is the *dispensing with the existence* of anyone who does not subscribe to the group's ideology. These people become "non-people" and have lost the right to existence, unless they remould their thought and take the necessary steps to adhere to the ideology. It has been noted that Muslim militant groups tend to demonise all non-Muslims as "infidels", "enemies of Islam and Muslims", and "allies of the United States".

This makes it easier for Muslims to de-humanise and attack non-Muslims in the name of armed jihad. That was evident in the case of 9/11 militant Muhammed Atta who carried with him a document where non-Muslims were branded as "allies of Satan and brothers of the devil".[14]

Strategies for Indoctrination

The third aspect of an indoctrinatory tradition refers to the strategies used. These strategies collectively provide the *cultural framing*: Mohammed M. Hafez defines it as the attempt to frame or rationalise collective action, high-risk activism, or extreme violence that disrupts normal living and brings tremendous hardship to participants as meaningful acts of redemption.[15] Cultural framing takes place through the text and context in formal, non-formal, and informal education.

The *text* refers to the interpretation of sacred writings, particularly on jihad and the proper relationship between Muslims and non-Muslims. It is no coincidence that Muslim militant preachers conscientiously refer to the Qur'an, hadiths, and writings of *Salafush Shalih* (pious predecessors) to implant their militant ideology in their victims. A reliance on the text is important as the indoctrinator needs to present his beliefs as sound religious doctrines that are consistent and comport well with the victim's existing belief system. By using ideas and language that fit into the victim's cognitive landscape through relevant association, the indoctrinator is able to convince the victim that they both share the same beliefs.[16] Skilful indoctrinators are able to give the impression that they are knowledgeable, likeable, sincere, respected, trustworthy, and charismatic. As Denise Winn points out, "Rather than impose new opinions, propaganda works if it articulates forcefully and graphically nebulous passions and fears and resentments that are constantly simmering below consciousness".[17]

That indoctrination is more effective if the victim has an affinity with the indoctrinator is evident in the case of Catholic priest Father Luca who was a prisoner of war in China. Despite his strong resistance, he caved in because of the influence of a young Chinese who spoke his language (Italian) and was kind towards him. Father Luca later testified that the young man's "questioning was objective and impartial. . . . He spoke in my own language. . . . It was easier for me to confess".[18] That is why Muslim militant groups are often fronted by charismatic and religiously learned leaders such as Omar Bakri Muhammad, Abu Hamza, and Abu Bakar Ba'asyir. Presenting his ideas as deeply religious yet simple to grasp, the indoctrinator adds credibility to these ideas by judiciously citing evidences that are valued by *the victim*, especially sacred writings, judgements of pious religious scholars, and historical events. Sacred writings are interpreted in such a way that the group's interpretation is the *only* correct interpretation for all believers. Concomitantly, alternative and competing interpretations of the religious texts are censored or dismissed as erroneous and corrupted.

Reinforcing and entrenching the control beliefs in the victim's cognitive landscape through text is the *context*—the social and political backdrop comprising internal and external factors against which cultural framing takes place.[19] The context is the stimuli manipulated by the indoctrinator to entrench the selected control beliefs. The context can take place in formal education (Islamic schools), non-formal education (Muslim militant organisations), and informal education (network of like-minded Muslims). Through various educational platforms, powerful external stimuli are repeatedly given with the help of external and internal factors. External factors are dependent on international developments such as political events affecting Muslims worldwide, while internal factors are linked to one's economic, social, religious, and political living conditions. All these factors are manipulated by the indoctrinator to stir up the victims' emotions to embrace the group's control beliefs and fulfil the group's mission.

These control beliefs are further strengthened through discursive and performative practices to remind and guide the believers to conduct their lives based on the teachings in the text. Culturally sanctioning and socially standardising the official interpretation of the text are repetitive symbolic behaviours through rituals and ceremonies of the tradition that aim to "communicate and declare identity, arouse emotions, deepen commitments, and inculcate the values of collective ethos".[20] These practices are part of the discourse of a tradition where shared meanings are constructed through textual transmission. Discursive and performative practices that are deliberately omitted or publicly rejected are as important as those that are selected and retained in influencing someone on what he should or should not accept. Given that religious framing is a competitive process whereby various religious authorities seek to promote their interpretations of sacred texts and practices, cultural elements that may hinder the strategic choices of the suicide bombers have to be carefully disregarded or de-emphasised.[21]

A common strategy is *total exposure* where all aspects of one's private life are potentially made public to the group. This follows from milieu control where the environment has total ownership of the person. The extent to which total exposure is demanded depends on the degree of indoctrination. A heavily indoctrinated victim is likely to expose all his thoughts, words, and actions to his indoctrinator through regimented daily activities, reports, and confession. In contrast, someone who is mildly indoctrinated may still retain the space to keep some of his thoughts or actions private. By demanding that the followers expose their thought, words, and actions, the indoctrinator is able to monitor, reinforce, and embed the control beliefs in them. One way to achieve the total exposure is to disrupt the victim's normal social life and isolate him from people and factors that promote inconsistent or competing beliefs. This is accompanied by creating an artificial environment where the indoctrinator has the victim's total attention and complete devotion. This environment is obtained by getting the victim to cast aside his time for family, job, or study and join a cell group that is usually clandestine and time-consuming. Other strategies include physical stress, fear or guilt manipulation, reward and punishment, regimented daily activity schedule, and carefully orchestrated social pressure.[22] It has been reported that indoctrinated Muslim militants are expected to live every detail of the religion based on instructions given to them.[23] In the words of Abu Bakr Naji, a militant Muslim scholar, his aim is to bring his followers to "servitude, obedience"; Omar Bakri Mohammed, the founder of militant movement Al-Muhajiroun, proclaims that his followers are "an identical copy of the way I think".[24]

There is one more condition of an indoctrinatory tradition, and it has to do with its impact on a person's rationality and autonomy. Given that the literature on indoctrination has traditionally focused on the relationship between indoctrination, rationality, and autonomy, it is instructive to discuss at length the relationship indoctrination has with these two educational ideals.

THE IMPACT OF AN INDOCTRINATORY TRADITION ON RATIONALITY AND AUTONOMY

Rationality

The first point to note is that rationality and its cognates such as critical thinking and higher-order thinking are not context-less and ideology-free. Standards of rationality are dependent on historically concrete languages and practices, and take place in specific contexts in response to particular situations.[25] Neither are human beings disembodied rational autonomous subjects; the community they belong to plays a defining role in socialising them and influencing the way they interact with each other and make choices in life. In short, we need to situate rationality in the context of a *tradition*. A person's tradition offers the developmental structure—a well-defined domestic space—for the child before she can begin to question.[26] Without a provisional acceptance of some framework of beliefs in virtue of which truth assessments can be made, a rational discussion of any issue is difficult, if not impossible.[27] A tradition-sensitive conception of rationality is recommended here, one that Elmer John Thiessen calls "normal rationality":

> Clearly normal rationality incorporates some elements of the traditional liberal ideal of rationality such as an understanding of the various forms of knowledge, a concern for evidence for beliefs held, and the acquiring of intellectual virtues like critical openness. . . . It also recognises the limitations inherent in our attempts to achieve objective rationality. . . . Normal rationality recognises that justification of

beliefs, while important, is intimately linked with the psychological and sociological conditions under which beliefs develop.[28]

We can further understand "normal rationality" by distinguishing a weak sense of rationality from a strong one. Here I find Joseph Runzo's distinction between *internal* and *external* questions regarding worldviews helpful.[29] According to him, internal questions refer to questions that must be decided on the basis of some particular worldview that is taken for granted. Internal questions are part of the "criticism internal to a tradition"—a process of examining the basis of our beliefs and values by assuming the truth of the other beliefs and values that we have acquired as a result of growing up within that tradition.[30] On the other hand, external questions are concerned with the acceptability of one's existing worldview against alternative worldviews. In line with these two types of questions, I propose that weak rationality refers to the ability and willingness to justify one's beliefs based on internal questions, whereas strong rationality refers to the ability and willingness to justify one's beliefs based on internal *as well as* external questions.

The distinction between weak and strong rationality helps us to debunk a common misconception that indoctrination is necessarily devoid of rationality or evidence. Back in the 1970s, Thomas F. Green argued that indoctrinated persons "will be unable to give *any* adequate reasons for them [beliefs held], *any* clear account for them, or offer *any* sound evidence in their support beyond logically irrelevant observation that they are commonly held beliefs".[31] His contemporary I.A. Snook contended that an indoctrinated person is one who disregards evidence, has a closed mind, and is not open to rational scrutiny. Snook defined "evidence" as "methods of assessing data, standards of accuracy, and validity of reasoning".[32]

Continuing the tradition in the 1980s was Harvey Siegel who claimed that a belief is an indoctrinated one if it is held "non-evidentially"—that is, "held without regard to evidence relevant to its rational assessment and held in such a way that it is impervious to negative or contrary evidence".[33] Testifying to the resilience of this view of indoctrination is a recent article by Eamonn Callan and Dylan Arena who aver that indoctrination is characterised by close-mindedness where the person is unable or unwilling to give due regard to reasons that are available for them to revise their current beliefs.[34]

The arguments by the above philosophers are not tenable if they are referring to *weak* rationality. This is because an indoctrinated person may be someone who remains willing and capable of engaging in internal questions—questions that examine one's beliefs on the basis of a worldview that she already subscribes to. Empirical studies also debunk the traditional link between indoctrination and the strict absence or suppression of rationality. Some researchers have rightly noted that suicide bombers and their organisations are rational in the sense that they are guided by a strategic logic to achieve their goal through violence.[35] Rationalist theories, according to Muhammad M. Hafez, maintain that "groups employing terrorism calculate costs and benefits of different courses of action, act with purpose, adapt to incentives and opportunities, and pursue means that are logically connected to their ends".[36] Suicide bombing, when projected as "martyrdom", is a rational choice that is made on the basis of available information. The individual is assured that her action, as an act of obedience to God, will reap salvation and reward in heaven for her. That is why a graduate of an Islamic school in Indonesia that is accused of indoctrinating its students points out that the suicide bombers "make a rational calculation about what they're doing".[37] Some readers may hesitate in calling indoctrinated terrorists "rational", as their form of "rationality" is a limited one that is largely instrumental in nature, much like a criminal who "rationally" plans his next bank heist. I agree with that objection, but my point here is that the assumption that indoctrinated persons are incapable of rational thinking and only capable of robot-like behaviour—like Ingrid in the television episode "The Tribe" mentioned in the previous chapter—is inaccurate and too simplistic.

To further illustrate how weak rationality may be present in the indoctrination process and indoctrinated persons, let us consider two examples. The first example is the testimony of Ed Husain, a British Muslim and author of *The Islamist*. He chronicles his experience of joining the radical Islamist organisation Hizb ut-Tahrir in Britain.[38] He admits that the "indoctrination of the Hizb was powerful and it was many years before I was completely free of it".[39] How was that achieved? The process was not without the use of evidence and reasoning process. Rather than learning by rote and memorisation, Husain details how he spent "hours in discussion with members of Hizb ut-Tahrir, questioning them on matters ranging from the dialectical materialism of Marxists to abstruse points in Muslim jurisprudence", and that "Hizb members always had answers".[40] He was later invited to join Hizb ut-Tahrir's *halaqah* (circle) or study group where a team of about five people gathered weekly to study the literature of selected Islamic scholars. Additionally, their beliefs are not bereft of evidential justification—the leaders of Hizb constantly referred to facts about the Afghans' struggle against the Soviets and the suffering of the Muslims in Bosnia and Iraq. Defensible and well-substantiated arguments are offered too; for example, Hizb ut-Tahrir's in-house economist argues that the solution to government debt in the Muslim world is for Muslim countries to withdraw from the World Bank, nationalise the oil wealth of Saudi, Kuwaiti, Iraqi, and Qatari, and use their oil to increase the wealth of the Muslim community.[41]

The second example comes from the arguments of a senior member of Jemaah Islamiyah, Aly Ghufron bin Nurhasyim (better known as Mukhlas). His writing demonstrates what Greg Fealy calls "jihadist logic"[42]. A senior Jemaah Islamiyah member and graduate of an Islamic school co-founded by Abu Bakar Ba'asyir, Mukhlas was convicted and sentenced to death by the Indonesian court on October 2003. The excerpts discussed are taken from his unpublished manuscripts that aim to provide a religious and moral justification for the Bali bombing.[43] Mukhlas asserts that the shar'iah commands Muslims to terrorise the enemies of God by causing them "to tremble, be afraid and be overwhelmed by fear".[44] He draws support from Islamic verses such as Al Anfal 8:60:

> And *prepare to face them with whatever force you can*, and *horses teth-ered for war* (which are part of those preparations), so that you make the *enemies of God your enemies and others whom you do not know of*, yet God knows of, TREMBLE. Whatsoever you expend in God's path will surely be repaid sufficiently to you and you will not be wronged.[45]

Furthermore, he endeavours to justify the Bali bombing such as the aim of the attack, choice of location, and target of attack, all the while grounding his arguments on the judgements of classical Islamic scholars, "the axioms of the Qur'an and Sunnah and the facts on the grounds".[46] He also considers possible objections to the Bali bombing such as the injury and death of fellow Muslims, women, children, and non-Muslim civilians. For example, he poses this question on the unintended killing of fellow Muslims: "Should our actions be considered an excessive deed because in the operation Muslims and other people who did not know they would be killed were forced to be included as targets?" He answers this question in the negative by substantiating it from historical events recorded in the Qur'an such as the Badar war where some Muslims were unintentionally struck by the Muslim army's arrows in their war against the polytheists.[47]

We see from our two examples above that Hizb ut-Tahrir and Mukhlas are open to addressing internal questions in the process of imparting their ideology to their members. They have referred variously to relevant historical evidence such as the encounters of Muslims during the Prophet Mohammad's time, the Qur'an, hadiths, and the works of classical Muslim scholars. But no provision is given for any member to ask *external* questions about the tradition itself, consider alternatives, or learn from other traditions, whether they are other Muslim traditions or non-Islamic traditions. Other examples of Muslim militants who rely on "jihadist logic" based on internal questions are Abdullah Azzam who is the founding father of the Arab Afghan movement, Sayyid Imam Abd al-Aziz Imam al-Sharif who is the ideologue of the Egyptian Islamic Jihad, and the Syrian al-Qaida theorist Mustafa bin Abd al-Qadir Sethmariam Nasar (better known as Abu Musab al-Suri).[48]

So *pace* Snook, Green, Siegel, Callan, and Arena, an indoctrinated person is not necessarily one who is unable to give any adequate reasons or sound evidence for his beliefs, unable or unwilling to give due regard to reasons that are available for them, and hold to beliefs in such a way that is impervious to negative or contrary evidence.

Autonomy

The acknowledgement of tradition-embeddedness applies to "autonomy" too. I follow Thiessen in emphasising "normal autonomy" where a person's freedom of thought and action is conceived within a contingent historical context, and is consistent with one's choice to submit to another person or God.[49] It is helpful to distinguish weak autonomy from strong autonomy.

Accordingly to John White, a weak sense of personal autonomy describes an "autarchic person" who freely engages in rational deliberation on the alternatives open to him within a tradition-directed society. A person with strong autonomy, on the other hand, is not just autarchic but is capable of critically reflecting on his own tradition and its basic social structures.[50] Arguing along the same line is Jan Steutel who posits that "minimal autonomy" (which corresponds to weak autonomy) refers to autarchic freedom where a person freely accepts, is motivated by, and orders his life according to a normative orientation (or tradition, as I have called it). "Maximal autonomy" (which corresponds to strong autonomy), on the other hand, is obtained when a person freely accepts, is motivated by, and orders his life independently according to a moral orientation *after* reflecting critically on the validity of these moral rules.[51] From the above discussion, we can conclude that a person with strong autonomy is one who not only consciously governs his life according to his tradition, but also critically reflects on his own tradition and considers the alternatives open to him. Such a person is autonomous in the sense of accepting and living a life that he has chosen for himself after a process of careful deliberation.

An indoctrinatory tradition is one that may grant its members weak autonomy but definitely not strong autonomy. This means that a member may be given the freedom to order his life within the boundary of the tradition and even decide the level of his commitment to the tradition (for example, as a community leader or just a follower). But no strong or maximal autonomy is given in the sense that the tradition deprives him the opportunity to critique his own tradition such as its basic social structures or the validity of its moral rules, and the options open to him outside his tradition. Any such attempt will be labeled as "immature", "unacceptable", "evil", and "sinful", thereby making the questioner feel guilty for having strayed from the "right" path.

Strong Rationality and Strong Autonomy

Putting together what we have learnt of rationality and autonomy, an indoctrinatory tradition is one that deliberately and consistently paralyses its members' development of *strong* rationality and *strong* autonomy. An indoctrinatory tradition is not necessarily one that undermines the conditions for its members to engage in internal questions about their tradition or exercise their weak autonomy. This is because an indoctrinated person need not be one who is unable to ask questions about the beliefs of the tradition or order his life according to a tradition he has accepted. While some deeply indoctrinated people may be so brainwashed that they have lost their ability to make decisions for themselves, this is not always the case for indoctrination. That is why, back to the episode "The Tribe" (refer to the epigraph in the previous chapter), the behaviour of Ingrid only represents one form of indoctrination, albeit an extreme one.

It should also be pointed out that a tradition that does not promote the activity of asking external questions about one's tradition is not automatically indoctrinatory. Neither is a tradition that does not encourage its members to critically reflect on their own tradition *ipso facto* an indoctrinatory one. Otherwise, many instances of enculturation (especially the upbringing of young children) and socialisation will be considered indoctrinatory (see additional comments in the next section). Rather, an indoctrinatory tradition is one that imperils its members' development in strong rationality and strong autonomy in a *deliberate, systematic, and sustained manner.* Furthermore, being a member of an indoctrinatory tradition does not automatically mean that that person is indoctrinated. What it means is that that there is a greater likelihood for her to be indoctrinated as compared to another person who lives in a non-indoctrinatory or educative tradition (I shall discuss an educative tradition in Chapter 5).

CONCLUDING REMARKS

In concluding our discussion on the theoretical framework for indoctrination, I would like to add two comments. The first comment concerns the difference between indoctrination and enculturation. Enculturation encompasses socialisation, upbringing of children, and other processes where a set of societal and cultural values are transmitted from one generation to another. The focus is not just on how human beings become members of their society, but members of their *cultural* community. This is in alignment with our conception of Islam as a cultural system of inherited conceptions expressed in symbolic forms for people to communicate, perpetuate, and develop their knowledge about and attitudes toward life.

The close association between "enculturation" and indoctrination was noted by Richard H. Gratchel half a century ago when he observed that some people regarded indoctrination as a necessary part of enculturation. He viewed enculturation as a complex process whereby a human society transmits its culture to its own members.[52] Enculturation is the process for a person to form what Pierre Bourdieu calls the "habitus"—a set of dispositions that structure perceptions of and actions toward the world but are themselves structured by the experience in the world.[53] In other words, the person is enculturated into a specific tradition with its own knowledge and knowledge representations. A distinctive feature of enculturation—one that may remind some people of indoctrination—is that the structuring during enculturation is unnoticed. In other words, enculturation necessarily involves "pedagogical partiality" where the control beliefs of one's culture are intentionally transmitted to members of that tradition.[54] This means that the habitus is associated with an acquisition of blind spots, ideologies, and prejudices of the field.[55] This uncritical acceptance of beliefs and values is especially applicable to young children where their limited perception and restricted worldview make them readily accept what is taught to and modeled for them by their parents.[56]

But the *mere* presence of pedagogical partiality, blind spots, ideologies, and prejudices of a field does not entail indoctrination. Conflating "enculturation" and "indoctrination" has the unintended consequence of making indoctrination unavoidable and enculturation undesirable. What is overlooked in enculturation by people who are fearful of indoctrinating children is that normal enculturation is not all about pedagogical partiality (unless one has an agenda to indoctrinate through enculturation). Rather, at the appropriate time, enculturation *should* include getting the children to understand the evidential basis for their beliefs, rationally reflect on their own beliefs as well as those of others, and order their lives autonomously as members of their tradition. In other words, the children need to be *educated* through strong rationality and strong autonomy.

Let me bring in the concept of control beliefs of a tradition to further explain the differences between enculturation and indoctrination. The process of enculturation requires the children or new members of a community to learn about that tradition's system of control beliefs. These control beliefs are held as psychologically strong beliefs in the sense that they define and frame the person's worldview and identity. These beliefs have become so habitual and automatised that they are taken for granted. But these beliefs should not be held in such a way that they become impervious to doubt: a healthily enculturated person should be one who proceeds to develop her strong rationality and strong autonomy. In other words, she is encouraged to inquire into, interrogate and even revise her control beliefs when the occasion arises (for example, when she is being questioned by someone from another tradition). This willingness and ability to critically reflect on one's tradition, however, cannot exist in an indoctrinated person because such a person holds to beliefs that are ideologically totalistic. In short, enculturation and education are necessary and desirable; indoctrination is not.

A related question is whether it is objectionable if an educator or parent extends enculturation to indoctrination by utilising indoctrinatory strategies for the good of the child, such as for him to be loving, kind, and disciplined. My answer is "yes" for two reasons. First, although the intention and outcome may be good, there is something disconcerting about the *manipulative* strategies used by the educator, such as social disruption, instilling fear and guilt, and censorship of contrary beliefs. Second, many of us would agree that an important educational aim is to nurture children to become moral beings who are capable of making informed and reflective choices for themselves. But the whole indoctrination enterprise contradicts this educational aim by having the educator make choices *for the child* (even if it is good for him), thereby paradoxically ensuring that one's child never grows up. That is why I recommend that we retain the pejorative connotation of indoctrination to remind ourselves that the problem of indoctrination is essentially a *moral* one.

My second comment concerns the concept of ideological totalism. First, a totalistic tradition is not necessarily one that demands total control in *every* aspect of the members' lives. That may describe brainwashing but not all forms of indoctrination. That is why I do not agree with Aziz Esmail who defines totalism as follows:

> [A] unifying system of thought that spells out everything, dictating everything, and makes, moreover, a very sharp distinction between its own world and other worlds, between what is deemed to belong inside and to lie outside its own sphere. Totalism insists that what belongs outside must not be let in, and what belongs to itself must not, at any cost, be left out. This rigid separation of the inside and the outside is a dichotomy found in all totalising ideologies.[57]

In my view, ideological totalism is not necessarily one that "spells out everything, dictating everything". As I have argued, an indoctrinated person that holds to beliefs in a totalistic manner may still be given room to make decisions for himself, albeit in a limited way, without the tradition spelling out and dictating everything to him. In addition, totalism need not insist that "what belongs outside must not be let in, and what belongs to itself must not, at any cost, be left out". Many totalistic traditions are willing to let in foreign theories and practices, such as the use of modern technology. What is true, rather, is that it prohibits foreign ideas and practices that are perceived to be antithetical to its own ideology.

Second, we should not confuse ideological totalism with *totalitarianism*. The latter refers to a political system where the ruler has absolute control over the people. This brings us back to George Orwell's *Nineteen Eighty-Four* and the television show *Big Brother*. While many totalitarian regimes tend to be ideological totalistic (based on our conditions of an indoctrinatory tradition), ideological totalism is not necessarily totalitarian. An (in)famous example is the Islamic school co-founded by Abu Bakar Ba'asyir in Indonesia, a non-totalitarian and vibrant democratic country governed by non-Islamic law. This school offers us an intriguing case study of an indoctrinatory tradition. This is the subject of the next chapter.

3   Indoctrination in Formal Education
The Case of Pondok Pesantren Islam Al Mukmin

I sat there feeling hot and uncomfortable. There was a strong sense of anticipation as everyone sat there waiting anxiously for the kyai (Islamic scholar) of a famous pesantren (Islamic boarding school) in Indonesia to arrive. I'd never met any kyai in my life and I wondered what the fuss was about.

Suddenly everyone jolted from their seats and stood upright in attention. An elderly man strolled into the living room. With a slight bow, he extended his hands gently to offer the traditional Javanese greeting to each one of us. When it came to my turn, I was so nervous I almost grabbed his hands—a social taboo no doubt. He carried himself with much ease and grace, as someone used to public adoration, and yet without a hint of being aloof or condescending. Half way through the interview—to my utter surprise—he stood up, took the plate of Javanese snacks from the table (we were all too shy to help ourselves to the food), and went around serving us. It was a humbling act that I did not expect from someone of his stature.

I was awed by him. There was something mysteriously special about him—a curious mix of spirituality and humanity. The experience was unforgettable.

When I later told an Indonesian friend that I have met the kyai, her first question was: "Did you feel his aura?" When I replied with a resounding "yes", she added: "That was how I felt when I met Abu Bakar Ba'asyir."

The above was one of my most memorable experiences in Indonesia. And what an apt way to introduce the appeal of Abu Bakar Ba'asyir to a non-Muslim like myself. Abu Bakar Ba'asyir is the co-founder of an Islamic school, Pondok Pesantren Islam Al Mukmin in Ngruki, Central Java. Despite his busy traveling schedule to other parts of Indonesia, he remains close to the school and has been a frequent preacher there. The International Crisis Group describes this school as an "Ivy League" for Jemaah Islamiyah recruits.[1] This reputation came about not just because of its association with Abu Bakar Ba'asyir. It is well known that a number of its graduates such as Ali Ghufron (also known as Mukhlas), Muhammad Musyafak, and Asmar Latin Sani were involved in the Bali bombing and other violent acts in Indonesia.[2] Abu Bakar Ba'asyir himself has been accused of being involved in a number of militant activities such as the 2002 Bali bombing and 2003 Jakarta bombing. At the point of writing this book, he has been arrested for allegedly leading a militant group in Aceh to assassinate the Indonesian President and carry out more violent activities.

Related to its link with militancy is the problem of indoctrination in the Islamic school, as noted by some writers.[3] The leading Indonesian Muslim scholar Azyumardi Azra asserts that this school, together with Pesantren Al-Islam in Lamongan, East Java, is responsible for sowing the "seeds of radicalism" in their students.[4] As we shall see, Abu Bakar Ba'asyir's role as a founding father and charismatic religious figure contributes significantly to the creation and perpetuation of an indoctrinatory tradition in the school. As Pondok Pesantren Islam Al Mukmin is situated in Ngruki and is more popularly known by that name, I shall refer to the school as "Ngruki" for the rest of the book.

This chapter (as well as the next one) reiterates and amplifies what we have learnt in the previous two chapters by focusing on Islamic education in Indonesia. It is helpful to recall that Islamic education is defined as any form of teaching and learning that is based on the principles and values of Islam. Formal education refers to schooling. Non-formal education refers to any organised educational activity outside the school system. Informal education refers to the teaching and learning that takes place through our daily experiences and interactions with our environments (see introductory chapter for details). This chapter will focus on *formal* education using the example of Ngruki, whereas the next chapter will explore non-formal and informal education using the case study of Jemaah Islamiyah.[5] Despite the classification of education into three categories (formal, non-formal, and informal), it is important to note that these three categories intersect and overlap in practice. As we shall see, these educational activities work together to provide a total and dynamic teaching and learning environment for the Indonesian Muslims, shaping Muslim traditions in the process.

In focusing on the indoctrinatory tradition of one Islamic school in Indonesia, it is necessary to make three qualifications. First, my concern is not so much on militancy but on indoctrination, that is, how the environment of Ngruki expresses the conditions of an indoctrinatory tradition. This means examining how the discourse in Ngruki seeks to implant control beliefs that result in ideological totalism in the students and others related to Ngruki. Second, I am not asserting that *every* student at Ngruki is indoctrinated, nor am I intending to identify who has been indoctrinated in Ngruki. My focus, rather, is on the *conditions* that create, sustain, and perpetuate an indoctrinatory tradition in the schooling context, in this case, in Ngruki. Finally, my spotlight on Ngruki does not imply that Ngruki typifies all the Islamic schools in Indonesia. A proper survey of the Islamic schools in Indonesia will be furnished in Chapters 6 and 7. But it suffices to note at this juncture that Islamic schools such as Ngruki that champion an ideology of armed jihad and antagonism towards non-Muslims comprise a "miniscule proportion of the whole".[6] Researchers put the figure of such schools at fewer than 20 out of a total of 50,000 Islamic schools.[7]

BACKGROUND INFORMATION OF NGRUKI

For a start, it is helpful to have a brief introduction to Indonesia and Ngruki. Indonesia is the most populous Muslim country in the world, with 203 million Muslims. However, it is not an Islamic state and Islam is not the state religion. Instead, the government officially recognises six religions: Islam, Protestantism, Catholicism, Hinduism, Buddhism, and Confucianism. The state ideology is *Pancasila* and contains five principles: belief in One Supreme God; just and civilised humanity; the unity of Indonesia; democracy that is guided by the inner wisdom through deliberation and representation; and social justice for the entire people of Indonesia. Islamic schools in Indonesia can be divided into three main types: pesantren (Islamic boarding school), madrasah (Islamic day school), and Sekolah Islam (Islamic school). I shall leave a detailed discussion of these schools to Chapter 6 and focus on Ngruki in this chapter.

History, Vision, and Mission

Ngruki is a pesantren and is classified by Jajat Burhanudin and Jamhari as an "independent pesantren".[8] This means that it is not associated with mass Muslim organisations such as Nahdlatul Ulama (NU) or Muhammadiyah who are the main providers of Islamic schools. Its independent status is also highlighted by the pesantren itself as it states on its website that it is an independent school that is not officially affiliated with any organisation.[9] Many independent pesantrens are known for adopting "Salafi" ideological beliefs. The term "Salafi" should not be confused with "salafiyah" in the Indonesian context. According to Martin van Bruinessen, the former refers to a Saudi-inspired Salafi movement where Islamic teachings are confined to the first three generations of Muslims in the time of the Prophet. The latter, on the other hand, also refers to "the way of previous generations" but extends the generations to the great ulama of more recent past based on the traditions of the Shafi'i *madhhab* (legal school).[10] Jajat Burhanudin and Jamhari elaborate on the ideological slant in Salafi pesantrens:

> From a religious doctrine perspective, these groups follow the earlier Salafi figures such as Ahmad ibn Hambal and Ibn Taymiyah whose

ideas were absorbed and developed by later figures such as Hasan al-Banna and Sayyid Qutb through Ikhwan Al-Muslimin in Egypt and Abu al-A'la al-Mawdudi through Jema'at Islami in the Indian sub-continent. The doctrines of Salafism as developed by these figures have become the main reference for these groups.[11]

Ngruki was founded in 1972 by Abu Bakar Ba'asyir, Abdullah Sungkar, and other associates. Originally located at Jalan Gading Kidul No. 72 A, in Solo City, Central Java, it moved to its current location in Ngruki in the village of Cemani. The school currently has about 1800 male and female students (*santri*) and about 250 teachers (*ustadz*). The students do not just come from the vicinity but from other provinces in Indonesia as well. They also come from diverse home backgrounds with their parents holding different jobs such as peasants, traders, state employees, and so on. Unlike a traditional pesantren that is led by a kyai (religious leader), Ngruki is controlled and managed by a director. Although Abu Bakar Ba'asyir is not officially on the school management, he is regarded as the spiritual leader of the school, and lives and preaches there whenever he is in town.

The school's teaching of shari'ah is modeled after a pesantren in Bangil that was established by an Islamist organisation Persis. What this means is that Ngruki replaces the teaching of classical *fiqh* (Islamic jurisprudence), which is common in many traditional pesantrens, with the Qur'an and hadith studies.[12] Following the practice of another pesantren, Pondok Modern Darussalam Gontor, where Abu Bakar Ba'asyir graduated from, the school expects all students, except those in the first year, to speak either Arabic or English, not Indonesian.

Describing itself as combining both traditional and modern educational systems, Ngruki claims that its goal is not to produce "*taqlid* Muslims", defined as Muslims who "accept and follow opinion/thinkings and religious practices without knowledge".[13] Rather, its aim is encapsulated in its motto of "Pious, Smart and Independent" (*Sholih, Cerdas and Mandiri*) and its vision to develop a generation of Muslims who are ready to accept and practise Islam universally.[14] The concept of "universal" (*kaffah*) underscores the vision that its graduates will obtain Islamic teaching that is comprehensive (*syumul*) and integrated (*mutakaamil*). It further states that its mission is to mould cadres who are scholars and intellectuals in the way of God; carry out educational and proselytising activities independently and responsibly to the people through its foundation YPIA; and implement an integrated learning process under the sole leadership of the director of the pesantren.

Curriculum

In terms of its curriculum, the school offers four main courses: Madrasah Tsanawiyah Islam (MTs); Madrasah Aliyah Al Mukmin (MA); Kulliyatul Mu'allimin (KMI); and Tkhasus (TKS). The core subjects for all students are *Aqidah* (Islamic faith), *shari'ah* (Islamic law), Arabic, and English language (see Table 3.1 for the subjects offered in the school). The first course, Madrasah Tsanawiyah Islam (MTs), is a junior high school level course that combines the school's educational curriculum with that of the Ministry of Religious Affairs (MORA). What is noteworthy is that this course is accredited by the state and prepares its students to sit for the national examinations. Besides religious subjects such as shari'ah and Arabic, students also study non-religious subjects (known as "general subjects" in Indonesia) such as English language, mathematics, physical science, social science, and economics. The school brochure states that this course aims to prepare students to have the basics of strong faith, science and technology, good morals, the ability to speak Arabic and English, and be ready to continue their education at the senior high school level.

Table 3.1 The Curriculum of Pondok Pesantren Islam Al Mukmin (Ngruki)

#	Madrasah Tsanawiyah Islam (MTs) (3 years)	Madrasah Aliyah Al Mukmin (MA) (3 years)	Kulliyatul Mu'allimin (KMI) (3 years)	Tkhasus (TKS) (1 year)
1	Aqidah (Islamic faith)	Aqidah (Islamic faith)	Aqidah (Islamic faith)	Aqidah (Islamic faith)
2	Syariah (Islamic law)	Syariah (Islamic law)	Syariah (Islamic law)	Syariah (Islamic law)
3	Durusulloghoh (basics of Arabic language)	Nahwu (Arabic grammar)	Nahwu (Arabic grammar)	Nahwu (Arabic grammar)
4	Nahwu (Arabic grammar)	Shorof (the morphology of Arabic words)	Shorof (the morphology of Arabic words)	Shorof (the morphology of Arabic words)
5	Shorof (the morphology of Arabic words)	Tahfidz (memorisation)	Tahfidz (memorisation)	Tahfidz (memorisation)
6	Tahfidz (memorisation of Qur'an)	Mutholaah (Arabic reading)	Mutholaah (Arabic reading)	Tajwied (rules of recitation of Qur'an)
7	Mutholaah (Arabic reading)	Insya' (Arabic writings)	Insya' (Arabic writings)	Tarikh Islam (Islamic history)
8	Insya' (Arabic writings)	Tafsir (Qur'anic interpretation)	Tafsir (Qur'anic interpretation)	Tafsir (Qur'anic interpretation)
9	Tafsir (Qur'anic interpretation)	Hadith (collection of stories on the words or deeds of the Prophet Mohammad)	Hadith (collection of stories on the words or deeds of the Prophet Mohammad)	Durusulloghoh (basics of Arabic language)

(continued)

Table 3.1   (continued)

#	Madrasah Tsanawiyah Islam (MTs) (3 years)	Madrasah Aliyah Al Mukmin (MA) (3 years)	Kulliyatul Mu'allimin (KMI) (3 years)	Tkhasus (TKS) (1 year)
10	Hadith (collection of stories on the words or deeds of the Prophet Mohammad)	Ushul Fiqih (principles of the Islamic jurisprudence)	Falaq (Astronomy)	Imla' (Arabic dictation)
11	Imla' (Arabic dictation)	Balaghoh (rhetoric)	Balaghoh (Arabic literature)	Mantiq (logical science)
12	Khot (Arabic calligraphy)	Khot (Arabic calligraphy)	Balaghoh (rhetoric)	Insya' (Arabic writings)
13	Tilawah (method of reading the Qur'an)	English	Tarbiyah wa ta'liim (teaching education)	Tarjamah (Arabic translation)
14	Tamrinat (Arabic exercises)	Mathematics	Tsaqofah Islamiyah (Islamic culture)	Muhadatsah (Arabic conversation)
15	Muhadatsah (Arabic conversation)	Physical	Various Tafsir (Qur'anic interpretation)	Femininity
16	Ushul Fiqh (principles of the Islamic jurisprudence	Biology	Ushul Fiqih (principles of the Islamic jurisprudence)	Indonesian language
17	Tarikh Islam (Islamic history)	Chemistry	Faroid (law on inheritance)	English language
18	English language	National history	Nidhomul Hukmi (manners in jurisprudence)	Sport
19	Mathematic	National citizenship	Tarikh Adab (History of Arabic language)	Know-how
20	Physical science	Know-how	Khot (Arabic calligraphy)	
21	Biology	Geology	Tarjamah (Arabic translation)	

(continued)

Table 3.1 (continued)

#	Madrasah Tsanawiyah Islam (MTs) (3 years)	Madrasah Aliyah Al Mukmin (MA) (3 years)	Kulliyatul Mu'allimin (KMI) (3 years)	Tkhasus (TKS) (1 year)
22	Indonesian language	Economy/ accountancy	Imla' (Arabic dictation)	
23	Sport	Indonesian language	Islamic history	
24	Social sciences	Arabic language	English language	
25	National citizenship	Quran and hadith	Indonesian language	
26	Akhlaq (Islamic morality)	Fiqih (jurisprudence)	Mathematics	
27	Fiqih (jurisprudence)	Akhlaq (Islamic morality)	Physical science	
28	Quran and hadith	Islamic culture and history	Biology	
29	Islamic culture and history	State structure	Sport	
30	Know-how	Anthropology	Know-how	
31	Femininity	Sociology	Social sciences	
32			Sociology	

Source: "Profile of Pesantren," August 2008, available at: http://almukmin-ngruki.com/index.php?option=com_content&view=article&id=46&Itemid=56 (accessed August 23, 2010).

Madrasah Aliyah Al Mukmin (MA) is a three-year senior high school level course and, similar to Madrasah Tsanawiyah Islam (MTs), adopts the state curriculum with a good spread of general subjects. Students are required to take the final state examinations set by MORA as well as the school's own final examination. This course aims to educate cadres, preachers, and Muslim intellectuals who are ready to continue their higher education in the university.

The third course is Kulliyatul Mu'allimin (KMI) where the goal is to educate cadres, preachers, and religious teachers who are ready to serve. Unlike Madrasah Aliyah Al Mukmin (MA) where general subjects constitute the bulk of the curriculum, this course comprises 70 percent of religious subjects and 30 percent of general subjects adopted from the national curriculum.[15] Graduates may apply to the Islamic University Medina Saudi Arabia where the certificate of KMI is recognised; alternatively they may sit for the state final examinations if they wish to continue their study at Indonesian universities. Assignments in the KMI course include analysing and submitting a report on various Arabic-text books (*Kitab Kuning*) in Arabic or English; teaching practice (*Amaliyatut Tadriis*) and public speaking in Arabic and English (*Al-Khutbah Al-Arobiyah wal Injiliziah*).

The final course, Tkhasus (TKS), is essentially a one-year bridging course for students who did not graduate from the school's junior high school. It is designed to prepare students for the Madrasah Aliyah Al Mukmin (MA) or Kulliyatul Muallimin (KMI).

AN INDOCTRINATORY TRADITION AT NGRUKI

The conditions of an indoctrinatory tradition are manifested in Ngruki. We can examine the school's aim to implant control beliefs in its students that result in ideological totalism in three aspects: the religious curriculum, the school's activities, and the school's hidden curriculum.

The Religious Curriculum

Although Ngruki follows the national curriculum for its junior and senior high school level courses, it is free to design and implement its religious curriculum and select its own teaching materials for its students especially during informal lessons. The school's religious content promotes ideological totalism through three inter-related control beliefs: the obligation to reject the secular state in favour of an Islamic state, carry out armed jihad, and be antagonistic towards non-Muslims. These teachings as well as the texts that support these teachings are not likely to be found in the majority of the Islamic schools in Indonesia.[16]

First, the students are taught to reject the secular state in favour of an Islamic state. This means that the students are not obligated to obey the Indonesian law or defend Indonesia as long as it is not based on Islamic law.[17] They are told that the state ideology of Pancasila should be rejected as it promotes democracy, which is regarded as a form of polytheism (*shirk*), a grievous sin in Islam. For example, the textbooks (1A and 1B of *Materi Pelajaran Aqidah*) state that:

> To act for reasons of nation is polytheistic idolatry, and polytheism destroys the values of the Islamic profession of the faith. Truly, a Muslim is forbidden to defend his country except if its rules and constitution are based on Islam.[18]

Correspondingly, the students are taught that they have a religious duty to establish an Islamic state. According to Robert W. Hefner, the same Aqidah textbook outlines three stages for Muslims to implement Islamic law: establish a community of believers that opposes the unbelievers; form a well-organised army; and learn how to use firearms.[19] The justification is drawn from Qur'anic verses, such as the following "Whoever does not follow God's law is an infidel".[20] Abu Bakar Ba'asyir who preaches regularly at the school also affirms the message that nationalism and democracy are violations of God's law.[21]

Second, the students are told that an Islamic state should be set up through armed jihad. Again, the justification is based on religious verses such as this hadith: "The core of human matters is Islam, while its pillar is prayer and the highest devotion is jihad (at-Tirmidzi)".[22] Works that exalt militancy and martyrdom such as *Tarbiyah Jihadiyah* by Abdullah Azzam, *Aqidah Islamiyah* by Abu Bakar Ba'asyir, as well as other works by leaders of the Ikhwanul Muslimin in Egypt such as Fatkhi Yakan, Syed Qutb, and Hassan al-Banna are introduced to the students during informal discussions.[23] One of the books is Syrian Brotherhood leader Sa'id Hawwa's *Jund Allah* on the Muslims' obligation to establish an Islamic state.[24] A graduate of Ngruki observes: "We were taught Islam is white or black, that it [armed jihad] is the only salvation there is, . . . the infidels and Jews would never stop fighting us till we followed their religion".[25]

Third, the students are also taught to maintain an adversarial relationship with non-Muslims. Textbooks such as *Al-wala wa-l-bara fi'l-islam* [Loyalty and Avoidance in Islam] by M. Sa'id al-Qahtani caution the students against befriending non-Muslims and even Muslims who are perceived to be less devout or belong to other persuasions.[26] An example of such a teaching is found in this textbook: "That is the reason God ordered Muslims to attack them [unbelievers] until truly the chaos that results from their actions can be wiped out, and truly the regulations that are applied to this world are only those of God's laws, *shari'a Islam*".[27] A graduate of the school points out that the students are constantly warned of foreign and Christian plots to harm Islam.[28] Abu Bakar Ba'asyir consistently propagates a "we versus you" mindset against the non-Muslims. For example, Muchammad Tholchah records what he heard from Ba'asyir in a speech at Ngruki on how Muslims should treat unbelievers:

> He said that there are only three possibilities for non Muslim: they obey our rule, they pay a huge amount of tax or they will be attacked. There's no other choice. For Muslims, he wrote, infidels are the enemy of God and believers. Accordingly, interaction and contact with them is based on vitriolic relationship. He stated that Muslims have to hate non Muslims and should not treat them as teammates, leaders or trustee.[29]

It should be acknowledged that Abu Bakar Ba'asyir has elsewhere added that Muslims may live peacefully with non-believers and even help non-believers in social matters. However, his caveat is that "those non-believers do not disturb the workings of shari'ah law, as long as those non-believers do not place obstacles before the implementation of shari'ah law and its proponents.[30] But what does he mean by placing "obstacles before the implementation of shari'ah law and its proponents"? For example, are supporting the current Indonesian government, singing the national anthem, or adhering to Pancasila considered acts of placing obstacles? The answers appear to be "yes" since Ngruki students have been taught not to support the current Indonesian government, not to sing the national anthem, and not to adhere to Pancasila. It follows that many actions of a law-abiding non-Muslim would be interpreted as placing obstacles before the implementation of shari'ah law and its proponents. It is therefore difficult, if not impossible, for the students at Ngruki to live peaceably with non-Muslims.

We can see from the above that the students at Ngruki are exposed to an indoctrinatory tradition that is underpinned by ideological totalism. A uniform monolithic ideology, based on the three control beliefs mentioned earlier, is consistently and deliberately imposed. *Thought-terminating and ultimate terms* such as "Islamic law", "infidel", and "polytheism" serve as thought stoppers to the students' development of strong rationality and strong autonomy. By pitting Muslims against "infidels" against a backdrop of an alleged conspiracy against Muslims, the students are obligated to *keep themselves pure* and separate. The division of "secular law" and "Islamic law" presents a bipolar worldview, coupled with the *mystical manipulation* of the students to believe that they are called to implement Islamic law through armed jihad. The religious language is likely to be accepted by the students as they are consistent with the students' Islamic faith and fit well into their existing cognitive landscapes.

The totalistic ideology is substantiated by *sacred science* to make it appear necessarily true, timeless, and universally applicable. This is achieved through carefully selected verses from the Qur'an and hadith, and writings of respected Muslim scholars including Abu Bakar Ba'asyir himself. It is noteworthy that Ba'asyir does not rely on his personal influence and authority in his teachings. Rather, he conscientiously justifies his every opinion with Qur'anic verses and hadith.[31] Such an approach serves to grant validity and universal truth to his proclamations. *Upholding doctrine over person,* the students are taught to interpret all events and experiences, especially those related to Americans, Jews, and non-Muslims, solely through the ideological lens of armed jihad and hostility towards them. The disparaging ways in which unbelievers are portrayed also incite the students to *dispense with the existence* of non-Muslims by vilifying them. The result is *milieu control* marked by a "single way of thinking among students", as noted by Muchammad Tholchah:

> They think that what the teachers teach them is the only truth. Since Islam teaches the followers to weight on [sic] truth, they will defend the "truth" that believe. For instance, Ngruki pesantren is known for the proponent of sharia implementation because they were taught that sharia is the only law should implement in the earth. Therefore, they will fight for the sharia by any means although they have to sacrifice their soul.[32]

The School's Activities

An ideologically totalistic ideology can be further translated into practice through the school activities. The criterion of *total exposure* is evident in Ngruki where all aspects of the students' lives are made public and accountable to their teachers. As a boarding school, Ngruki requires the students to abide by a very rigorous schedule. The day begins at 2.30am and ends only at 10pm, with every hour marked by a bell. Strict discipline is enforced; the students need a permit if they wish to leave the dormitory, are denied access to newspapers, radio, and television most of the time, and meet their parents only once in two weeks.[33]

The students are also strongly encouraged to join extracurricular activities, especially jungle activities such as hiking, mountain climbing, and camping. The purpose is for the students to internalise and apply what they have learnt through the physical and mental training.[34] While such a regimental schedule and demanding lifestyle are not uncommon for Islamic boarding schools, they provide excellent opportunities for the school leaders of Ngruki to implant their control beliefs and shield them from the outside world. In other words, the round-the-clock monitoring of and interactions with the students strengthen the privileged control beliefs and remove any beliefs that are inconsistent or do not comport well with the Ngruki's ideology.

The isolation of the students is helped by the decision of Ngruki's management not to participate in the activities organised by MORA for the Islamic schools. This decision is not surprising, given the historically hostile relationship between Ngruki and the state. Since the time of President Suharto, the school has been under the intensive surveillance of State Intelligence Agency (BIN). The involvement of its graduates in the Bali bombing and Abu Bakar Ba'asyir's run-in with the state further deepened the rift between Ngruki and the state. I have personally experienced the tense and suspicious atmosphere when I visited Ngruki in May 2010. Unlike the rest of the Islamic schools that I visited where I was greeted by friendly staff and allowed to move freely in the school, the security was very tight at Ngruki. All visitors have to be screened at the guard house manned by a muscular and fierce looking man who wears a perpetual scowl. After registration, visitors are directed to a holding room to wait for further instruction and prohibited from touring the school without permission.

The School's Hidden Curriculum

The third aspect of Ngruki that makes its environment ideologically totalistic is the school's hidden curriculum. This refers to "those things which pupils learn at school because of the way in which the work of the school is planned and organised, and through the materials provided, but which are not in themselves overtly included in the planning or even in the consciousness of those responsible for the school arrangements".[35] We can analyse Ngruki's hidden curriculum in three ways: the learning culture, the teacher-student relationship, and the influence of Abu Bakar Ba'asyir.

The Learning Culture

First, the control beliefs of the Muslims' obligation to implement an Islamic state, carry out armed jihad, and be antagonistic towards non-Muslims are reinforced through a specific learning culture. It is a learning culture where the students are not expected to question what they have been taught. A graduate of the school noted that the atmosphere at the school is "one of unquestioning obedience" and the students were trained "to be robotic and not to question".[36] It is easy to see how the development of strong rationality and strong autonomy is suppressed in such an environment.

Furthermore, the school environment is planned and organised in such a way that the totalistic ideology is transmitted both inside and outside the classroom. Posters and songs in Arabic, Indonesian, and English glorifying armed jihad are prominently displayed in various parts of the school. They are found, for example, on the walkways leading to the classrooms, on the walls in the classroom, at the mosque, dormitories, and even at the lockers. Some examples of the messages are "Allah is our Aim, Jihad is our Way"; "Death in the Way of Allah is the Highest Aspiration"; "Prophet is our Leader, Live in Prosperity or Die in Martyrdom"; "Jihad, Why Not?"; and "No Prestige without Jihad".[37] Reporters who visited the school noted that anti-Western and anti-American sentiments are infused into the school's daily teachings and routines. Not only are the students spotted wearing T-shirts with images of Osama bin Laden, Saddam Hussein, and the Chechen militant leader Shamil Basayev (such behaviour may be harmless in itself), they are encouraged to publicly express their desire to uphold strict Islamic law and defending their faith from attacks by infidels.[38]

Overall the school ethos is comprised of culturally sanctioned, socially standardised, and repetitive symbolic behaviours that serve to entrench the control beliefs of Ngruki's ideology. These discursive and performative practices also include what is deliberately omitted, such as the refusal to fly the national flag and sing the national anthem. Such deliberate omissions send out powerful signals to the students to delegitimise the Indonesian state and increase their resolve to implement Islamic law. Such a learning environment has a tendency to discourage and ultimately paralyse the students' capacity to question the religious content, consider alternative interpretations, and learn from other Islamic and non-Islamic traditions. Any student attempt to do the above is invariably viewed as "immature", "sinful", or "un-Islamic". Through the above strategies, the existing control beliefs are further embedded and new information from outside is dismissed.

The Teacher-Student Relationship

The second aspect of Ngruki's hidden curriculum is the nature of the teacher-student relationship. Referring to the major influence of pesantren teachers on their students, a graduate from Ngruki asserts that "indoctrination of jihad" comes through personal contact with some of the teachers.[39] He explains that these teachers keep a lookout for potential recruits who are religious, smart, and physically fit to join militant organisations.[40] He adds that he himself had been approached by a teacher to join Darul Islam, a clandestine movement devoted to establishing an Islamic state. His schoolmates who joined the movement went on to attend military training camps in Afghanistan and the Philippines as part of a Jemaah Islamiyah programme. These short-listed students were also invited to attend extra classes where their teachers would introduce and entrench the control beliefs on animosity towards the Indonesian government, the United States, and its allies.[41]

To further appreciate the influence of the teachers at Ngruki, we need to understand the traditional perception of Islamic teachers in the pesantrens. The first evidence of the high regard for Islamic teachers is seen in the Indonesian term *wong pinter*. Literally meaning "educated man", it was used historically to refer to a person who was educated in a pesantren. That was the norm until the 1950s when the term began to be applied to someone who had received a general education at secular universities.[42] Second, Islamic teachings instruct students to respect their teacher as highly as their father. For example, a hadith states, "And indeed, the man who teaches you only a word of religious knowledge is your father in Islam".[43] A pesantren graduate Zamakhsyari Dhofier elaborates:

> Within the pesantren tradition, students' respect for their teachers is absolute and everlasting, and must be expressed in all aspects of life— religious, social and personal. It is contrary to their religious values for a student to forget his tie to his teacher. . . . The student must show his complete respect and obedience to his teacher, not because of an absolute surrender to his teacher, who is regarded as having authority, but because of the student's belief in his teacher's sanctity; the teacher is a channel of God's grace for his student in this world and in the hereafter.[44]

Of special mention is the unique role of a kyai in a traditional pesantren. A kyai is a Muslim scholar who usually directs a pesantren and teaches classical Islamic texts to his students. The title of kyai is not self-conferred but bestowed by the community. It represents a public recognition of the authority of his knowledge and his status as an Islamic teacher.[45] Believed to be the inheritors of *Wali Songo* who were the nine saints who brought Islam to Indonesia, the kyais are regarded as the spiritual successors of the prophets.[46] The high status of a kyai is exemplified in the saying among Muslims: "Kyai should not pay homage to the government, the government should pay homage to kyai".[47] It is believed that some kyais are endowed with *karamah*, which are supernatural power or charismatic gifts possessed by pious persons; the kyais become the sources of *barakah* (holiness, virtue as inherent spiritual power) for their followers.[48] The concept of karamah may explain why some kyais possess an aura, the charisma to inspire awe and respect. That was my personal experience, mentioned at the start of this chapter, when I met a kyai who is famed for his aura.

A kyai is not just a religious teacher but a spiritual guide and model of the ideal Muslim for the santri (students) and community. He is effectively a little king (*raja kecil*) in his small kingdom (*kerajaan kecil*). He is given absolute power and authority and no santri can challenge the authority of the kyais except another greater kyai. A reverential attitude towards and unquestioning obedience to the kyai is one of the first values installed in every student of the pesantren.[49] This makes it easy for the pesantren to impose strict rules and regulations and ensure discipline and moral nurture in the santri. That the santri live in a boarding school where they are being supervised around the clock enhances the power of the kyai. The influence of the kyai goes beyond the pesantren; he possesses immense moral authority in the community who turn to him for advice on religious and personal matters such as property, marriage, divorce, and inheritance.[50] So influential is the kyai that he can shape the identity of the community through his ethical conduct and vision for the pesantren and community.[51] The emotional bond the students share with their teachers at Ngruki is also fostered through the yearly reunion for graduates, parents, students, and teachers.

Zamakhsyari Dhofier qualifies that the student's absolute obedience to the kyai and other religious teachers precludes following orders that are contrary to Islamic teachings.[52] However, most students studying in a pesantren are not knowledgeable or mature enough to discern whether their kyais' teachings are in alignment with Islamic teachings. Besides, many religious teachers including Abu Bakar Baa'syir himself are careful to justify their teachings based on religious texts. This means that many pesantren students are not equipped with the wherewithal to critically reflect on and evaluate their teachers' teachings within a learning environment that does not sanction critical questioning and thinking. Therefore, they are likely to accept what they have been taught and obey their religious teachers unconditionally.

The Influence of Abu Bakar Ba'asyir

Embodying the esteemed position and tremendous influence of an Islamic teacher is Abu Bakar Ba'asyir. He represents the third aspect of the hidden curriculum of Ngruki that contributes towards an indoctrinatory tradition. I am aware that Ba'asyir is not a kyai, and that there is no kyai in Ngruki (kyais are usually found in traditional pesantrens under Nahdlatul Ulama [NU]). As an adherent of a Saudi-inspired Salafi ideology, Ba'asyir holds that Islamic teachings should be taken only from the first three generations of Muslims in the time of the Prophet. Consequently he and his associates at Ngruki strongly object to the devotional and mystical beliefs held by traditional pesantrens, including the age-old belief that some powerful kyais possess supernatural powers that remain even after their death. But the point here is that Ngruki enjoys the cultural values and benefits the Indonesian Muslims attribute to pesantrens in Indonesia, such as the high status of its religious teachers and unquestioned obedience from their students. Having a highly respected, magnetic and likeable leader is crucial to successful indoctrination, as noted earlier. And here is where Ba'asyir's role is integral in cultivating and promoting the indoctrinatory tradition at Ngruki. In fact, I would argue that Ba'asyir's popularity and influence exceed those of many kyais in other pesantrens.

That Ba'asyir is charismatic and venerated is undeniable. He appears to possess an aura that is reserved only for special individuals who have the ability to attract and inspire. Muchammad Tholchah who has met Ba'asyir while living at Ngruki testifies to Ba'asyir's appeal. He observes how people who meet him were "kissing his hand while shaking"; they respect him as the "most honorable figure among the teachers", and most Ngruki students and teachers profess that they are willing to die for him.[53] An Indonesian who has met Ba'asyir told me that she was awed by his charisma—"It's like meeting your prime minister or the pope", she gushed. In my interaction with Muslim Indonesians, I have also noticed a widespread affinity for him, ranging from a quiet support and empathy for him as a perceived victim of American conspiracy and state persecution, to an outright aggressive defence of him and his school. For example, an innocent question from me on whether Ba'asyir or Ngruki was advocating armed jihad or militant teachings was often met by uncomfortable silence or vocal support for him and his school. Ba'asyir's influence extends beyond the school compound. His public sermons at Ngruki are usually attended by hundreds of people from the vicinity as well as faraway towns such as Klaten.[54] Ba'asyir is able to sway the public's opinion not only with his words but his actions as well. For example, by presiding over the funerals of militants who were killed by the Indonesian police, Ba'asyir indirectly legitimises their ideology and actions.

Adding to Ba'asyir's attraction is his humble demeanour and simple lifestyle. Parents who were interviewed asserted that they did not believe in the government's allegation that Ba'asyir was linked to any militant activities.[55] They pointed out that he was just a simple religious teacher with neither money nor property, incapable of possessing the sophisticated knowledge needed to lead others in militant operations. The parents were certain that he was just a victim of an international conspiracy led by the United States against him, of which the Indonesian government is an accomplice. The parents' loyalty towards Ba'asyir is strengthened by the help they have personally received from him. They noted that Ba'asyir had assisted them in addressing their religious questions and resolving their life problems, as well as educating their children in religious knowledge. All the above factors contribute towards Ba'asyir playing a central role in promoting and entrenching the ideological totalistic conditions in Ngruki.

CONCLUDING REMARKS

We have seen that what makes the tradition of Ngruki indoctrinatory is its intention to implant control beliefs that result in ideological totalism. This tradition is created and sustained through the religious curriculum, the school's activities, and the school's hidden curriculum. But not *every* student, graduate, staff, and parent is indoctrinated in Ngruki or indoctrinated to the same extent. While there are those who are successfully indoctrinated and ended up joining Jemaah Islamiyah, receiving training in Afghanistan or becoming suicide bombers, there are many others who are not indoctrinated. How do we explain the discrepancy?

I have earlier noted that the embeddedness of control beliefs depends on, among other factors, the existence and influence of beliefs that are not consistent or do not comport well with the control beliefs. Effective indoctrination requires the removal of all external stimuli and inputs from various sources that have the potential to be held as control beliefs by the victim. As much as Ngruki tries to control the students' thought and movements, they are unable to shield them *totally* from alternative ideas and influences. There are two specific factors that pose a continuous challenge to Ngruki's attempt to remove new and incompatible beliefs from its students: the incorporation of general subjects into the curriculum, and the expectations and demands of the parents.

First, Ngruki accepts the curricular guidelines from MORA for its general subjects. I have earlier outlined the main courses offered by Ngruki and noted that both religious and general subjects are offered. The inclusion of general subjects based on the state curriculum means that its courses, especially at the junior and senior high school levels, are similar to those in the public schools. Robert W. Hefner rightly observes that its curriculum and pedagogy are "fairly conventional modernist".[56] It follows that Ngruki is unable to censor new information that arises naturally from the study of general subjects. In fact, for students who take the national exams seriously so that they could obtain good results and be admitted to a secular university, they are likely to devote more time, attention, and interest to the general studies than religious studies. Hence, the implanting and entrenching of the control beliefs (the obligation to reject the secular state in favour of an Islamic state, to carry out armed jihad, and to be antagonistic towards non-Muslims) have to be done mostly outside the formal curriculum time. This makes the process of indoctrination challenging in Ngruki.

That Ngruki is willing to accept the guidelines from the state is due to the expectations and demands of parents. It has been noted that many Muslim parents, including those that are religiously inclined, steer clear of Islamic schools that do not provide knowledge and skills that prepare their children for social and economic mobility.[57] Official statistics since the late 1970s confirm that young people prefer mixed curricula madrasahs to religion-only pesantrens.[58] In the case of Ngruki, students and parents have opted for Ngruki not necessarily because of its Salafi ideology; a number are attracted to the school due to its generous scholarships and good reputation in the teaching of Arabic, English, and computer software in Central Java.[59] The school leaders of Ngruki are pragmatic enough to know that the school needs the continual support of the community in sending students to the school and participating in the school's activities.

Its desire to attract parents and potential students to the school is demonstrated first in its colourful banner at the entrance of the pesantren to recruit new students (see Figure 3.1). The image of Ngruki as a modern and IT-savvy school is seen in its provision for potential students to register online, printed in its brochure. Visitors to the school are likely to be impressed (as I was) by the glossy posters and 3-D model of the school's

Figure 3.1 A banner on student recruitment at the entrance of Ngruki.

Figure 3.2   A glossy poster of Ngruki's new building.

Figure 3.3   A 3-D model of Ngruki's new building.

future new and modern building as part of its expansion plans (see Figures 3.2 and 3.3). Ngruki also highlights the fact that most of its high school graduates have successfully furthered their studies at various state universities in Indonesia. It adds that most Ngruki graduates are accomplished in their chosen professions and "could be found at any sector such as multinational companies, banking industries, universities, business, engineers, doctors, consultancies, etc.", demonstrating that its graduates possess "broad knowledge of religion, science and technology (*Mustaqofu'l Fikri*)".[60]

The above two factors challenge Ngruki's control beliefs and vitiate the indoctrinatory efforts at the school. However, Ngruki is not the only site where indoctrination can take place. Abu Bakar Ba'asyir's influence is also not confined to formal education. After all, he is the spiritual leader of one of the most potent trans-national Muslim militant groups in the region—the Jemaah Islamiyah. The indoctrinatory tradition of Jemaah Islamiyah, and its relationship with Ngruki, is the topic for the next chapter.

4 Indoctrination in Non-formal and Informal Education
The Case of Jemaah Islamiyah

My love, death surely will come. What is important is how to die. A death blessed by Allah or a death that is a loss. I am doing this jihad because I fear God if I do not obey him. Pray for me to die as a martyr because to die as a martyr is the most blessed of death. When I tasted martyrdom this means I will bring 70 of my family to paradise. This is because when one is martyred Paradise will be filled with 70 of his family.

This love note is at once touching and perverse. It was written by Dr Azahari Husin to his wife and found only after his death.[1] An intelligent man, Dr Azahari had earned a doctoral degree in statistical modeling from Reading University. He subsequently returned to Malaysia to work as a university lecturer. After the arrest of Abu Bakar Ba'asyir in 2002, he co-led the Jemaah Islamiyah (henceforth JI)—the Muslim militant group that claimed responsibility for the Bali bombing 2002 that killed more than 200 people.[2] An expert in bomb-making and key player in the Bali bombing and other violent acts, Dr Azahari was killed in 2005 in a police raid in East Java. Many people find it hard to believe that a highly educated, socially respected, financially stable, and loving family man, in other words, "a regular guy", could be so taken in by the ideology of JI that he was willing to be a suicide bomber (or what he calls a martyr). The best explanation is that he has been indoctrinated.

That JI relies on indoctrination has been noted by a number of researchers. For example, Zachary Abuza states that JI "remains a strong organisation that, despite arrests of much of its leadership, is able to recruit and indoctrinate new members".[3] Kumar Ramakrishna claims that "ordinary young Muslim men are transformed into indoctrinated JI militants".[4] Rohan Gunaratna adds that "the group of JI's members was psychologically predisposed to indoctrination and control by JI's leaders".[5] Some family members of convicted militants in Indonesia also believed that their relatives had been victims of indoctrination.[6] The influence of JI went beyond the shores of Indonesia to other parts of Southeast Asia. For example, groups of Singaporean JI members were arrested in Singapore for their plots to attack key installations in Singapore. It has been reported that these members "had been indoctrinated by a charismatic preacher during religious classes in the privacy of JI members' homes".[7]

This chapter continues our application of an indoctrinatory tradition for Islamic education in Indonesia. While the previous chapter focuses on formal education, this chapter directs our attention to *non-formal* and *informal* education. JI offers a good example of non-formal education as it is a movement that offers organised educational activity outside the school system. Informal education is also present as JI is part of a loose network of like-minded Muslims who interact with, influence, and support one another in non-structured settings. I shall analyse JI in terms of its ideology, strategies used, network, and existing socio-political context.

I would like to preface the discussion by qualifying three points. First, I am not asserting that *every* member or associate of JI is indoctrinated by virtue of his membership. While research has shown that many members have indeed been indoctrinated, we should acknowledge others who are not victims of indoctrination. These people, especially the relatives of JI members, may have chosen to join the movement to support their family members.

Second, by discussing JI as a "group" or "movement", I am not thereby assuming that it is unified and monolithic. Noor Huda Ismail and Carl Ungerer correctly point out that JI is "no longer a cohesive organisation with a clear, unified leadership structure" due to pressure by police and security operations since the first Bali bombings.[8] It has also been noted that the leaders of JI themselves do not always agree or cooperate with one another. For example, Iman Samudra, when asked whether his understanding of jihad had been influenced by Abu Bakar Ba'asyir and four other JI leaders, replied: "I've never thought of the five people as being leaders or idols; and I've never consulted any of those five".[9] It is also unclear what specific role Abu Bakar Ba'asyir played in the militant activities of JI as he has denied any direct involvement in the Bali bombing and other violent activities. His associates claimed that the JI members who had carried out these militant activities actually belonged to breakaway factions and are not directly under Ba'asyir's command.[10]

I shall therefore treat JI not as a cohesive organisation under one leader but as an *ideological organisation* with decentralised but interconnected webs of groups, factions, local leaders, members, and other supporters. In tandem with this understanding of JI, I shall use the term "member" broadly to include both formal members who have been initiated into JI as well as associates and supporters. Despite the heterogeneity and internal divisions within JI, it is still possible to identify the core beliefs and practices shared by JI members that collectively express the conditions of an indoctrinatory tradition. The ideology of JI can be gleaned from a document "General Guide for the Struggle of Al-Jama'ah Al-Islamiyah" (PUPJI; Pedoman Umum Perjuangan Al-Jama'ah Al-Islamiyah), as well as the writings of key figures of JI.

Third, my focus on JI does not imply that Indonesia is controlled by JI or faces a grave "Islamist threat".[11] The majority of the 203 million Muslims in Indonesia do not support Muslim militant groups such as JI; a survey of public opinion conducted in 2004 shows that only 13.4 percent of Muslim respondents supported JI's programme.[12] Nevertheless, we cannot deny that JI has its supporters and that it employs indoctrination to recruit and control its members. It is therefore instructive to examine the conditions for the indoctrinatory tradition of JI.

NON-FORMAL EDUCATION: JI AND IDEOLOGICAL TOTALISM

JI was formed in 1993 by Abdullah Sungkar with his close ally, Abu Bakar Ba'asyir. Both had ties with Darul Islam, a militant group that aspired to establish an Islamic state in Indonesia in the 1950s.[13] There is no need for me to rehearse the details on the origin, growth, organisation, and activities of JI; interested readers may consult the corpus of literature on JI and other militant groups.[14] I shall instead examine the extent to which the environment of JI reflects an indoctrinatory tradition. In other words, I am interested in exploring the social process that results in ideological totalism through the text and context.

First, the JI ideology is characterised by *thought-terminating and ultimate terms* that aim to *mystically manipulate* its members. In her analysis of PUPJI, Elena Pavlova highlights its emphasis on the establishment of an Islamic state (*Daulah Islamiyah*) as a stepping stone to realising a global Islamic Caliphate through armed struggle (*jihad musallah*).[15] JI members are told that martyrdom for the sake of jihad is the ultimate obligation (*fardh 'ain*). So sacred is their obligation to perform armed jihad that it trumps even four of the five pillars of Islam. The only pillar of Islam that is not trumped by the obligation of jihad, according to the teaching of JI, is the confession of faith that none has the right to be worshipped but God (*Allah*) and Muhammad is God's messenger. (The other four pillars are to offer the five compulsory prayers (*salat*); to pay the obligatory charity (*zakat*); to perform pilgrimage to Mecca (*hajj*); and to fast during the month of Ramadan.[16]) Scott Atran, from his interviews with potential JI suicide bombers and their supporters, reports that these people believe that their duty to armed jihad cannot be postponed and surpasses all other commitments in life.[17] We witness this belief in Dr Azahari. Despite his great love for his wife, he chose to be a "martyr" because, in his words, "I fear God if I do not obey him". That he was willing to put his own life on the line based on his belief that he could bring 70 family members to paradise demonstrates the *milieu control* of the ideology over him.

It is no coincidence that Dr Azahari was greatly influenced by Abu Bakar Ba'asyir whom he has met. The *demand for purity* through a binary worldview is underscored in a sermon by Ba'asyir in Solo, Indonesia, October 18, 2002:

Allah has divided humanity into two segments, namely the followers of Allah and those who follow Satan. The party of God, and the party of Satan, God's group, and Satan's group, and God's group are those who follow Islam, those who are prepared to follow his laws and struggle for the implementation of Sharia, that is [Hisbullah]. . . . There is no non-believer who allows the development of Islam, who will allow Islam to be free, non-believers must work hard to threaten Islam and the laws thereof. This is the character of non-believers. Non-believers will always expend their wealth to impede the way of God, to impede the law of Islam. Non-believers will expend not insignificant sums to destroy Islam. This is the character of non-believers.[18]

In accordance with a "Us versus Them" mindset, Abdullah Sungkar and Abu Bakar Ba'asyir also contend that alternative systems such as democracy, socialism, Pancasila, capitalism, other religions, and even more moderate forms of Islam such as Sufi-influenced Islam are un-Islamic and destructive.[19] Adopting a similar bipolar perspective is Bali bombing mastermind Iman Samudra who proclaims that fellow Muslims are "our brothers and sisters" and "blood relatives" but Israel and America are "Draculas spawned by Monsters".[20]

This binary worldview has serious implications for morality—what is ethical boils down to what is dictated by one's ideology. It makes it easy for an indoctrinated person to *dispense with the existence* of other human beings. Every act, including killing civilians at tourist sites, and non-Muslim children and elderly persons, is deemed morally justified as long as it is endorsed by JI. As argued by Iman Samudra, Muslims are obligated to wage war against and kill the non-Muslims until they convert to Islam and the Islamic law is completely instituted. This reasoning extends to killing fellow Muslims. For example, when asked if it was right for his brother Iman Samudra to kill Muslim civilians who happened to be at Paddy's club in Bali, Kamaluddin defended his brother's action as such: "What they were doing in the immoral place like Paddy's club, it was their fault for being engage [sic] in immoral activity".[21] Another example is the case of robbery. Iman Samudra was suspected of robbing from a bank operated by Chinese non-Muslims to fund the bombing. He justifies the act of robbing from non-Muslims based on the Islamic principle of *al-fai*: booty taken by Muslims from the infidels in war though means other than combat.[22] Since Muslims are in perpetual war with non-Muslims, Iman Samudra argues the former are entitled to rob from non-Muslims as part of the war booty. He also encourages Muslims to engage in other criminal acts such as hacking and carding against Americans based on the same moral justification.[23]

The condition of *sacred science* is evident in the speeches and writings of key figures associated with JI. Let us examine the arguments of Iman Samudra based on his book *Aku Melawan Teroris* (literally "I Fight

Terrorists").[24] Iman Samudra prefaces his discussion by deferring to religious experts and authority. He carefully reminds his reader that his views on jihad do not originate from him but from those who have earned the right to do so. Using the argument by analogy, he explains that it is logical for any sick patient to consult the right medical specialist. For example, a person with a toothache will see a dentist, whereas one with problems in obstetrics will see an obstetrician. He then claims that "[w]e can carry this logic over into the context of jihad" and consult only specialists who are the "holy-war religious scholars (*ulama mujahid*)"—Muslim scholars who have fought on the battlefield of jihad themselves.[25] He substantiates this point by identifying "holy-war religious scholars" and historical events where such "holy wars" had been fought, such as the first attack on World Trade Centre by Ramzi Yusuf in 1993, September 11, 2001 attack, and the 2002 Bali bombing.

He then proceeds to expound the meaning of jihad, again by claiming that his definitions are legitimised by the consensus of the "pious ancestors" from the four schools of legal thought (Shafi'i, Hambali, Maliki, and Hanafi). He even lists some classical books written by Muslim scholars as additional references for readers who wish to read up more or perhaps to verify his teaching. He scrupulously cites verses from the Qur'an and hadiths to justify his argument that the Bali bombing is an act of jihad in the path of God. He relies on the principles of justice and the reciprocity argument to argue that the Bali bombing represents the Muslims' proportionate and reasonable response to the perceived years of oppression by America and its allies. He also refers to historical evidence such as the experiences of Muslims during the Prophet Muhammad's time. At the same time, he cleverly preempts objections to his views by raising the question of whether it is justified to attack civilians in the Bali bombing. He rejoins that the tourists killed in Bali are not really innocent civilians but active contributors to the war against Muslims. This is because they had voted for their governments that had initiated the war in Afghanistan and paid taxes that were used to employ the military personnel for the war.

Another related condition is to *place doctrine over the person* where all events and experiences are interpreted solely through ideological lens. For example, Iman Samudra interprets the whole of human history based on the various stages of jihad. That led him to conclude that we are now at the final stage of perpetual hostility and war between Muslims and non-Muslims—a state that is universal and binding for all Muslims. He also reduces complex political events such as the U.S. government's military actions in Afghanistan and Iraq to purely religious wars targeting Muslims. This dismisses a host of historical, political, social, and economic events and factors that influence political decisions and international relations. The arguments of Iman Samudra demonstrate what we know of deeply embedded control beliefs—they control and distort reality by rejecting new beliefs that are not consistent or do not comport well with the existing beliefs, and form new control beliefs to explain away the new inputs.

Total exposure is ensured by requiring, as a prerequisite to membership, potential members to pledge their allegiance (*Al-Bai'ah*). The pledge obligates the JI members to obey their leaders or risk committing a sin by dishonouring his pledge.[26] Specific discursive and performative practices such as using esoteric language ("JI-speak") and code names within a climate of secrecy add to a sense of sharing and empowerment vis-à-vis outsiders.[27] Further censoring new beliefs and fortifying the existing control beliefs are strategies such as physical isolation from one's community, regimented daily activity schedule, manipulation of emotions especially fear and guilt, reward and punishment, and carefully orchestrated social pressure. All these serve to culturally sanction and socially standardise the ideological totalism of Jemaah Islamiyah.

Likewise, the paralysis of one's strong rationality and strong autonomy is evident in the JI tradition. Such a tradition does not necessarily disallow weak rationality and weak autonomy. JI allows its members to ask internal questions such as questions on what jihad means and how it should be carried out by Muslims. That is why key figures such as Iman Samudra and Abu Bakar Ba'asyir attempt to delineate and justify their ideology. JI also grants weak autonomy to their members in deciding the extent to which they wish to be involved in its militant programmes. A noteworthy technique used in JI is psychological contracting. A leader, after a fiery speech, would ask members who have been all stirred up to indicate their preferred choice of responsibilities and capabilities, such as contributing ideas or dying for the cause (*istimata*).[28] This technique acknowledges that different JI members have different levels of commitment and willingness to make personal sacrifices for JI. The presence of weak rationality and autonomy reminds us that not all JI members are indoctrinated, and if they are, they are not indoctrinated to the same extent. Not everyone is prepared to be a Dr Azahari Husin.

However, what JI does *not* endorse is strong rationality and strong autonomy. JI deliberately and systematically shields its members from the outside world by strongly discouraging them from engaging in a critical reflection on its ideology, exploring alternative traditions, and ordering their lives autonomously based on such an informed and comparative process. On the contrary, the members' thought and movements are being monitored and they are taught that any attempt to question the JI ideology is to stray from the "right" path and would jeopardise one's chance of entering paradise.

Last but not least, the JI network is fronted by a charismatic, respected, and likeable leader. Abu Bakar Ba'asyir became the spiritual leader of the JI network upon the death of his close collaborator Abdullah Sungkar in early 1999. I have already noted the aura and impact of Abu Bakar Ba'asyir in the previous chapter. That Ba'asyir consistently advocates ideological totalistic beliefs, backed by religious justification, has been highlighted earlier. Furthermore, he established the Mujiheddin Congress of Indonesia to push for an Islamic state in 2000.[29] He also founded the Jemaah Anshorut Tauhid (JAT) in 2008 for the same purpose of implementing Islamic law across Indonesia.

Given the above conditions for an indoctrinatory tradition, it is not surprising that many JI members have been culturally framed to accept collective, high-risk, or violent action as meaningful acts of redemption. Having looked at the ideology and strategies of JI, we shall move on to see how informal education plays a big part in sustaining and extending the JI network. I shall specifically examine a network of like-minded Muslims and the socio-political context that facilitates the acceptance and growth of militant organisations such as JI.

INFORMAL EDUCATION

A Network of Like-Minded Muslims

An informal and loose network of like-minded Muslims is crucial to the existence and continual growth of JI. This network is formed, expanded, and sustained through kinship ties, educational institutions, social and political organisations, small discussion groups, and other social media. It is facilitated by new technologies such as password-protected websites and web forums, coded SMS messages, secure e-mail, and audio-visual resources.[30] Brek Batley claims that "most of the [JI] group's members have been recruited and indoctrinated through Islamic boarding schools (pesantrens), Islamic high schools (madrasahs), Islamic study groups (halaqahs), militant Islamic training camps, religious battlefields, and Islamic charities".[31]

Historically, Ba'asyir, Sungkar, and their associates had set up an underground structure of cells (*usrah*) modeled after the Muslim Brotherhood thought. The aim was to recruit members for ideological training and clandestine activism, and bring members together to guide and support one another.[32] The cell members who were united in opposing the Suharto regime in the early years became known as the Jama'ah Islamiyah. So important is networking that the PUPJI, which is the unofficial constitution of JI, underlines the need to "establish relations with other parties that may benefit the Jama'ah".[33]

The relationship between the underground structure of cells and Ngruki is an informal one. van Bruinessen avers that "some of the more serious students at Ngruki were also recruited into the usrah movement and some alumni played a part in extending the usrah network into other regions".[34] What is of significance is the creation and accumulation of network resources or "social capital" to connect the students and graduates to similar organisations and projects while remaining immersed within a specific Islamic orientation.[35] It should be noted that not all members of the cell share the same ideology or political inclination. Most of the group members are quietist and apolitical, as they are more interested in individual self-improvement; others however share Ba'asyir's vision in the establishment of an Islamic state and imposition of the shari'ah on fellow Muslims.[36]

Other examples in the network are organisations such as the Front Pembela Islam (Islamic Defenders Front), Majelis Mujahidin (Mujahidin Council), and Hizbut Tahrir Indonesia (Hizbut Tahrir of Indonesia), government officials, and student organisations such as the Kesatuan Aksi Mahasiswa Muslim Indonesia (Indonesian Muslim Students Action Front, or KAMMI) where its members have publicly supported Abu Bakar Ba'asyir.[37] As a form of informal education, the network of like-minded Muslims is potentially more powerful than formal and non-formal education. This is because it transcends the rigid boundary of organised educational institutions and structured activities to encompass the continuous daily experiences and interactions of a person with his environment. It is common knowledge that Muslim militants disseminate their ideologies and recruit members through various sites such as the mosques, universities, and especially the internet. An example is popular Muslim preacher Anwar Al-Awlaki whose sermons are readily available on YouTube (so are Abu Bakar Ba'asyir's).

It is necessary to highlight the role of family background, kinship ties, and community support to support and strengthen an indoctrinatory tradition. Research on the family background of militants shows that a majority of them come from a cloistered religious upbringing. It is no coincidence that both Iman Samudra and Mukhlas grew up in a predominantly Islamic environment and received a largely religious education, with very limited exposure to non-Islamic traditions and non-Muslim acquaintances.[38] Many militants also come from families with a history of resistance against the state and plots to establish an Islamic state, such as Darul Islam (DI) and Jihad Command (Komando Jihad) during Suharto's era.[39] It has been reported that militants on the run often married local women in order to fall back on family ties for protection.[40] A recent example is the case of Putri Munawaroh whose husband harboured slain militant Noordin Top. Her husband was shot dead in a police raid together with Noordin and other militants. When Putri was interrogated, she supported her husband's action and said that she had intended to die as a "martyr" by protecting Noordin.[41] Beyond the family support is that of the community. The ideology of an organisation is often spread to the villagers through the networks of Islamic schools, Islamic preachers, economic projects, and social services. A director of a pesantren that is linked to a reform movement that espouses Salafi doctrines explained how his organisation consciously identifies and establishes links with villages:

[F]or the function as a *dakwah* [propagation] centre, we would scout for villages that have not been represented by us and we would recruit students from these area and we would provide them with scholarships to study in this pesantren. And we would also send our graduates to these villages, for examples, we had sent our graduates to North Sumatera, Jembara, Bali, Tete, Sulawesi, Kalimantan, Irian Jaya. . . . In addition, we also have the social welfare and economic functions, where we have the Salam Co-operatives, which we use to help the economy of community. . . . We provide small capital to the community to set up their own business, especially to the members of the cooperatives. We have agriculture, businesses, etc. We also have a polyclinic where we provide health education, health management, medicines, etc.[42]

It is helpful to see how the conditions of an indoctrinatory tradition are manifested in the outlook and actions of the family members and community of convicted militants.[43] First, the family members believe that they have been chosen by God to be a *mujahid* family (*mujahid* means "struggler" or one who engages in armed jihad). For example, the wife of an Al-Qaeda's representative for Southeast Asia said that she believed she has been elected to show all Muslims that the truth of Islam is not merely about praying, giving alms, or fasting but most importantly, fighting in the way of Allah (*jihad fi sabilillah*)—a thought-terminating and ultimate term.

Accompanying mystical manipulation is the demand for purity. This binary view of "us" from "them" is seen in them rejecting the secular government and arguing for the setting up of an Islamic state. For example, a family member of convicted militant Hambali said that "if we obey the government's rules means we ignored and neglected God's rule, no place except hell for us".[44] The demand for purity also serves to censor new information that challenges their control beliefs and form new control beliefs to protect and further entrench the existing beliefs. Many family members refuse to accept that their kinsman has done anything wrong or has been indoctrinated. They defend their actions with new control beliefs such as "we are different from them [Muslims who do not support militancy] because we knew better about Islam" or "people did not realise their obligation of being Muslim that they have to conduct jihad as similar as my relative's did".[45] Through these defensive responses, all external questions, criticisms, and blame are brushed aside and viewed as originating from Muslims who are immature or inferior. This also makes it convenient for them to dispense with the existence of those who do not share their belief in militancy.

The condition of sacred science is also evident as many of them are quick to substantiate their belief in militancy through religious sources and moral arguments. A typical response to justify the violent attacks against non-Muslims is to cite the alleged example of the Prophet Muhammad in his war against the infidels; they also refer to Qur'anic verses that advocate "jihad as a blessing terror", such as the following:

Fight those who believe neither in Allah nor the last day, nor hold that forbidden by Allah and his apostle, nor acknowledge the religion of truth, (even if they are) of the people of the Book until they pay the jizya [tax] with willing submission, and feel themselves subdued (Sura 9: 29:72).

An accompanying condition is "doctrine over the person" where all events and experiences are interpreted solely through ideological lens. A number of family members justify the Bali bombing by noting that their sons/husbands/relative are helping fellow Muslims who are trapped in vices such as prostitution, human trafficking, and drug abuse. For example, the father of convicted terrorist Andri Octavia said, "Without the efforts from my son, perhaps many mothers will loss [sic] their daughters, therefore, people properly thank to my son for helping and solving the problem".[46] Or the family members will refer to the moral duty to fight for their fellow Muslims in Afghanistan, Iraq, and other parts of the world who are believed to be oppressed by the United States and its allies.

The existence of a network of supporters from the community also plays a significant role in strengthening and embedding the control beliefs in the minds of the family members of militants. Many of them pointed out that they have received empathy, support and even admiration from the community. A father of a militant said that his business flourished after his son's arrest due to sympathy and assistance from the community; Kamaluddin who is the brother of Imam Samudra said that many people hailed his brother as a hero in the tradition of Ki Wangsit who fought against the Dutch during the colonial period.[47]

It is important to note that the network of like-minded Muslims is not official, structured, and well-differentiated. Instead, it comprises overlapping circles and multiple traditions with heterogeneous members subscribing to and supporting ideological totalism in different ways and to varying extent. It is also necessary to point out that individual Muslims and Muslim groups may choose to connect and cooperate with militant Muslim groups, but they may not share the same ideology or motivation. Some may be a case of what Azyumardi Azra calls *nikah mut'ah* (marriage of convenience).[48] Hence, although it is important to highlight the network of like-minded Muslims, we should also acknowledge their internal differences, contestations, and negotiations, all contributing to the evolving nature of Muslim traditions.

The Socio-Political Context for Ideological Totalism

Besides a network of like-minded Muslims, the indoctrinatory tradition of JI is also enhanced by the social and political context. This refers to the backdrop that comprises the external and internal factors against which cultural framing takes place. Major external factors that affect the Indonesian Muslims include the negative impact of globalisation and modernisation on Muslims' lives, and the sufferings of Muslims in Afghanistan, Iraq, Palestine, and other parts of the world. Azyumardi Azra explains how many Muslims, when confronted with continued Western political, economic, and cultural domination and hegemony, "were afflicted by a kind of defensive psychology that led to, among others, the belief of the so-called 'conspiracy theory'".[49] Rapid industrialisation and modernisation have acted as catalysts to prompt many Indonesian Muslims to turn to Islam to make sense of a rapidly changing social and economic environment.

In response, Muslim organisations of various Islamic orientations have risen to the occasion and mobilised these Muslims to achieve their social and political objectives.[50] A key factor for the successful indoctrination of Muslims by militant organisations such as JI is its skilful manipulation of relevant socio-political factors affecting Muslims.[51] The goal is to induce fellow Muslims to accept the control beliefs of an internal conspiracy and war against Muslims (thereby explaining the global suffering of Muslims), and the corresponding obligation to carry out armed jihad for the sake of Islam. Noting that Iman Samudra has capitalised on the worldwide hardships of Muslims to incite terrorism, Muhammad Haniff Hassan avers that terrorist leaders will be less successful in gaining support from the people if there is no conducive context for their ideas to blossom.[52]

On the other hand, the main internal factors relevant to the Muslims are the general unhappiness with and distrust of the state, coupled with vexation over economic difficulties, social problems—especially rampant corruption—and the moral degeneration of young people. The Indonesian scholar Zakiyuddin Baidhawy asserts that the laws enacting decentralisation and eradication of corruption in 1999 have ironically been "the basis for new opportunities for corruption and abuse of power" in Indonesia through "the pursuit of personal benefits over the communal good and a lack of information, transparency and public accountability".[53] This concern with the moral degeneration in Indonesia is a recurring theme arising from my interviews with the religious leaders of the Islamic schools. A majority of them, when asked about the challenges the school faces, cite their struggle with inculcating religious and moral values in the young people today. A typical comment came from a director of a pesantren:

> [W]e know that the lifestyles of the society in Indonesia are becoming too liberal, too ostentatious, and too secular. Our current government is secular, there is no control and no boundaries, everything is possible. All these are extremely harmful for the students. . . . [W]e have to acknowledge the contradictions between the ideals in educational goals and what is happening in the society. You could just look at the drinking problem in the society—there are drinking binge among youth in

many places, in Cirebon, in Tingerang, and in Cianjur and even here in Garut. We know of the sexual crimes where a 14 year old girl was gang-raped by 14 assailants, etc.[54]

Another pesantren's director frankly acknowledges that the instilling of moral character "is still very weak" in his pesantren: "We claim ourselves to be religious but our behaviour is not religious. . . . [I]t's the biggest challenge".[55] Linking the rise of militancy to the social problems in Indonesia, a director of a pesantren opines that it is due to "the people feeling marginalised and feeling frustrated with the government. . . . [W]hen they see the injustices and corruption, there is some kind of vengeance inside their hearts".[56]

Worsening this worry is the general perception amongst the Muslim community, especially the Muslim parents, that the public schools are not doing enough to imbue moral values in their students. Consequently, an increasing number of Muslim parents prefer to send their children to Islamic schools that place a premium on religious and moral cultivation.[57] Islamic boarding schools (pesantrens) are especially valued by busy parents who are assured that their children are being supervised around the clock. This same reason was given by many parents who enrolled their children in Ngruki.[58] In a recent interview, they said that they are unhappy with the harmful effects brought about by modernity and technology such as pornography and promiscuity. At the same time, they have little faith in the public schools, particularly those in the big cities, as these schools have purportedly failed to prevent their students from turning to fighting, drug abuse, and free sex. Given their work commitments that make it difficult for them to keep a close watch on their children in the day, they appreciate the strict control, regimental lifestyle, and religious teachings provided by Ngruki.

The above external and internal factors have, to a large extent, contributed to more Muslims in Indonesia turning to their religion for the answer, represented by their desire for the implementation of an Islamic state. This is reflected in a recent national survey on 960 respondents from 64 pesantrens and 16 Islamic schools in eight provinces throughout Indonesia.[59] Expectedly, the survey points to the general low trust of the state and its institutions. Only a small minority trust the police performance (17.5 percent), the court (19.3 percent), the People's Representative Council (21.9 percent), and political parties (16.1 percent). On the other hand, there has been a steady increase in the number who support Islamic governance, from 57.8 percent in 2001 to 72.2 percent in 2006. The number of respondents who support government enforcement of shari'ah has also risen from 61.4 percent in 2001 to 82.8 percent in 2006. The respondents have interpreted the support of shari'ah as essentially that of the *hudud*, which is the penal code for public crimes. This is demonstrated in their support, in the same survey, for the government enforcement of hand amputation for thieves: an increase from 28.9 percent in 2001 to 51.9 percent in 2006.

CONCLUDING REMARKS

It is important to clarify that we should not conclude from the survey findings that shari'ah is equivalent to the hudud, or that all Muslims confine the scope of shari'ah to the hudud. On the contrary, the shari'ah goes beyond the penal code to refer "generally to the commands and prohibitions not just as they are found in the Qur'an and Sunnah but as they have been interpreted and elaborated in fiqh [jurisprudence] to be acted upon in everyday life".[60] This was attested to in the Gallup World Poll on more than 35 nations with significant Muslim populations conducted between 2001 and 2007; John Esposito and Dalia Mogahed report that there is "widespread support for shari'ah" as a "spiritual mental map that offers a sense of meaning, guidance, purpose, and hope": the shariah is viewed as a "moral compass of a Muslim's personal and public life", not a "harsh and primitive code of law".[61]

This broad and moral view of the shari'ah is echoed by a recent report by the Centre of Islamic Studies of the University of Cambridge. It avers that the shari'ah is a way of life, based on an ethical code that seeks to serve both a Creator God and His Creation. It adds that there is "a great deal in common between human rights declarations and the underlying objectives of the Shari'ah (*maqasid al-Shari'ah*), which seek to establish dignity, equity, and justice for all".[62] Rejecting the project by some Muslims to set up an Islamic state, Ishtiaq Ahmed argues that the Qur'an does not interfere in political questions nor does it lay down specific rules of conduct in the Civil law; the basis for an Islamic state is purely based upon "an interpretation of history rather than upon a strict interpretation of the core Islamic faith".[63] What the above shows is the different and competing interpretations of the shari'ah based on a plurality of shari'ah traditions. Just as there is no single jihad tradition, there is no single shari'ah tradition held by all Muslims across the globe.

This chapter highlights the indoctrinatory tradition of JI through nonformal and informal education as epitomised by Dr Azahari Husin, mentioned at the start of our chapter. A graduate of secular and non-Islamic education, he met Abdullah Sungkar and Abu Bakar Ba'asyir in informal settings and was subsequently indoctrinated by their totalistic ideology. His control beliefs of martyrdom and armed jihad were reinforced and entrenched when he joined the network of JI-linked Muslims and travelled to Mindanao in the southern Philippines and Afghanistan in 1999–2000 for bomb-making training. His control beliefs became so embedded that they replaced his previous control beliefs acquired when he received a secular education in Australia and Britain. And these very beliefs unfortunately led to his demise and the loss of many lives in Bali.

Our case studies of Ngruki and JI show that indoctrination is fundamentally about holding to control beliefs that result in ideological totalism. The approach to counter and avoid indoctrination, therefore, is to challenge and ultimately replace these control beliefs. Doing so will help students in schools such as Ngruki and movements such as JI to break out of an indoctrinatory tradition marked by a binary worldview, milieu control, demand for purity, paralysis of strong rationality and strong autonomy, and so on. While state legislation and tough legal enforcement against militants continue to be necessary, what is more efficacious in the long run are measures targeting not just behaviour but deeply held beliefs. After all, our behaviour is shaped by our control beliefs that function to interpret our "reality" and determine our relationships with others. What then is a better and more effective solution to counter and avoid indoctrination? We shall come to grips with this question in the next chapter.

5 Weaving a Different Net
An Educative Tradition

The astronomer Arthur Eddington once told a parable about a fisherman who had for many years used a net with a three-inch mesh. After never catching any fish shorter than three inches he concluded that there were no such fish in the ocean.[1]

We may find this anecdote amusing, but there's an important truth in it. We're all fishermen with our own conceptual nets. This net is our belief system underpinned by our control beliefs. Our net shapes our worldview, guides our interactions with people and phenomena, and ultimately defines our reality.

We have seen in the previous chapters that Ngruki and JI have used a similar net—the net of indoctrinatory tradition. This net has been weaved to catch the fish of ideological totalism. Like the wrong net used by the fisherman in our story, the net of indoctrinatory tradition distorts the reality for an indoctrinated person. Just like the fisherman who dismisses the existence of any fish shorter than three inches, the students at Ngruki and members of JI have cast aside important beliefs about non-Muslims, non-Islamic traditions, and their own rationality and autonomy. In short, they are trapped in an impoverished worldview with their rationality and autonomy imperilled.

To stop and avoid using the wrong net, we need to weave a new one—a net of *educative tradition*. Such a net is tightly and strongly constructed to catch fishes of all shapes and sizes in the ocean, providing a balanced diet and nourishment to the fisherman. In other words, an educative tradition seeks to nurture educated persons who live purposeful and self-directed lives within a religious worldview. In this chapter, I shall first discuss the salient features of an educative tradition, followed by an application of such a tradition in the Muslim context.

Although I will only focus on and contrast two traditions in this book (an indoctrinatory tradition and an educative tradition), I am not implying that all traditions fall neatly into one of the two traditions. In reality, there is an array of traditions along a continuum. Some may tend towards an indoctrinatory tradition because they express many conditions of such a tradition (see Chapter 2 for details). Others may tend towards an educative tradition for manifesting most of the conditions of such a tradition. Yet there may be others that lie in the middle of the continuum and are neither distinctly indoctrinatory nor educative. My purpose of limiting our discussion to two traditions is to provide a broad theoretical framework for us to understand the essential characteristics of both traditions.

AN EDUCATED PERSON VERSUS AN INDOCTRINATED PERSON

Let us begin by contrasting an educated person with an indoctrinated person.[2] We have already learnt that an indoctrinated person is one who holds to control beliefs that result in ideological totalism. In contrast, an educated person, while subscribing to control beliefs that she cherishes and seldom doubts, is not trapped in an ideologically totalistic worldview. Let me elaborate on the antithetical ways in which an indoctrinated person and an educated person hold their control beliefs.

The first difference concerns the *number of control beliefs* held by a person. An educated person necessarily holds to a greater number of control beliefs than an indoctrinated person. Rather than clinging to control beliefs that are confined to a "We versus You" binary perspective, an educated person holds to control beliefs that encompass multiple perspectives from a variety of disciplines. The greater number of control beliefs for an educated person ensures that no single control belief is held so strongly that it is beyond doubt and revision. The greater number of alternative paths for the flow of neutral activity from input stimulus to output response means that the individual synapse for the control belief is likely to be weaker.

The second difference concerns the *extent of embeddedness* for the control beliefs. We have noted that the control beliefs of an indoctrinated person are so deeply embedded and psychologically intense that they have dominated her entire cognitive landscape. To be sure, an educated person, like an indoctrinated person, holds to her control beliefs in a psychologically strong way too. This is inevitable as all human beings naturally acquire control beliefs that are strongly embedded in their cognitive landscape. These beliefs are often shielded from doubt and change, functioning as habitual and automised beliefs to shape our outlook and behaviour. However, what makes the control beliefs for an educated person non-indoctrinatory is that they are not so entrenched and held so tenaciously that they are impervious to question, doubt, and revision. In other words, they have not colonised a person's cognitive landscape to make her a "one-issue fanatic".

The last contrast relates to *one's response towards new information*. The control beliefs of an indoctrinated person are able to withstand external challenge, distort reality by filtering all incoming stimuli, and re-interpreting new information in alignment with and support of her control beliefs. While it is the natural characteristic of control beliefs to attempt to (re)interpret new beliefs in a way consistent with the existing belief structure, control beliefs are not necessarily unchanging and unchangeable. By being less entrenched than the control beliefs of an indoctrinated person, the control beliefs of an educated person do not stubbornly and repeatedly filter and censor all new information. Rather, an educated person, when persistently confronted with contradictory theories and evidence, is willing to engage with, reflect, and question her control beliefs. In the process of theory devising and theory weighing, an educated person may reach a point where she is prepared to revise or discard her existing control beliefs.[3] In short, the control beliefs of an educated person, rather than limiting her horizon, open up her intellectual vistas. She strikes a balance between holding to her control beliefs rationally and autonomously, and remaining open to alternatives and changes.

AN EDUCATIVE TRADITION

Let us understand an educative tradition by referring to the conditions of an indoctrinatory tradition discussed in Chapter 2. First, a typical member of an educative tradition may subscribe to *ultimate terms* such as "God" and "Truth" but they are not *thought-terminating* concepts that lead her to a personal closure. She is not a victim of *milieu control* where her control beliefs have drained the energy from all other beliefs and taken over her entire being. She does not cling to a simplistic and narrow binary worldview of "for us or against us" or *demand purity* by exalting herself and fellow believers as superior to those outside her group. There is no *dispensing with the existence* of others by virtue of their non-membership. Her ideology does not *mystically manipulate* her to see herself as chosen by God or some other forces to accomplish a "higher purpose". She is not a victim of *sacred science* and *doctrine over the person* as she is able to exercise her strong rationality by critically considering her beliefs, events, and experiences based on relevant evidence. At the same time, she is not a victim of *total exposure*; she exercises her strong autonomy by choosing and regulating her life based on a personal and active reflection. Overall, her development of strong rationality and strong autonomy are not jeopardised or paralysed. I shall further explain how an educative tradition is weaved by using three control beliefs: pluralism, strong rationality, and strong autonomy.

Pluralism

An educative tradition is one that deliberately and consistently develops a pluralist mindset in its adherents. Pluralism is a broad term that may be applied to different fields, such as political, religious, cultural, or epistemological. It is instructive to understand what pluralism is *not*. Pluralism is not *mere* tolerance: it presupposes but goes beyond tolerance to necessitate an appreciation of and active engagement with other traditions. Such interaction goes beyond superficiality to explore the similarities and differences between traditions.[4] Second, pluralism is not about compromising, being doubtful of, or indifferent to one's convictions. As noted by Nicholas Rescher:

> The fact that others may think differently from ourselves does nothing as such to preclude us from warranted confidence in the appropriateness and correctness of our own views. . . . Pluralism holds that it is rationally intelligible and acceptable that others can hold positions at variance with one's own. But it does not maintain that a given individual need endorse a plurality of position—that the face that others hold a certain position somehow constitutes a reason for doing so oneself.[5]

Finally, pluralism is not a theoretical knowledge or mere description of multiplicity; it also includes an attitude and a corresponding action to celebrate such multiplicity in life.[6] In short, pluralism influences a person in her cognitive, affective, and behavioural domains.

A pluralist tradition is an open tradition in the sense that it is *anti-totalistic*. This does not mean that an educative tradition does not subscribe to *any* ideology.[7] All traditions have their own ideologies that inform their adherents about themselves and the world, and govern their individual and collective lives. The tradition's ideology is transmitted through enculturation, schooling, and other forms of socialisation. But while an educative tradition privileges a specific ideology, it encourages its adherents to reflect critically on their ideology as well as consider alternative ideologies. Open to engaging in and learning from other traditions, it is adaptable to changing times and places.[8] Underpinned by pluralism, an educative tradition ensures that its beliefs are not impervious to doubt and revision and remain open to new inputs and external stimuli. This pluralist mindset is closely related to and supported by the control beliefs of strong rationality and autonomy.

Strong Rationality and Strong Autonomy

An educative tradition is one that deliberately and consistently develops its adherents' strong rationality and strong autonomy. It is necessary to reiterate that what is advocated here are "normal rationality" and "normal autonomy". Such an approach rejects treating rationality and autonomy as abstract and *a priori*. Instead, it situates these concepts within a convictional community from which beliefs develop, and emphasises human beings' dependence on others and/or some supernatural being.

I have already explained in Chapter 2 that strong rationality refers to the ability and willingness to justify one's beliefs by addressing internal *as well as* external questions. Internal questions are questions about one's own tradition which assume the truth of a set of beliefs that we acquire as members of a particular tradition. External questions, on the other hand, are questions directed at the beliefs we have taken for granted when we are addressing internal questions. Such questions critically inquire into the acceptability of our worldview against alternative worldviews.

A person with strong autonomy does not just freely accepts, is motivated by, and orders her life according to her tradition. She also critically reflects on her own tradition by considering, for example, its basic social structures and the validity of its moral rules. She exercises her human agency by being intrinsically motivated by the norms of her educative tradition. These norms are by definition broad, flexible, and open to interpretation, rather than specific, rigid, and dogmatic in interpretation.[9] These norms encourage her to define who she is and how she wants to live her life as a member of her community. There is no contradiction between her adherence to a tradition and her exercising strong autonomy. Her decision is based on a life she has chosen for herself after careful deliberation and thoughtful reflection of her own tradition and alternatives open to her. More can be said about the concepts, types, and processes of reflection, but space does not allow me to discuss these topics at length. I have argued elsewhere that reflection needs to go beyond technical rationality to include what Donald Schon calls "reflection in action". This form of tacit and intuitive reflection is salubrious for us to exercise our human agency and arrive at practical wisdom (*phronesis*). Terence H. McLaughlin describes this form of reflection as involving the "engagement of persons in activity with others which is non-instrumental in that it is not intended to realise goods 'external' to the persons involved but rather excellences characteristic of a worthwhile form of life".[10]

It follows from the preceding that a tradition is highly educative if it manifests strong evidence of pluralism, strong rationality, and strong autonomy. It is necessary, at this juncture, to make some qualifications about an educative tradition. First, not every adherent of an educative tradition becomes an educated person by virtue of her membership in that tradition. This same point was noted in our earlier discussion of indoctrinatory tradition: adherents of an indoctrinatory tradition are not indoctrinated just because they are members of that tradition. The point here is that an adherent of an educative tradition is *more likely* to be educated due to the favourable conditions that predispose her to education rather than indoctrination. Whether or not she is ultimately educated, and the extent of her education, depends on a host of contingent factors such as her family upbringing, the country she lives in, the type of school she attends, and so on. Second, educative traditions, like indoctrinatory traditions, come in varying forms and degrees. Distinguishing features, as I have highlighted, are the control beliefs of pluralism, strong rationality, and strong autonomy. Despite their differences, all educators of educative traditions are united in seeking to balance the needs to enculturate their members in their own tradition *and* equip them with the wherewithal to judge between different traditions at the same time.[11]

A question arises: how can one go about evaluating and judging different traditions? If standards of rational justification originate from and are imbedded in a specific tradition, does it mean that all standards of rational justification are equally valid and incommensurable? Responding to this question, John Wilson recommends that "transcendental principles of reason" be introduced for the child to evaluate the various traditions.[12] But what do we mean by "transcendental principles of reason"? If we are referring to principles of reason that are context-less and ideology-free, such principles do not exist. I have argued that rationality cannot exist in a pure form independent of a specific social milieu. James M. Jasper rightly posits that one's culture not only bounds rationality but defines it by providing the context and criteria for recognising and judging rationality.[13]

A better interpretation of "transcendental principles of reason", in my view, is to see them as principles of reason that are shared by ("transcend") two or more traditions. These principles should be both procedural and substantive. Procedural principles are rules that tell us whether an argument is valid and acceptable. Examples are principles to help us to construct deductive and inductive reasoning, identify fallacies, and so on—in short, what undergraduates typically learn in a course on logic. On the other hand, substantive principles are concerned with the content of the argument. They tell us what "moral values" are (e.g. justice, fairness, and goodness), and how these values should be interpreted and put into practice. Procedural principles in themselves are insufficient for members of different traditions to engage in deep, meaningful, and sustained intellectual discourses. Often, when two opposing traditions collide, it is not because they disagree on *procedural* principles, such as whether analogical reasoning is used or whether perceptual evidence is employed. Rather, their fundamental disagreement is about the *content* of the arguments. More precisely, they differ not on whether moral values such as "justice" and "goodness" are important (almost all traditions would agree that they are), but on the precise meanings of these values (e.g. is a "just society" equivalent to an Islamic state?) and the application of these values (e.g. is killing civilians by Muslim militants an act of justice?).

That is where substantive principles come in to build bridges between traditions. I propose that we supplement procedural principles with substantive principles that *already* exist between two traditions. It is in this sense that these principles are "transcendental principles of reason". Let me give an example. Muslims from two different jihad traditions may disagree on the meanings and application of jihad. However, they are likely to rely on the same authoritative texts and use the same "theological and juristic approach" in interpreting the Qur'an and hadiths. According to Muhammad Haniff Hassan, this methodology is based primarily on three important sciences popularly known as *Usul Fiqh*, *Usul Tafsir*, and *Usul Hadith*.[14] The two jihad traditions may also share relevant substantive principles, such as agreeing that jihad refers to defensive and not offensive struggle and does not apply to non-combatants. Mediated by "transcendental" procedural, and substantive principles, the Muslims from these two traditions could then engage in a critical study of jihad and resolve any disagreements between them. The same may apply to Muslim and non-Muslim traditions that share transcendental principles of reason.

EDUCATIVE MUSLIM TRADITIONS

Against a backdrop of an educative tradition, let us turn our attention to the Muslim context. Muslims have always placed a high premium on Islamic education. Islamic education through the learning of the Qur'an can be traced back to the Prophet Muhammad's time. Subsequently, informal religious instruction took place in sites such as mosques, palaces, and homes of learned people, leading to the rise of organised schools with established curricula in the eleventh century.[15] An *educative Muslim tradition* is an open tradition that deliberately and consistently develops its members' pluralist mindset, strong rationality, and strong autonomy. Let us look at these three control beliefs in the Muslim context.

Pluralism

Pluralism means not insisting that one's Muslim tradition has the monopoly of truth. Rather than castigating other traditions (Muslim and non-Muslim), a pluralist Muslim tradition is open to alternatives and is adaptable to changing times and places. Leading Muslim scholars who have advocated pluralism include Fathi Osman, Khalid Abu El Fadl, Mahmoud Ayoub, Azyumardi Azra, and M. Fethullah Gulen. A Muslim educative tradition may be pluralist in different aspects, such as in the political, social, and religious spheres. An example of political pluralism is democratic pluralism where Islamist political parties of an educative tradition campaign for votes through peaceful means.[16] Another example is epistemological pluralism where a Muslim tradition embraces knowledge from all sources and encourages its students to study both religious and non-religious subjects. Epistemological pluralism is not new in Muslim traditions. Khaled Abou El Fadl points out that Islamic epistemology has traditionally accepted discordant views and Islamic civilisation has "produced a moral and humanistic tradition that preserved Greek philosophy, and generated much science, art, and socially benevolent thought".[17] Historical examples of pluralism between Muslims and non-Muslims include the city of Baghdad in the eighth and ninth centuries, and Cordoba in Muslim Spain in the ninth and tenth centuries.[18] I shall return to the topic of epistemological pluralism in Indonesia in the next chapter.

In this section, I would like to focus on *religious pluralism* as it is most relevant to our discussion on religious indoctrination. Abdulaziz Sachedina elaborates:

Religious pluralism calls for active engagement with the religious other not merely to tolerate, but to understand. Toleration does not require active engagement with the other. It makes no inroads on mutual ignorance. In a world in which religious differences historically have been manipulated to burn bridges between communities, recognition and understanding of religious differences require us to enter into knowledgeable dialogue with one another, even in the face of major disagreements. A morally and spiritually earnest search for common undertakings within our particular religious traditions can lead the way for society as a whole. Religious pluralism can function as a working paradigm for a democratic, social pluralism in which people of diverse religious backgrounds are willing to form a community of global citizens.[19]

A pluralist mindset should be inculcated in Muslims for them to be open to other Muslim traditions as well as non-Islamic traditions. The former means that Muslims should be tolerant and appreciate other religious orientations and schools of thought within the Islamic faith. For instance, Sunni Muslims could go beyond their usual Ash‘ari theology and Shafi‘i legal school of thought (*madhhab*) to explore alternatives such as the Hanafi law school, the theological school of Maturidis, Sufism, Shi’i, and Mu’tazila schools of thought. For example, in the case of rituals, Muslims in the Shafi‘i school generally believe that the recitation of the chapter called the "Opening" is an obligation in every ritual prayer, including congregational prayers. But the recitation of any liturgical passage in a congregational prayer comes close to invalidating one's prayers for the Hanafi law school.[20] A pluralist perspective is exemplified by jurist Imam al-Shaf’i who asserted: "My opinions are correct but can be wrong while another imam's opinions are wrong but may be true".[21]

It is also important for Muslims to consider and learn from non-Islamic traditions. Irfan Abubakar avers that Islam is a religion sent by God as proof of His mercy to humanity and the entire creations (*rahmatan lil ‘alamin*); hence it should reject a closed attitude towards those who hold differing opinions on the basis.[22] Azyumardi Azra asserts that Islam, as a religion of compassion, is "hospitable and peaceful to all groups—teaches a human ethic that strongly stresses universal humanity (*al-ukhuwwah al-insaniyyah*)".[23] Kemal Ataman points out that an attitude of religious pluralism finds support in Qur'anic verses, such as the following:

Those who believe [Muslims], the Jews, the Christians, and the Sabeans—whosoever believe in God and the Last Day and do good deeds, they shall have their reward from their Lord, shall have nothing to fear, nor shall they come to grief. (Qur'an 2:62)[24]

A report by the Islamic centre of the University of Cambridge makes the same point, citing this verse:

> Let there be no compulsion in religion: Truth stands out clear from Error: whoever rejects evil and believes in Allah hath grasped the most trustworthy handhold, that never breaks. And Allah heareth and knoweth all things. (Qur'an 2: 256)[25]

Another Muslim scholar is Nurcholish Madjid who maintains that religious pluralism is "consistent with the idea of progress, is an open mental attitude, in the form of a readiness to accept and to take (temporal) values from *whatever source* as long as they contain truth".[26] Madjid even goes as far as arguing that Muslims should accept "people of the book"—defined by him as comprising Christians, Jews, Hindus, and Buddhists—as brothers in faith with equal rights.[27] Ataman adds that the Hanafi school of law has implicitly included Hinduism and Buddhism within the category of the "people of the book" in legal practice.[28] It should be qualified that such a radical stand by Madjid and others, although salutary for religious harmony, is not necessary for religious pluralism to take place in a Muslim educative tradition. In the context of avoiding indoctrination, what is required, at the minimum level, is to eschew hostility and violence towards non-Muslims, and promote religious pluralism that propels Muslims to establish peace and harmony with non-Muslims.

Pluralism in Action: Back to Jihad

To further understand how the control belief of pluralism functions in an educative tradition, it is helpful to give an example by returning to the topic of the justifiability of the Bali bombing (see Chapter 1 for details). I shall explain how the control belief of pluralism functions to direct Muslims to accept a conclusion of jihad that is diametrically opposite to that of Iman Samudra.[29] I shall refer to the views of Muhammad Haniff Hassan, a trained Islamic religious teacher (ustaz) in Singapore who has written a book *Unlicensed to Kill: Countering Iman Samudra's Justification for the Bali Bombing*.[30] Hassan's views epitomises an educative Muslim tradition that promotes religious pluralism between Muslims and non-Muslims.

As shown in Table 5.1, Hassan rejects the theory that the Bali bombing is justified. He does not view the Bali bombing as an example of fighting in the way of God (jihad fi sabilillah). Rather, he regards it as an unjustified violent act that is un-Islamic. The tourists who were attacked should not be regarded as enemies of and conspirators against Islam and Muslims, but as innocent civilians.

Hassan's data beliefs are conditioned by his data-background belief on what jihad fi sabilillah is. He maintains that the primary function of jihad is "not to fight non-Muslims because of difference in faith but to establish justice and eradicate oppression and jihad in Islam can only be waged against

Table 5.1   A Comparison of Two Jihad Traditions on the Justifiability of the Bali Bombing

Theory: The Bali bombing is justified.

Accepts the theory	Rejects the theory
Data beliefs: Data about the Bali bombing such as: what happened where it happened when it happened how it happened why it happened (a case of jihad fi sabilillah: fighting in the way of God) who were being attacked (Americans and their allies who are guilty of attacking Muslims in Afghanistan in 2001) who were the attackers (martyrs)	Data beliefs: Data about the Bali bombing such as: what happened where it happened when it happened how it happened why it happened (a violent act committed by professed Muslims who have the wrong understanding of jihad fi sabilillah) who were being attacked (innocent tourists who are civilians) who were the attackers (perpetrators of violence/suicide bombers)
Data-background beliefs: Belief about jihad fi sabilillah: an Islamic act of retaliation against infidels who have transgressed the limit, and contributed to the war against Muslims.	Data-background beliefs: Belief about jihad fi sabilillah: war against non-Muslims to be carried out only under specific conditions, and should not involve civilians such as tourists.
Control belief: The relationship that should exist between Muslims and non-Muslims is armed jihad and war.	Control belief: The relationship that should exist between Muslims and non-Muslims is peace and harmony.

those who wage war".[31] This war against non-Muslims is to be carried out only under specific conditions. For instance, armed jihad can only be decreed and carried out by *Ulil Amri* or persons of appropriate authority, not by individuals such as Iman Samudra or militant groups such as JI. It should also not be directed at civilians and non-combatants such as tourists, and certainly not targeted at all non-Muslims. Hassan cites this hadith to support his view on the prohibition of killing non-combatants such as the elderly, the sick, young children, and women:

> The Prophet said; "Do not kill the elderly who are sick, young children or women and do not behave excessively, accumulating the spoils of war. Be kind, for Allah loves those who are kind." (Narrated by Abu Daud)

His data-background beliefs are in turn conditioned by his control belief on religious pluralism. Hassan avers that the principle of pluralism is based on God's will in allowing a plurality of faiths and cultures so that human beings can get to know one another and do good for one another. He cites these verses:

O men! Behold, We have created you all out of a male and a female, and have made you into nations and tribes, so that you might come to know one another. Verily; the noblest of you in the sight of God is the one who is most deeply conscious of Him. Behold, God is all-knowing, all-aware. (The Qur'an, 49:13)

As for such [of the unbelievers] as do not fight against you on account of [your] faith, and neither drive you forth from your homelands, God does not forbid you to show them kindness and to behave towards them with full equity: for, verily, God loves those who act equitably. (The Quran, 60:8)

According to Hassan, Islam is a religion that loves peace, is revealed as a mercy to all creations, and honours and respects all mankind. Some supporting verses quoted by him are:

But if they incline to peace, incline thou to it as well, and place thy trust in God: verily, He alone is all-hearing, all knowing! (The Qur'an, 8:61)

And [thus, O Prophet,] We have sent thee as [an evidence of Our] grace towards all the worlds. (The Qur'an, 21:107)

Those who do not love his fellow mankind, Allah does not love him. (Narrated by Al-Bukhari and Muslim)

Now indeed, We have conferred dignity on the children of Adam. (The Qur'an, 17:70)

Guided by his control belief of religious pluralism, he refutes Iman Samudra's proposition of a perpetual hostility and war between non-Muslims and Muslims. He maintains that Muslims should show kindness towards non-Muslims unless they are being attacked, based on verses such as the following:

As for such [of the unbelievers] as do not fight against you on account of [your] faith, and neither drive you forth from your homelands, God does not forbid you to show them kindness and to behave towards them with full equity: For, verily, God loves those who act equitably. God only forbids you to turn in friendship towards such as those who fight against you because of [your] faith, and drive you forth from your homelands, or aid [others] in driving you forth: And as for those (from among you) who turn towards them in friendship, it is they, they who are the wrongdoers! (The Qur'an, 60:8–9)

Hassan of course is not the only Muslim scholar who argues for a pluralist attitude towards non-Muslims. Azyumardi Azra emphasises the same point in his interpretation of jihad:

> Islam urges its community of believers to struggle to create peace, justice and respect. But that struggle must not be undertaken by means of violence, terrorism and war. Each struggle for justice, peace and harmony must start from the premise that justice and peace are universal values which have to be upheld and defended by humankind.[32]

The preceding shows that a person's control beliefs directly influence and define his worldview and actions. These beliefs prompt members of a tradition to accept or reject certain beliefs, and provide the conditions for them to view other beliefs as data beliefs and data-background beliefs on a given occasion. It is therefore crucial for Muslims to adhere to a Muslim tradition that is educative—an open tradition that deliberately and consistently nurtures Muslims who embrace the control belief of pluralism.

Strong Rationality and Strong Autonomy

Going hand in hand with pluralism are strong rationality and strong autonomy. In line with our notions of "normal rationality" and "normal autonomy", we need to situate rationality and autonomy within a Muslim tradition. Zafar Alam avers that a spirit of inquiry is important for Muslims to observe and learn from the phenomena around them, but it should be located "within the fold of the Islamic law".[33] Muslim leaders who convened at four world conferences on Islamic education from 1977 to 1982 recommended that Muslim students should "think precisely and logically but let their thoughts be governed by their spiritual realisation of truth as found in the Qur'an and the Sunnah so that their intelligence is guided in proper channels and does not stray".[34] Muslims support the value of rationality based on an Islamic view of human beings as rational. Syed Muhammad Naquib al-Attas states that Islam defines a human being as a rational being with "the capacity for understanding speech, and the power responsible for the formulation of meaning—which involves judgement, discrimination, distinction and clarification, and which has to do with the articulation of words or expressions in meaningful pattern".[35] Commenting on the need for the development of intellectual abilities, Tariq Ramadan asserts that "to be Muslim entails struggling to increase one's abilities, seeking tirelessly to know more, to the extent that one might say in the light of the Islamic sources that, when it comes to the cultural dimension 'to be Muslim is to learn'".[36]

Strong rationality is cultivated when Muslims are able and willing to justify their beliefs by addressing both internal and external questions about their tradition. In the case of schooling, an Islamic school should provide a learning environment where the students do not learn just by rote or memorisation but actively understand and interrogate what they have learnt. They need to be equipped with the intellectual tools of inquiring, reflecting, questioning, and deliberating. These tools empower them to search for the evidential justification for their beliefs, integrate their knowledge in a conceptual scheme, and compare their worldview against alternative worldviews.

Besides rationality, the value of autonomy is in tandem with the Islamic belief that Muslims are to fulfil their role as vicegerent. The Qur'an states that "It is He Who has made you [His] agents, inheritors of the earth (khala'if); He has raised you in ranks, some above others, that He may try you in the gifts He has given you".[37] The very concept of vicegerent presupposes the exercise of one's free will to execute God's intent and rules on earth, as noted by Abd al Majid al Najjar:

> Trust on the basis of free will is the only path for growth and perfection. Being given the choice to follow the self's desires and be subjected to base (lower) motives, or to pursue the divine instructions and long for higher aspirations, enables individuals to overcome the soul's *hawa* [vain or egotistical desire, individual passion, and impulsiveness] and achieve sublimation. It is a kind of psychological jihad leading to gradual growth and perfection through interacting with the universe, during which human beings observe Allah's injunctions by enjoining right or refraining from wrong. This jihad climaxes with the realisation of *khalifah* [stewardship].[38]

An educative Islamic tradition fosters strong autonomy by encouraging its members to making their own choices and ordering their lives based on a critical reflection of their tradition. Intrinsically motivated by norms rather than purely external rewards and punishments, an educative Muslim tradition encourages its members to define their own identity and life goals. Within this context, Islamic education should aim at helping "all Muslims to enter into personal growth and, consequently, to become autonomous in their lives, their choices, and more generally, in the management of their freedom".[39]

CONCLUDING REMARKS

The contrasting views among Muslims on jihad represent the diversity and contestations of views within Muslim traditions. Such disagreement is not new: there has been no consensus, from the past to the present time, among Muslim scholars on a number of other key Islamic issues such as the final stage of jihad, *amaliyat istisyhadiyah* (martyrdom operation) and *harbis* (non-Muslims at war).[40] That a plethora of incompatible views from Muslim scholars exist, demonstrates the dynamism, conflicts, and power struggle within and across the Muslim traditions. It also shows that Islamic texts are "polyvocal" with Muslim scholars disagreeing with one another and propagating their privileged interpretations and application of Islamic beliefs and practices, due to different control beliefs at work.[41]

We have spent this chapter weaving a new and better net. I have explained how the net of an educative tradition is undergirded by the control beliefs of pluralism, strong rationality, and strong autonomy. Two caveats should be added on the characteristics of an educative Muslim tradition. First, the willingness to learn from different and competing alternatives should not extend to Muslim traditions that are indoctrinatory. While Muslims should be informed of these traditions, they should not accept ideologies that undermine the *very* condition that enables them to learn from other traditions. This point is related to another question of whether the control beliefs of pluralism, strong rationality, and strong autonomy themselves should be questioned and revised. My first response is that these beliefs certainly should be questioned. Doing so demonstrates the *very* attributes of being rational, autonomous, and open to alternatives. This situation is similar to the question of whether one should think critically about critical thinking, and my answer is yes. But I do not agree that the control beliefs of pluralism, strong rationality, and strong autonomy should therefore be jettisoned. They should be retained to function as control beliefs to protect a person against indoctrination and guide her to become an educated person.

Second, while all Muslims are invited to exercise their rational and autonomous faculties to critically reflect on their Islamic beliefs, the *extent* to which they should be encouraged to do so is circumscribed by the particular Islamic tradition they are in. To appreciate this point, it is helpful to look at the different views Muslims have on *ijtihad* (independent reasoning). Used by jurists in adjudicating legal matters, ijtihad involves interpreting the Islamic law as revealed in the Qur'an and the Sunnah. This ensures that the jurists' judgements are in line with the intellectual, political, economic, legal, technological, and moral developments of a society.[42] Ijtihad is a process of forming judgements through human reasoning and personal effort by elaborating the laws either on the basis of the revealed texts or formulated in the light of them.[43] It is used mainly under the following conditions: when there is evidence in the primary sources of the shari'ah, but neither the meaning of the evidence nor its authenticity is certain; the meaning of the text is certain, but the authenticity is not; the authenticity of the text is certain but the meaning is not; or there is no text at all relevant to the matter.[44] As a legal term, ijtihad is commonly exercised by an Islamic scholar qualified to solve a legal problem or derive a ruling from the revealed texts. A person needs to be professionally trained to meet the strict requirements of an Islamic scholar. These requirements include competence in Arabic, knowledge of the sciences of the Qur'an and hadith, mastery in the principle and methodology of analogical reasoning (*qiyas*), etc. But there are Muslims who argue that ijtihad should not be confined to the *ulama* (religious scholars) and that ijtihad should be open to all Muslims. The contrasting views stem from different Islamic traditions.

For example, there are Islamic traditions that are closely aligned with specific legal schools, such as the Hanafi, Maliki, Shafi'i, and Hanbali. They generally hold that only the specialists in the shari'ah sciences are qualified to exercise ijtihad in interpreting the revealed texts, and their rulings had already been codified between the eighth and eleventh centuries. These Muslims believe that there is now limited scope for ijtihad to reread and reinterpret the revealed texts since the "gates of ijtihad" are closed. However, there are other Islamic traditions that call for the "democratisation" of ijtihad by allowing non-scholars to perform ijtihad.[45] Their argument is that any faithful Muslim of sound mind is capable of using ijtihad to interpret the revealed texts, rather than relying on blind acceptance (*taqlid*) of the teachings of the ulama.[46] Irrespective of the position one takes on ijtihad, all educative Islamic traditions are committed to developing their members' rational autonomy in their daily lives. Having weaved our net of an Islamic educative tradition, let us proceed to use it by casting it into the Indonesian ocean in the next chapter.

6 Islamic Schools in Indonesia
Islam with a Smiling Face?

The label "Islam with a Smiling Face" was used by international magazines such as *Time* and *Newsweek* to describe the form of Islam in Indonesia: inclusive, progressive, and modern.[1] By extension, an Islamic school that embodies "Islam with a smiling face" would be one that is inclusive, progressive, and modern. Such a school would be inclusive by being pluralist, progressive by emphasising strong rationality and strong autonomy, and modern by preparing its students to meet the challenges of a globalised world and knowledge-based economy. It follows that an Islamic school with a smiling face is one that resides in an *educative tradition*.

We have learnt in the previous chapter that an educative tradition is one that fosters the development of pluralism, strong rationality, and strong autonomy in its students. An Islamic school that adheres to an educative tradition is one that offers a broad-based curriculum. Such a school is willing to learn from various traditions and sources, and is adaptable to changing times and places. Its students not only master the facts but are equipped with the capacity and willingness to critically inquire and provide the evidential justification for these facts in an age-appropriate manner. The corresponding pedagogy should promote engaged learning: this entails the construction of knowledge (not only transmission of knowledge), understanding (not only rote memorisation), social constructivism (not only individual study), self-directed learning (not only teacher-directed), and learning about learning (not only learning about subjects).[2] The students should be exposed to a variety of learning methods such as lectures, group discussions, experiments, and independent research. The school's programmes, activities, and learning environment should nurture the students' freedom of thought and action. The students should be encouraged to order their lives based on a Muslim tradition that they have chosen reflectively for themselves.

So do the Islamic schools in Indonesia fit the bill of "Islam with a smiling face"? We have already looked at Ngruki in Chapter 3. But Ngruki is a mere drop in the ocean—one out of about 50000 Islamic schools in Indonesia. Do the rest of the Islamic schools reside in an indoctrinatory or educative tradition? We shall answer this question by analysing the Islamic schools in Indonesia in terms of their curricula, pedagogy, and extra-curricular activities. Given the vast number and variety of Islamic schools in Indonesia, it is impossible to give a detailed discussion of all these schools. Instead, I shall provide a broad overview of the Islamic schools, identify some common trends, and highlight some examples.

AN OVERVIEW OF ISLAMIC SCHOOLS IN INDONESIA

Of the 50,000 Islamic schools in Indonesia, 16,015 of them are pesantrens (Islamic boarding schools), 37,000 of them are madrasahs (Islamic day schools) and a small minority are Sekolah Islams.[3] The enrolments in Islamic schools have been increasing since the late 1980s. Currently about 5.7 million or 13 percent of the 44 million students enrolled in the formal educational system are enrolled in madrasahs.[4] As noted in Chapter 3, Islamic schools in Indonesia can be divided into three main types: pesantren, madrasah, and Sekolah Islam.

Pesantren

Among the three types, the pesantren is the oldest form of Islamic school in Indonesia. As the most traditional type of Islamic school, it caters mostly for children from the rural areas. Maintaining their status as private educational institutions, pesantrens are the bastion of Islamic knowledge and the main provider of Islamic scholars and teachers.[5] They focus on the transmission of the classical Islamic sciences, including the study of the Qur'an and hadith, jurisprudence, Arabic grammar, mysticism (*tasawwuf*), and the Arab sciences (*alat*).[6] Traditionally, the pesantren students learn classical Islamic commentaries, known as *kitab kuning* (literally, yellow books). According to Martin van Bruinessen, the traditional Islamic contents in the pesantrens are based on "the Ash'ari doctrine (as mediated especially by Sanusi's works), the Shafi'i madhhab (with nominal acceptance of the other three Sunni madhhab), and the ethical and pietistic mysticism of Ghazali and related writers".[7] Although pesantrens started with teaching purely religious subjects, pesantrens today supplement their religious studies with a general elementary education. This change was partly due to state reforms in the late 1970s.[8] Besides non-religious subjects, many pesantrens have also offered vocational courses such as agricultural skills, vehicle repair, and business enterprising skills.

Pesantrens can be further divided into three types: traditional, modern, and independent.[9] A "traditional pesantren" tends to focus on traditional Islam and is likely to be ideologically affiliated with Nahdlatul Ulama (NU). NU, which commands a huge following, is an association of kyais—Muslim scholars who usually have their own pesantrens and teach classical Islamic texts to their students.[10] A traditional pesantren is characterised by its endorsement of devotional and mystical beliefs and practices. An example is visits to the graves of local saints and great kyais to obtain blessings and barakah (holiness, virtue as inherent spiritual power) (see Figure 6.1). Other practices include chanting religious formulae (*zikir*, literally means remembrance of God) and specific devotions and mystical exercises imparted by the kyai to their followers.[11] The second type is a "modern pesantren". As its name implies, it modernises pesantren education by introducing a structured grade system, classrooms, textbooks, and an ethos of reform and progress.[12] Most modern pesantrens are affiliated with Muhammadiyah, which is a mass-based Muslim association like NU. But unlike NU, it is "reformist" in the sense that it rejects the mystical and devotional beliefs and practices endorsed by NU and found in traditional pesantrens. Muhammadiyah views these beliefs and practices as syncretistic and un-Islamic.[13] The third type is "independent pesantren" that is not associated with NU or Muhammadiyah and tends to adopt Salafi ideological beliefs. I shall not elaborate on this type, as it has already been covered in Chapter 3 and illustrated by the example of Ngruki.

Madrasah

The second type of Islamic school is madrasah. Although a madrasah is historically known as an Islamic college or Islamic institution of higher

Figure 6.1   Muslims praying at the graves of great kyais.

learning, it refers to an Islamic day school in Indonesia.[14] Introduced by the first president of Indonesia, Soekarno, this type of school combines traditional religious education with a broad general component.[15] The majority of madrasahs are privately owned, with state-owned madrasahs comprising between 6.4 percent and 13 percent from the primary to the senior secondary levels.[16] Besides being a non-boarding school, the madrasahs are distinguished from the pesantrens in their mission and modern approaches to the school setup, curriculum, and pedagogy. Unlike pesantrens that primarily aim to nurture religious scholars, madrasahs are set up to create "learning Muslims" who are ready for secular professional jobs.[17] Similar to Dutch government and Christian missionary schools, the madrasahs offer their students different levels of graded instruction, modern classrooms with blackboards, textbooks, and structured assessments. All madrasahs today adopt a government-approved madrasah curriculum consisting of 70 percent general subjects and 30 percent religious subjects. Recognised as on par with the public schools in the Educational Act of No 2/1989, madrasahs follow the national curricula fully and their graduates may continue their studies at both Islamic and secular public universities. While public schools offer only two hours of Islamic religious studies (*Pendidikan Agama Islam*) per week, the madrasahs offer about five or six hours per week. Furthermore, the madrasahs offer additional Islamic subjects such as *Aqidah* (theology), *Akhlak* (virtue), and Islamic history.[18]

Sekolah Islam

The third type of Islamic school is Sekolah Islam (Islamic school). Although "Sekolah Islam" literally means "Islamic school", I will refer to the Indonesian term so as not to confuse this type of school with the generic term "Islamic school". As stated in the introductory chapter, "Islamic school" is used to refer to any educational institution that emphasises the transmission of Islamic knowledge and inculcation of Islamic values and ethos. Many Sekolah Islams are found in urban areas and cater largely for Muslim students from middle-class family background. This contributes to the general perception that they are elite Islamic schools. Their popularity is due to the desire of middle-class parents who wish to provide a modern Islamic schooling for their children that offers a high academic standard in general subjects within an Islamic environment. Charging relatively high school fees compared to pesantrens and madrasahs, these schools are well-equipped with modern facilities such as air-conditioned classrooms, libraries, language labs, science labs and computer labs, and multimedia facilities. They are also staffed by teachers and managers who are generally highly qualified and competent.[19] Examples of such schools are Yayasan Pesantren Islam (YPI) Al-Azhar, Madrasah Aliyah Negeri Insan Cendikia Serpong, and Pesantren Ibnu Salam Nurul Fikri Boarding School.[20]

The students in Sekolah Islams do not concentrate on learning Islamic subjects such as Islamic jurisprudence or Islamic theology. Rather, their attention is on general subjects such as science, history, social studies, and foreign languages. At the same time, Sekolah Islams surpass the public schools by allocating more hours to religious instruction: an average of four or five lesson hours as compared to two lesson hours per week in the public schools. On top of that, they include Arabic language and Qur'anic studies in their curriculum. Sekolah Islams are known for combining a quality general education with Islamic ethos and morals; importance is placed on Islamic practices such as prayer, and attempts are made to infuse Islamic principles and values into the curriculum. For example, one Sekolah Islam includes additional religious instruction after school hours such as getting the students to recite the Qur'an after *Maghrib* (the prayer after sunset), and engage in research activities based on religious themes such as basic jurisprudence.[21] This type of school is also known for offering its students a rich variety of extracurricular activities so as to inculcate Islamic values through these activities.

Islamic Higher Education

Although my focus is on Islamic schools from the primary to the senior secondary levels, I would like to briefly add a note on Islamic higher education. Of special mention is the expansion and development of State Islamic Institutes (IAINs) and State Islamic Universities (UINs), as they have facilitated the continual study of graduates from Islamic schools. Adopting an integrated approach, these institutions offer both Islamic sciences as well as general subjects such as psychology, education, and languages. They also attempt to foster independent and critical thinking in their students, and are open to new ideas within and outside the Islamic faith. (I shall give an example in Chapter 8.)

Having looked at the broad educational landscape of Islamic schools in Indonesia, let us see whether these schools generally reflect an educative tradition. I shall highlight three noteworthy trends of Islamic schools in Indonesia: the inclusion of non-religious subjects, the adoption of student-centred pedagogies, and the provision of a variety of student activities.

INCLUSION OF NON-RELIGIOUS SUBJECTS

The Islamic educational system in Indonesia has been described as "among the most open and innovative in the world" for the willingness of Indonesian Muslim educators to go beyond religious studies to offer marketable skills and general education.[22] Most Islamic schools in Indonesia encourage their students to study both religious subjects and non-religious subjects (known as "general subjects" in Indonesia). By being open to new ideas and latest inventions from a variety of traditions and sources, including from the United States and other Western countries, the Islamic schools remain adaptable to changing times and places.

Since the 1920s, some pesantrens have incorporated general subjects such as Dutch language, mathematics, geography, and history into their curricula. By the 1950s, the majority of pesantrens have included general subjects for their students. The incorporation of general subjects is also due to the decree in 1952 by the Ministry of Religious Affairs (MORA) that requires madrasahs and other Islamic institutions that wish to obtain state financial support to allocate 30 percent of their curriculum time for general subjects. Many pesantrens since 1960s have set up public schools in their school complexes, such as Sekolah Menengah Pertama (SMP, junior high schools) and Sekolah Menengah Atas (SMA, senior high schools). It is important to note that the adoption of general subjects is not a knee-jerk action from the pesantrens in response to the challenge of the Dutch government or pressure from the Indonesian government. Rather, as noted by Ronald Lukens-Bull, the pesantrens are engaged in a process of negotiation in which they actively (re)invent modernity—one that is subject to traditional morality in accordance with their Islamic traditions.[23]

So important is the goal to juggle religious and general studies that almost all the Islamic educational leaders I interviewed, when asked about the proportion of religious subjects vis-à-vis general subjects, replied that it is equal. Technically, with the exception of the pesantrens, madrasahs and Sekolah Islams devote a larger part of their formal school hours to general subjects. But it is also true that the weighting between religious and general subjects is at parity when we consider the religious activities *outside* the formal curriculum. This is especially applicable for pesantrens where, as boarding schools, they have the students with them around the clock. It is notable that some Islamic schools, especially the Sekolah Islam, have gained a reputation for academic excellence in general subjects that rivals that of the top private schools in the country. For example, schools such as Madrasah Aliyah Negeri Insan Cendikia Serpong and Pesantren Ibnu Salam Nurul Fikri Boarding School are known for producing top students who ace the national exams and win trophies in national and international competitions (see Figure 6.2).

Pondok Pesantren Tebuireng

To further understand the pluralist attitude of the pesantrens towards general subjects, it is helpful to examine the efforts of one pesantren, Pondok Pesantren Tebuireng (or Tebuireng for short). Founded by Kyai Hasyim Asy'ari in 1926 who also established Nahdatul Ulama (NU) in the same year, this pesantren is arguably one of the most famous and established pesantrens in Indonesia. Almost all the major pesantrens in Java were founded by disciples of Kyai Hasim Asy'ari based on the Tebuireng model.[24] The former Indonesian President Abdurrahman Wahid (Gus Dur) is

Figure 6.2   Some trophies on display in an Islamic school.

the grandson of the founding father and brother of the current kyai. The influence of Tebuireng extends to the community as well, where the villagers would seek advice and blessings from the kyais. A tour of the community reveals paintings and even merchandise associated with the kyais and Gus Dur for sale (see Figure 6.3).

Educational reforms began with the opening of a six-grade system consisting of a preparatory grade for one year, followed by a madrasah grade for six additional years in the 1930s. In the 1950s, general subjects such as Dutch language, history, geography, and mathematics were fully incorporated, together with the adoption of the madrasah system as the main model of education.[25] However, the early reforms at Tebuireng were not without opposition; some Muslims charged that 'Abdul Wahid Hashim, then kyai of Tebuireng, had "contaminated the pesantren with worldly affairs".[26] Nevertheless, the progressive attitude of Tebuireng's leaders ensures that the pesantren continues its quest to keep up with the changing times. Its desire to integrate religious and general knowledge is evident in Tebuireng's educational objective to nurture students to be *ulama intellektuil* (Islamic scholars who master secular knowledge) as well as *intellektuil ulama* (scholars of modern knowledge who master Islamic knowledge).[27] Besides being book-smart, the students are given opportunities to participate in

Figure 6.3   A bag with the name "Gus Dur" for sale near Pondok Pesantren Tebuireng.

extracurricular activities and other student activities after school hours (see Figure 6.4). That the leaders are positive about general studies such as the sciences is testified to in a book written by its founder KH. M. Ash'ari Hashim ("Adabul 'Alim Wal Muta'allim") where he details the benefits of science for society.[28]

Today, its students may choose to study in a madrasah (Madrasah Tsanawiyah for junior high school level and Madrasah Aliyah for senior high school level) or a sekolah (SMP A. Wahid Hasyim at junior high school level and SMA A. Wahid Hasyim at senior high school level). Students who wish to specialise in religious studies may opt for Madrasah Mu'allim that will lead them to the level of Ma'had Aly. Both the madrasahs (except

Figure 6.4 Students of Pondok Pesantren Tebuireng participating in a student activity.

Madrasah Mu'allim) and sekolah devote most of the curriculum time to general subjects. This means that a dual system is implemented where students study general subjects during the formal curricular time and receive religious instruction after school hours within a pesantren environment.

ADOPTION OF STUDENT-CENTRED PEDAGOGIES

The Islamic schools' adoption of the national curriculum has a direct impact on their pedagogies. While the traditional didactic teaching methods of *bandongan* and *sorogan* are still widely used in the pesantrens (I shall elaborate on them in the next chapter), many pesantrens have expanded and diversified their teaching repertoires. They have incorporated more student-centred pedagogies so that their students do not simply learn by rote or memorisation.[29] Since the general subjects are based on the national curriculum, the teaching methods for these subjects are similar to those used in the public schools. Through activities such as laboratory experiments and project work, the students acquire not just facts but learn about the scientific inquiry and evidential justification for the facts. It is also increasingly common for Islamic schools to capitalise on information and communication technology (ICT) and multimedia resources in promoting engaged learning (see Figures 6.5, 6.6, 6.7, and 6.8).

Compared to pesantrens, student-centred pedagogies are more prevalent in madrasahs, as they follow the national curriculum fully. The director of a popular madrasah notes that his school encourages active learning through "cooperative learning, discussion, experiments, enquiry, exploratory learning" with the teacher serving as a facilitator "to give many opportunities for the students to be highly active in class".[30] An example, he adds, is for his teachers to use CDs to explain the concept of light in physics and other abstract concepts in mathematics.

Among the three types of Islamic schools, Sekolah Islams stand out for leading the way in pedagogical innovations. A senior staff member of a Sekolah Islam explains that the pedagogies used in his school have been carefully designed to enhance the cognitive, psycho-motor, and affective developments of the students:

> We have a variety of methods because they need to follow the curriculum that has been standardised, where we have the affective, psycho-motor and cognitive aspects. For cognitive, we normally would use tests, either written or oral depending on the subjects. For psycho-motor, we would have the practicum, presentations, etc. For

Figure 6.5   Female students taking a computer lesson.

Figure 6.6   A modern and well-stocked library in an Islamic school.

affective, we could assess these from presentation, or practicum, etc. For example we could observe their attitude and behaviour based on the tools, so for each subject, we would have components that we want to assess in the students. The same goes for religious studies, when they are learning how to perform *solat* (prayers), they will have practical lessons in solat. If they are to learn how to wash the corpse, then there would be a mannequin and the whole process will be done and practised.[31]

Another Sekolah Islam prepares its students to do project work with the objective of preparing them for tertiary education.[32] Its students conduct in-depth research on a topic, followed by a presentation and a write-up. Another noteworthy pedagogical approach used in Integrated Islamic Schools (a type of Sekolah Islam) is an active learning method known as *sentra*. It is conceptualised to encourage students to learn independently by giving them the freedom to develop interests and conduct their own experiments based on themes such as creative arts, mathematics, and language. Each sentra has a small laboratory for the students' practices.[33] Other Sekolah Islams such as those run by the Prosperity Justice Party (PKS) and the Hidayatullah schools are known for providing plenty of opportunities for the students to participate actively in class and engage in exchanges with guest speakers.[34]

Figure 6.7   Some science equipment in an Islamic school.

Student-centred pedagogies also extend to religious subjects in Sekolah Islams. For instance, students in one Sekolah Islam carried out their own research on various aspects of Islamic jurisprudence.[35] A corresponding change to support student-centred pedagogies is the production of learner-centred textbooks for religious subjects. For example, the Islamic textbooks produced by Persis for the junior high school level have been carefully designed to engage the learners. Each lesson comes with stated lesson objectives, clear learning points, pictures, contemporary examples, and religious justification for these points through relevant verses

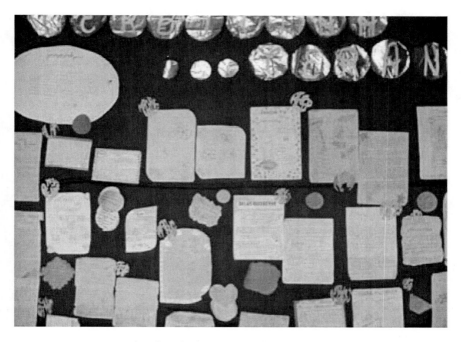

Figure 6.8 An example of student-centred pedagogy: Students to pen down their thoughts and display them.

from the Qur'an and hadiths. The lesson on what is *haram* (forbidden) for Muslims, for instance, is systematically explained, accompanied by selected Islamic verses, and amplified with concrete examples such as the consumption of liquor.

PROVISION OF A VARIETY OF STUDENT ACTIVITIES

Another striking feature of Islamic schools is their provision of a variety of student activities to develop the students' life skills and leadership abilities. This goes towards helping students to internalise and put into practice the principles and values they have learnt. Students are encouraged to be involved in a cornucopia of activities both during and outside the official school hours. Basic extracurricular activities in a pesantren include silat, wushu (martial arts), and basketball (see Figures 6.9 and 6.10).[36] Additionally, students in some pesantrens are encouraged to take part in *jam'iyyah*, which are student political organisations. Students receive practical training on forming an organisation, speaking in public, recruiting members, organising activities, interacting with other groups, and developing leadership

Figure 6.9   Students enjoying a game of football.

Figure 6.10   Students learning wushu.

qualities.[37] One Sekolah Islam offers a programme, *Programme Pendidikan Bela Negara* (PPBN; National Defence Educational Programme), to inculcate leadership skills and love for one's country and fellow countrymen. A pesantren gives its students the opportunities to organise various activities through its *Ikatan Pelajar Muhammadiyah* [IPM; Muhammadiyah Student Society]. The director explains that the students "actualise in practice the theories that they have learnt in class. . . . [T]hey are exposed to being independent without being dictated and closely monitored by us here".[38]

Pesantren Darussalam Gontor Ponorogo

A good example of a pesantren that underlines not just classroom teaching but dynamic student activities is Pesantren Darussalam Gontor Ponorogo (or Gontor for short). Established in 1926, it is the first pesantren to embrace modernity in its educational reforms, thereby inspiring its graduates to set up pesantrens (known affectionately as "the Alumni's Pesantren") based on the same model.[39] Its vision is to nurture "intellectual ulama"—leaders for the community who can contribute to the spread of religious and general knowledge. Stressing the importance of Arabic as the language of the Qur'an and English as the language of modernity, its students are obliged to communicate in either Arabic or English (and not the Indonesian language) (see Figure 6.11). This emphasis on bilingual competency was also introduced to Ngruki by Abu Bakar Ba'asyir who graduated from Gontor.

Figure 6.11 Posters in Arabic and English in Gontor.

Rather than a dual system where religious and general subjects are offered under different units, Gontor offers its own unique integrated six-year programme. Known as Kulliyatul Mu'allimin Islamiyah (KMI = Islamic Teacher Education Programme), it is equivalent to a combination of a junior and high school level education. The KMI curriculum has two components: formal education conducted during the school hours and "student development" (*Pengasuhan Santri*), which covers all extracurricular activities. Students need to pass both components in order to graduate from the school. The "student development" aims to harness and develop the students' character, which is a central focus of Gontor. The students are given ample opportunities to develop their leadership skills by running the hostels under the supervision of the teachers. Opportunities include being in charge of the security, co-operatives (for example, the bookshop and canteen), sports, and the arts. Other student activities include scouting, martial arts, painting, calligraphy, music (both *nasyid* [Islamic songs] and popular music), gymnastics, body building, and speech training. These activities are facilitated by the sprawling compound of Gontor equipped with facilities such as a sports hall (see Figure 6.12). A senior staff member of Gontor elaborates:

> Because the students here are given responsibilities, training in leadership, cooperation, etc. and it can be said that most of the development

Figure 6.12   A sports hall for the students in Gontor.

of the students' emotional quotient and spiritual quotient are done more outside class. All students have to go through this. They are self-governed, which means that the students themselves do the planning, organising, and implement the activities and we only do supervision.[40]

Another unique feature of Gontor is its aim to nurture students who are "free-minded". This means they should be "free in thought and act" by determining their own future, choosing their way of life, and being unencumbered by negative influences from society.[41] Being free-minded also entails eschewing extremist religious views and following the moderate way. The objective of free-mindedness is expressed by one of Gontor's founding fathers, Imam Zarkasyi, who emphasised the need to implement madhhab (legal school) flexibility, freedom of thought, and modern ideas of progress (*kemajuan*).[42] Post-secondary students enrolled in the teacher's college (*Institute Islam Darussalam*) are also exposed to diverse Islamic traditions through the course *Perbandingan Mazhab* (Different Sects) and non-Islamic traditions through the course *Perbandingan Agama* (Comparative Religion).[43] Not surprisingly Gontor does not align itself with either NU or Muhammadiyah. This ideological neutrality and nonpartisan stance explains its openness towards various traditions. For example, its religious teaching materials include classical fiqh text by Ibn Rushd's *Bidayat al-mujtahid* that compares various legal schools.[44]

Freedom in action is also achieved through its inculcation of a self-directed and entrepreneurial spirit. This independent spirit is shaped by the pesantren's past: the school itself has been surviving and thriving without any government assistance from the beginning. This school ethos was put to me succinctly by a Gontor graduate who is currently a university lecturer: "We can survive anywhere". A senior staff member of Gontor, also a graduate of Gontor, explains:

> The students are all trained and they are encouraged to be innovative and creative, which would eventually lead them to be able to survive living amidst the community. They are also trained in "survival skills", such as the ability to solve problems, the ability to survive in any situations.[45]

To engage the minds of the students and develop their rationality and autonomy, various teaching methods such as lecture, demonstration, discussion, project work, and practical sessions are used. These methods are aided by the use of computer, internet access, language laboratories, and science laboratories. An example of a project work is to give the level 5 students a problem such as the legal ruling on reading the *qunut* in *fajr* prayers [morning prayers].[46] The students are expected to do their own research by consulting relevant classical books and subsequently write a report on it. Unsurprisingly, Gontor cultivates a lively intellectual atmosphere and has produced many educated and progressive Muslim thinkers such as Nurcholish Madjid.[47]

DISCUSSION

We can see from our survey of Indonesian Islamic schools that they generally do not reside in an indoctrinatory tradition. On the contrary, they are pluralist in the sense that they embrace non-religious subjects and promote rationality and autonomy through their student-centred pedagogies and student activities. With the teaching and learning of general subjects such as English, mathematics, and sciences, the control belief of *epistemological pluralism* is introduced to the students. Students are exposed to knowledge from various disciplines and sources. They no longer learn purely Islamic subjects (unlike students in pesantrens of old), but general knowledge such as the history and geography of countries outside Indonesia, as well as the language and culture of English-speaking countries. A pluralist attitude opens the students' vistas to the rest of the world and keeps them abreast of modern knowledge and skills integral for success in a globalised and digital world. Such a broad-based education encourages the students to acquire a body of control beliefs from various sources.

A focus on modern knowledge and skills through the learning of general subjects also broadens the students' aspirations and goals in life. Whereas students in the past simply stopped school early for work or became religious teachers (a noble aspiration in itself), they are now more likely to aspire to seek higher education locally or overseas, and become professionals in secular fields such law, medicine, or business. This new aspiration is reflected and highlighted in the visions and missions of many Islamic schools as they are aware of the demands from parents and students for marketable and twenty-first-century skills. This orientation is especially evident in the Sekolah Islams, as they are elite and high-achieving schools with students whose parents who are themselves high-flying, working professionals.

The implanting of a greater number of control beliefs through a broad-based and holistic educational experience has a direct implication for indoctrination. We have learnt that an educated person is one who holds to control beliefs strongly but not in such a way that they are immune to doubt and change. By being exposed to many forms of knowledge, the students in the Islamic schools form more control beliefs in their cognitive landscape, thereby ensuring that no one control belief dominates. At the same time, the demand of the national examinations means that a large chunk of the curriculum time is spent on general subjects. The students' wide exposure to new ideas, information, and influences makes it challenging for an exclusive indoctrinatory tradition to take root. An indoctrinator no longer has the monopoly of the students' attention and time, and will find it difficult to shield them from beliefs that are not consistent or do not comport well with ideological totalism. This point also explains why not all the students in Ngruki are indoctrinated, as noted in Chapter 3.

The adoption of student-centred pedagogies also serves to reduce the likelihood of indoctrination. By enabling students to engage in more self-directed activities such as conducting scientific experiments and writing research papers, these teaching methods reinforce the control beliefs of strong rationality and strong autonomy. These activities motivate the students to go beyond rote learning and memorisation to explore and construct the evidential justification for the facts learnt. In the process of working with their teachers and peers on group discussions and projects, the students also develop the confidence to speak up, draw their own conclusions, and support their arguments with evidence. With their teachers serving not purely as content experts but facilitators, the students also learn to relate to their teachers in a more egalitarian and consultative environment. This scenario is a far cry from a teacher-centred environment of a traditional pesantren where the kyais and religious teachers focus on textual transmission and expect unquestioned obedience from their students. Besides giving them choices to participate in an array of programmes and events, these activities potentially cultivate their leadership qualities, an independent spirit, and other life skills such as working with others and resolving group conflicts. Of course, the extent to which a student is given the opportunity to do the above varies from school to school. A big and modern pesantren such as Gontor is likely to be more successful in enhancing its students' strong rationality and strong autonomy than a small traditional pesantren that is cash-strapped with limited resources for the students.

That most of the Islamic school leaders, teachers, and other educational stakeholders in the Muslim community are open to the learning of non-religious subjects should not surprise us. Theoretically, "religious" and "secular" knowledge are integrated in Islamic thought under two main types: rational sciences (*al-'ulum al-'aqliyyah*) or intellectual sciences, and the traditional sciences (*al-'ulum al-naqliyah*) or revealed knowledge. Syed Farid Alatas explains that rational sciences refer to knowledge that arises from man's capacity for reason, sense perception, and observation, whereas traditional sciences refer to knowledge that is devolved to man via revelation. Traditional sciences, he adds, include disciplines termed "modern" today: logic, physics, metaphysics, geometry, arithmetic, medicine, geography, chemistry, biology, music, astronomy, and science of civilisation.[48]

It is also important to note that the inclusion of non-religious subjects is not foreign to the Islamic heritage. The madrasahs during the Ottoman Empire incorporated "specific sciences," which were mathematics (*hisab*), geometry (*handasah*), astronomy (*hay'ah*), and practical philosophy (*hikmah*). Far from mere memorisation, the madrasahs also included "instrumental sciences" where students learnt, among other things, the art of rhetoric in terms of eloquent elocution, literary style, and artful composition.[49] It should also be pointed out that student-centred pedagogies are not new to the Islamic traditions. I have elsewhere argued that student-centred pedagogies such as problem solving, dialogue, discussion, disputation, and application have been propagated by Muslim scholars and implemented in Islamic institutions since the medieval times.[50]

At the ground level, many pesantren leaders do not see a strict dichotomy between religious studies and secular studies. Pointing out that one needs to integrate both religious and general knowledge to understand the Qur'an, a pesantren director quotes the following examples from the Qur'an:

> *Afala yanzuruna ilal ibili kaifa khulikat?* ["Do they not look at the Camels, how they are made?" from Surah Al-Ghashiyah 88:17]. That is biology. If you do not study biology, psychology, sociology, it would be difficult to understand this. Another verse: *'wailas samai kaifa rufia'at* ["And at the sky, how it is raised high?" from SurahAl-Ghashiyah 88:18]. It is talking about the sky, stars, the moon, and without studying physics and such subjects, it will be difficult. There are so many other examples. About the creation of man; *'hua anshaakum minal ardhi wasta'makum feeha'* ["It is He Who hath produced you from the earth and settled you therein" from Surah Hud 11:61]. . . . Seeking knowledge is compulsory, both religious studies and general studies but they should not be separated because when they are separated, it would be secular. . . . We cannot simply know how to recite the Qur'an, we need to learn how to read and write, we need to study history, mathematics.[51]

The integration of religious and general subjects is achieved by alerting the students to their educational duty of knowing Allah and linking all lessons to relevant Islamic sources, principles, and values. For example, a pesantren director explains that his biology teacher, when teaching about fruits or creation of man, will bring in the Qur'an and hadiths on these matters.[52] The infusion of religious values is also actualised through the hidden curriculum such as displaying religious teachings in various parts of the school compound (see Figure 6.13).

While it is clear that there is a strong potential in infusing Islamic principles and values into the teaching of general subjects, such integration is difficult in reality. A successful integration is more likely to take place in Sekolah Islams rather than in pesantrens and madrasahs. This is because Sekolah Islams generally have better facilities, high-tech equipment, more qualified teachers, and other resources needed for an integrated curriculum and educational innovations. Of special mention is a type of Sekolah Islam known as Integrated Islamic school (ISS; Sekolah Islam Terpadu). Rather than restricting religious instruction to one or two religious subjects, the priority in ISS is to infuse religious principles and values into the total curriculum across the entire school day.[53] This integration is usually achieved in two ways: the formal curriculum by infusing Islamic ideas and values into the teaching of general subjects, and the informal curriculum through the school ethos and activities outside the formal school hours.[54]

Notwithstanding the potential of and endeavours at integrating religious and general studies, many Islamic schools face an uphill task in doing so. The first challenge is that there is a conceptual difficulty in finding a direct link between general subjects and Islamic teachings all the time. As noted by Wardi Isman, the chairman of curriculum development of Al-Azhar's curriculum, the Qur'an is not a scientific book where

Figure 6.13 Religious teachings are displayed along the school corridor.

one can consult to confirm every scientific fact or theory.[55] The second challenege is the capacity of the teachers, as pointed out by a teacher of a madrasah:

> In terms of the teachers' capacity to integrate the subjects with religion, we have yet to have this capacity fully in our teachers. We have some teachers who properly understand this, but there are others who do not have the capacity, especially when they need to find relevant Qur'anic verses that relate to the concepts or issues that they are teaching to the students.[56]

A consequence of a lack of integration between general subjects and religious subjects within a coherent conceptual framework is "educational dualism". This refers to "the existence of an Islamic educational system with little if any general educational content alongside a secular educational system with little if any Islamic content".[57] Highlighting the "knowledge dichotomy" between Islamic schools and public schools, the Indonesian academic Rusydy Zakaria asserts that the Islamic educational system produces graduates who have a strong religious knowledge base and moral attitudes but lack a methodological approach, while general education produces graduates who are strong in methodological approaches but lack a religious knowledge base.[58]

CONCLUSION

I have argued in this chapter that the majority of the Islamic schools in Indonesia are not rooted in indoctrinatory traditions, unlike Ngruki. They fit the description of "Islam with a smiling face" in the sense that they welcome knowledge from non-Islamic sources and seek to enhance their students' rationality and autonomy through their mission, curriculum, and pedagogy. However, we have been talking about epistemological pluralism but not *religious pluralism*.[59] Similarly, we have been discussing rationality and autonomy, but not *strong rationality* and *strong autonomy*. Without these three control beliefs of an educative tradition, there is no guarantee that one can prevent the seed of indoctrination from being sown in the Islamic schools. In other words, the *mere* inclusion of non-religious subjects, adoption of student-centred pedagogies, and provision of a wide choice of student activities are not sufficient for these schools to reside securely in educative traditions. To effectively counter and avoid indoctrination, the tradition of Islamic schools needs to be rooted in the control beliefs of religious pluralism, strong rationality, and strong autonomy.

We need to ask a few pertinent questions here. In terms of religious pluralism, are the students of an Islamic school given the opportunity to engage in a genuine understanding of and active engagement with other Islamic and non-Islamic traditions? In terms of strong rationality and strong autonomy, are the students invited to ask and seriously consider both internal and external questions? Are they equipped and empowered with the where-withal to reflectively examine their own traditions, critically consider other traditions (both within and outside the Islamic faith), and be motivated to order their lives after such an examination? The answers to these questions will determine the extent to which the Islamic schools in Indonesia are grounded in educative traditions. The prognosis, unfortunately, is not good, as the next chapter will explain.

7 Whither Religious Pluralism, Strong Rationality, and Strong Autonomy?

"I was not too keen to send our graduates to America . . . a country which has strong Jewish influence, with liberal values."

—Director of a pesantren in Indonesia[1]

"The United States is behind this. . . . [T]his arrest is a blessing . . . I will be rewarded by Allah!"

—Abu Bakar Ba'asyir[2]

One thing that struck me in my interactions with the school leaders, staff, alumni, and other key stakeholders of Islamic schools is their aversion to the word "liberal". "Progressive" is fine. So is "open" or "free", but not "liberal". Describing someone, an action, or an institution as "liberal" is to insult that person, action, or institution. I know that, having ignorantly committed that *faux pas* in Indonesia. It appears that "liberal" is treated as a code-word to represent all things American and, by implication, "immoral" and "un-Islamic".[3] I also sense a general anti-American sentiment in Indonesia. An alien who has just landed on Indonesia would probably conclude that the United States is a morally bankrupt Jewish country that masterminded grand terrorist attacks against Muslims worldwide. It was no coincidence that Abu Bakar Ba'asyir pointed a finger at the United States when he was arrested by Indonesia's anti-terrorism unit in August 2010.

But what I find intriguing and paradoxical is that this general anti-American and anti-Western mindset is paired with an eagerness by the Islamic educational community to embrace modern and cutting-edge knowledge, scientific inventions, and technological breakthroughs that originate largely from—you guessed it, the United States and other Western countries. This interesting coupling of hate and love towards the United States and the West deserves our closer examination. In the previous chapter, we looked at how the majority of Islamic schools in Indonesia are open to non-Islamic studies and have designed their curricula and pedagogy to enhance the students' rationality and autonomy But to reside in and express an educative tradition, these schools *also* need to subscribe to and promote the control beliefs of religious pluralism, strong rationality, and strong autonomy. Whereas religious pluralism ensures that we are open to and engaged with other religious traditions, strong rationality and strong autonomy guide us to interpret and assess existing and new beliefs, and order our individual lives deliberately and reflectively. To what extent have the Islamic schools in Indonesia achieved that?

RELIGIOUS PLURALISM?

Religious pluralism presupposes tolerance, inclusiveness, and openness. It rejects the insistence that one's own religious tradition has the monopoly of truth. Rather than condemning alternative traditions, it is willing to critically explore and learn from other traditions, both within and outside one's religious faith. Such a pluralist mindset enables the students to be open-minded and adaptable to changing times and places—an outlook essential in an inter-connected, globalised, and multicultural world.

Despite the development of the students' rationality and autonomy through an enthusiastic implementation of general subjects, student-centred pedagogies, and student activities, most of the Islamic schools do not emphasise the value of religious pluralism. Most pesantrens, madrasahs, and Sekolah Islams appear to be uninterested in or unwilling to getting their students to learn about or learn from other religious traditions. In fact, some pesantrens, especially the independent and Salafi ones, draw the students' attention to other religions for the purpose of denouncing them. The director of a pesantren said that he gets his senior students to watch videos of Ahmad Deedat—a popular Muslim apologist who was known for his incendiary attacks against Christianity.[4] Muchammad Tholchah, in his interviews with teachers and parents in Ngruki, reported that they evince an anti-non-Muslim attitude. They are convinced of a plot by non-Muslims to subjugate the Muslims based on verses from the Quran such as this verse: "Never will the Jews or the Christians be satisfied with Thee unless Thou follow their form of religion."[5]

The same trend is evident in the Sekolah Islams where some are known to inculcate in their students anti-pluralist attitude and behaviour. It has been observed that students in Sekolah Islams run by Prosperous Justice Party (PKS) are "regularly reminded that non-Muslims are different, they're doomed to go to hell, and they shouldn't be in positions of authority over Muslims."[6] Noorhaidi Hasan asserts that the founders of a type of Sekolah Islam, Integrated Islamic Schools (ISS), are motivated to build such schools because they believe that Islam is under attack by what Islamists describe as a "U.S.-led Zionist-Christian imperialist plot".[7] Accordingly, the way to defend Islam against this plot is to "instill Islamist framework into the students' young minds and nurture their commitment to Islam as a preparation in the long-term process to implement the shari'ah".[8] This strategy of using formal and informal education (*tarbiyah*) is influenced by the Muslim Brotherhood ideology. Students in these schools learn about Salafi-Wahhabi ideology through books such as *Kitab al-Tawhid* by the Wahhabi founder Muhammad 'ibn Abd al-Rahman al-Su'udi.[9] Within such an anti-pluralist climate, any mention or discussion of other religions is likely to be carried out in a defensive and disparaging way using polemical materials.

The general apathy and hostility towards religious pluralism is reflected in and aggravated by a *fatwa* (religious verdict) issued by the Council of Islamic Scholars (Majelis Ulama Indonesia, MUI) in 2005. The fatwa stated that pluralism, together with liberalism and secularism, is prohibited (haram) in Islam.[10] Although the fatwa is not binding on Muslims, its release by a group of respectable and conservative Islamic scholars has a major impact on the Indonesian society.[11] As the country's highest Islamic authority, MUI has a significant influence over the country's mosques and enjoys important representation from major Islamic organisations including the NU and Muhammadiyah.[12]

Here I need to qualify that I am not asserting that *all* the Islamic schools are apathetic or antagonistic towards other faiths. Noorhaidi Hasan rightly points out that the principle of tolerance to non-Muslims is taught in some Sekolah Islams based on the Qur'anic message of *Lakum dinukum waliya din* (for you your belief and so goes for me) and the exemplary behaviour of the Prophet Muhammad.[13] Nevertheless, these are the exceptions. Most Islamic schools, even when they encourage their students to go beyond their own tradition to consider other traditions, confine the scope to other mainstream Islamic traditions. It is highly unlikely for any Islamic school to be open to controversial Islamic sects such as the Ahmadiyah that was denounced by MUI, or non-Islamic traditions such as the Christian or Buddhist traditions. A pervasive anti-pluralistic mindset among Islamic educational community members has been attested to in two national surveys discussed in the next section.

National Surveys

Two recent national surveys were conducted by the State Islamic University (UIN) of Jakarta (now known as the Syarif Hidayatullah State Islamic University, Jakarta). The first is a survey published in 2006 based on 960 respondents from 64 pesantrens and 16 Islamic schools in eight provinces throughout Indonesia.[14] The objective of the survey is to gauge the social and political attitudes of religious leaders (kyai), teachers (ustadz), and students (santri) of the Islamic educational community in terms of their support for shari'ah, democracy, tolerance, pluralism, gender, sentiments towards the West, and education.

On their perceptions towards the United States and its war on terror, the majority agree that Western countries, primarily the United States and Great Britain, are the root cause of religious violence in Muslim countries (77.6 percent). The majority agree that the U.S. invasion of Afghanistan and Iraq is an attack on Islam (67 percent), and only 10.7 percent agree that Osama bin

Laden is the actor of violence in the world. However, only 18.8 percent agree that the 2002 Bali bombing is justified as a movement against the West. On the impact of Western culture, a high proportion of them (87.3 percent) agree that Western culture has a potential negative impact on the life of Indonesian Muslims, and that Westerners who travel to Indonesia bring with them negative behaviour that may eradicate the Islamic elements of Indonesian culture (79.7 percent). However, they do not reject the adoption of Western knowledge, science, and technology, with an overwhelming majority supporting such an adoption (94.1 percent).

The survey also reveals that a majority of the Islamic education community in Indonesia do not demonstrate tolerant attitudes. For example, only a small minority of Muslims surveyed agree that non-Muslims are allowed to do the following: hold their religious services in Muslim areas (20.1 percent); build their religious sites in Muslim areas (36.2 percent); become the president of Indonesia (6.5 percent); and become teachers in public schools (19.9 percent). The low support for non-Muslim school teachers and president is due to the general belief that these positions are strategic and only Muslims are capable of transmitting religious and moral values needed by the students who are mostly Muslims.[15]

Another national survey conducted by the same university in 2008 focused on the socio-religious attitude and behaviour of religious teachers in Java.[16] A total of 500 religious teachers and 200 high school Class Level 3 students in public schools throughout Java were interviewed. The findings show that most of the respondents are intolerant of non-Muslim communities having the same status and socio-political rights as Muslims in Indonesia. More than half of the respondents object to non-Muslims being their school principal (68.6 percent) or their leader (62.4 percent), while about one-third object to having non-Muslims as their teachers (33.8 percent).

On the need of children to learn about another religion (apart from their own), only 18.5 percent agree and strongly agree with the statement. Three quarters of them object to pluralism (75 percent) and forbid their students from celebrating events that are associated with Western tradition (85.6 percent). Only 10.4 percent of respondents report that their Muslim students learn about non-Islamic religions, and only 25.9 percent of them state that their schools conduct inter-religious dialogues. Correspondingly, in terms of the most important goal in their teaching, a small minority agree that the value of tolerance is the most important goal (3 percent) or second most important goal (11 percent) in their teaching. The top two goals are "noble virtue" and "obedient in worshipping".

On the other hand, there is a high support for Islamic governance: a majority support the election of people's representatives that will fight for Islam (65 percent), agree that people who committed adultery must be stoned to death (87.9 percent), and support the Islamic penalty of chopping off one's hands (74.6 percent). About a third agree that Muslims who have turned away from the faith must be killed (32.7 percent). Commenting on the survey results, Noorhaidi Hasan concludes that they point to the growing influence of Islamism, anti-pluralism, and religious intolerance among practitioners of the formal education.[17] Martin van Bruinessen also observes that the Indonesian mainstream Islam has shifted from a relatively open and tolerant culture to one that is marked by an anti-West attitude, religious conservatism, and intolerance towards other faiths.[18] Fred R. von der Mehden argues that the characterisation of Islam in Indonesia as tolerant and nonviolent was "overly simplistic", as it "ignored major movements in the post independence era that showed some elements of the country's Muslim community that were prepared to employ violence in the name of Islam and were highly critical of other religious and ethnic minorities".[19]

The survey results resonated with me when I mingled with the Muslims during my visit there. Some Muslims I have met told me that they object to religious pluralism. A Muslim father told me that he and his wife chose to send their children to Islamic schools rather than public schools because he does not want his children to mix with non-Muslims. Another Muslim father who bravely enrolled his daughter in Madania—an elite school known for its promotion of religious plurality and harmony—told me that he has been criticised by other Muslim parents who reminded him of the fatwa by MUI against pluralism.

At the same time, I have encountered Muslims who are sympathetic towards or supportive of militant Muslims. I have met Muslim graduates of Islamic schools who reacted angrily and defensively when I asked them about the allegations of terrorism by Abu Bakar Ba'asyir and in Ngruki. Many Muslims I spoke to also do not support the government's tough actions against militant Muslims. A Muslim who graduated from an Islamic school told me that her father, who is currently an Islamic teacher in a public school, said that he would gladly harbour Noordin Top, a convicted militant involved in the Bali bombings, due to "religious reasons". When asked why there is such a pervasive albeit silent support for militant Muslims, a Muslim explained to me that it is probably because many Muslims are upset with the perceived moral degeneration of the Indonesian society and believe that the only or best solution is the establishment of an Islamic state and implementation of hudud (penal code for public crimes) in Indonesia. That may explain the rising support for Islamic governance in the survey.

STRONG RATIONALITY AND STRONG AUTONOMY?

Besides limited religious pluralism, there is also little evidence to suggest that most Islamic schools emphasise the development of strong rationality and strong autonomy. To do so requires the students to address not just internal questions about their Islamic tradition but external questions about their tradition and alternative worldviews. The aim is for the students to freely order their lives based on a tradition that they have chosen for themselves after critical reflection. The result is an educated person who is open to new beliefs, willing and able to question and even replace her control beliefs if necessary. Although it is true that most Islamic schools have adopted more student-centred pedagogies, this applies largely to general subjects and *not* religious subjects. The absence of a learning environment that fosters the development of strong rationality and strong autonomy is especially evident in the traditional pesantrens.

The Sorogan and Bandongan Methods

Many pesantrens rely primarily on two traditional teaching methods: *sorogan* and *bandongan* (or *weton*).[20] The sorogan method is a form of individualised tutorial where the teacher reads and translates some passages of the Qur'an or some Arabic texts into Javanese; this is followed by the student repeating and translating the same passages as correctly as possible.[21] The bandongan method, on the other hand, is intended for intermediate and advanced students, and is attended by students ranging from a handful to a few hundred. In such a system, a teacher reads, translates, and explains an Arabic text aloud while the students, armed with their own copies, listen to his reading and take notes on the proper vocalisation and the teacher's explanations.[22]

Both the bandongan and sorogan methods do not require the student to show that he has understood the lesson. The priority for the teacher is to complete the reading and translation of the texts and for the students to take notes. Although the students are allowed to ask questions, these questions are primarily limited to the linguistic aspects of the texts, and the teacher usually does not offer critical comments on the applicability of the text.[23] A senior member of a pesantren said that his pesantren chooses to rely on rote-learning and memorisation, as they are the methods passed down from centuries and have proven to be effective for the students to learn the grammar of Arabic and master the Qur'an and kitab kuning (classical commentaries).[24] That memorisation is exalted in the Islamic tradition is seen in the traditional belief among Javanese Muslims that a person who knows the Qur'an by heart is more blessed and is always looked after by God.[25]

It should be qualified that the adoption of the bandongan and sorogan methods does not necessarily mean that the students lack understanding or are unable to think for themselves. Furthermore, these methods are useful in laying the foundation for the students to proceed to review and discuss the meaning of the text with others.[26] Critical discussions and debates may also take place at a higher level among senior students who sit around to analyse the texts in their historical and cultural contexts and relate them to the modern world.[27] I should also add that Islamic schooling has not always been characterised by memorisation without higher-order thinking. George Makdisi, commenting on the methodology of learning in medieval education in Islam, states that memorisation was "not meant to be unreasoning rote learning" but was "reinforced with intelligence and understanding".[28]

Nevertheless, the intellectual climate in many pesantrens today is one that does not encourage their students to question their own Islamic traditions and exercise independent and critical thinking. Muslim reformists have criticised traditional pesantren education as underlining rote learning without critical understanding.[29] The graduates of these schools have also described the pedagogy used in traditional pesantrens as a "largely passive" approach that does not allow the development of critical thinking.[30] Abdullah Saeed concludes that the due reverence shown to early authorities has led to "a mentality among the graduates . . . of narrow-mindedness, pedantry, and pride in the skill of memory".[31]

Although the bandongan and sorogan methods are associated with pesantrens, the madrasahs have also been criticised for using a "textual and normative approach" that stresses the learning of Islamic knowledge and norms and marginalises "social sciences, economy, law, humanistic, and religious studies".[32] To be sure, rote-learning and memorisation themselves do not necessarily lead to indoctrination. However, a closed tradition where students are discouraged from questioning their own tradition and exploring other traditions—in other words, engaging in *external* questions—is more susceptible to indoctrination. Rote-learning and memorisation without understanding are likely to fortify the existing control beliefs in the learner's cognitive landscape. The entrenchment is further helped by the absence of critical inquiry, which deprives the learners of new ideas and control beliefs that are not consistent with or challenge the existing control beliefs.

Asking External Questions

Most Islamic schools do not seek to develop their students' strong rationality by encouraging their students to ask external questions. In other words, the students are often not given the opportunity to critically ask questions about their own tradition and comparing it with other traditions. The "other traditions" could be other Islamic traditions or non-Islamic traditions. Many Islamic schools do not go beyond one Islamic school of thought (madhhab); apart from the Shafi'i school, the students often do not learn about other legal schools of thought such as Hanafi, Hanbali, Maliki, and Ja'fari law. Even less common is the move for the students to progress beyond the dominant Ash'ari theology to explore non-mainstream Islamic literature such as Shi'i and Mu'tazila schools of thought. Neither is there a trend among Islamic schools to refer to the works of contemporary Muslim scholars such as Fazlur Rahman and Muhammed Arkoun.

There are of course exceptions that I should highlight, besides the example of Gontor that was discussed in the previous chapter. A senior staff member of a Sekolah Islam said that "the students are trained here to be open to any religious sects and not be narrow in their religious outlooks until they are tolerant and not be too exclusive and be too strict".[33] A director of a pesantren gives the example of teaching solat (prayer) to his students. Students at the junior high school level will not just learn how to memorise and pray, they also learn the *dalil* (arguments) for all the actions related to prayers. When they proceed to the senior high school level, they will be introduced to the practices of the different legal schools of thought. During the discussion, the students will explore the reasons from the different schools of thought and critique the arguments under the guidance of the teacher. The rationale for such exposure, according to the director, is that "we now live in a global world, so every student must know about the different schools of thought".[34] Another director of a pesantren likewise encourages his students to compare the different schools of thought on qunut (special supplications made while standing):

> For the higher level, they [students] may discuss about fiqh issues—for example why do we read qunut in our prayers and why some others argue that we do not have to read qunut in our prayers. So, they would go into the comparison between different madhhab.[35]

If learning about other Islamic traditions is not pervasive in the Islamic schools, learning about *non-Islamic traditions* is even rarer. This has already been noted in our previous section on religious pluralism. If students are discouraged from critically inquiring into their own tradition and comparing it with other traditions, they will not be motivated to regulate their life based on a tradition they have chosen for themselves. This makes it easy for them to be indoctrinated, and adversely affects their human agency and ability to deal with their daily problems. Rusydy Zakaria, a former policymaker at the Ministry of Religious Affairs in Indonesia, comments on this problem faced by Islamic schools in Indonesia:

> The form of teaching is characterised by one-way direction in which the teacher is a dominant party, the teacher is the only owner of knowledge and a student is an "empty box" to be filled. The learning process occurs in the narrative way in which a teacher gives a teaching instruction that needs to be accepted and memorised by students in order to pass their examinations. This "Banking Concept of Education" has significant consequences, not the least being a strong barrier against developing critical skills and creativity in students. As a result, most graduates from Islamic schools have lacked self-confidence and are unable to create a valuable response in term of resolving their daily problems.[36]

The preference for rote-learning and memorisation with a corresponding limited opportunity for students to ask external questions is not confined to the Islamic schools in Indonesia. Commenting on Islamic educational

institutions in general, Aziz Talbani observes that "authoritative acceptance of knowledge is stressed, with learning often based on listening,
memorisation, and regurgitation" and "greater emphasis is placed on listening to a teacher, who is active as a transmitter of knowledge, while the
student is passive".[37] Tariq Ramadan asserts that one can observe Muslim systems and methods that kill critical thinking and reinforce rote-
learning in Africa, Asia and the Middle East.[38] On the general trend of
pedagogy in Islamic schools, especially in non-Arabic countries, Rukhsana Zia claims that an "[i]mpeccable recitation of the Qur'an, committed to memory came to be prized and according to some, understanding
of the text or questioning became not only unnecessary but a hindrance
to successful memorisation", with the result that the need for such high-
order skills as analysis and discussion is neither expected of students
nor developed.[39]

DISCUSSION

Modernity and the West

At the start of the chapter, I have noted the paradoxical phenomenon of
key Islamic educational leaders holding to a general anti-American and
anti-Western mindset with a concomitant eagerness to acquire modern
knowledge from the West. Put simply, the de-emphasis on religious pluralism is accompanied by an emphasis on epistemological pluralism. The
development of the students' rationality and autonomy applies *only* to
epistemological, not religious, pluralism. This puzzling state of affairs
can be demystified when we understand the Indonesian Muslims' views
towards modernity.

Muslims, like every one else, live in a modern world—a world that is
characterised by constant creation and exploitation of knowledge, technical breakthroughs, and scientific advancements in a dynamically
changing future. Against the backdrop of a knowledge-based economy,
modern knowledge, especially in the sciences, technologies, and humanities, is highly valued and transmitted in many schools today. More than
ever before, human beings need to go beyond their own parochial tradition
to welcome useful knowledge from multiple sources. Historically, Muslims have contested over the "proper" attitude towards knowledge from
non-Islamic sources and traditions. On the one hand, scholars such as
al-Farabi, al-Baqillani, Ibn Sina, al-Juwayni, and al-Ghazali have argued
for an acceptance of knowledge regardless of religion and ethnicity; on
the other hand, scholars such as al-Shaf'i, Ibn Hanbal, Ibn Salah, and Ibn
Taymiyya have countered that knowledge that originated from non-Islamic
cultures and civilisations "had a corrupting influence on the legacy of the
pious ancestors of early Islam".[40] The rejection of non-Islamic philosophy

and methodology has prompted some Muslim scholars to champion the "Islamisation of knowledge" so that Muslims can participate in modernity within an Islamic worldview. The Islamisation project, conceived by Abdul Hamid Abu Sulayman in the late 1960s, aims at "a systematic reorientation and restructuring of the entire field of human knowledge in accordance with a new set of criteria and categories derived from and based on the Islamic worldview".[41] This internal debate among Muslims on non-Islamic sources and traditions demonstrates the evolving and contested nature of knowledge (re)construction within Muslim traditions.

How then do Indonesian Muslims respond to modern knowledge in a globalised world and digital age? That most Muslims in Indonesia are open to epistemological pluralism is attributed to their Islamic belief that all knowledge comes from God; Muslims are obligated to seek knowledge even if it means going to China. Many Muslims are also aware of the outstanding achievements of Muslim scientists and intellectuals in the past such as Ibn Rushd, al-Farabi, and Ibn Sina. However, the openness of the Islamic educational community towards knowledge from non-Islamic sources is mostly confined to the technical know-how, and does not extend to non-Islamic *cultures and values*. In other words, many Muslims distinguish between modernisation and "Westernisation": the latter is generally unacceptable, as it is perceived to be un-Islamic and robbing the ummah (Muslim community) of its religious and cultural heritage.[42] This explains the love-hate relationship between Indonesia and the United States/West. Such a view is expressed by a senior member of a Sekolah Islam:

> Knowledge such as science comes from Islam and the others borrowed or took it from us. So, as long as we make use of the knowledge in the proper way, it belongs to Muslims, so we are not being Westernised. What differs is in terms of the Western culture and customs, but in terms of knowledge, it belongs to Allah and we should seek and apply it, especially if we were to see that the West apply the knowledge in the wrong or improper way, then we have to ensure that when we apply the knowledge, it should be towards something that is better.[43]

As long as the adoption of "Western knowledge" is kept to its utilitarian purpose to equip the students to meet the challenges of a knowledge-based economy, it is "safe" for Muslims to learn from the West. That is why most Muslims regard general studies, information and communications technology, and modern equipment and facilities positively as part of the modern discourse they need for the progress and success of Muslims and the Islamic schools. This particular interpretation of "modernity" is evident from my interviews with the Islamic school leaders. For example, when asked how the school understands "modern", a senior staff member of a Sekolah Islam said, "The essence is that the students should be able to make use of the current technology. For example, the use of internet: they should make full use of it. These could be observed from their achievements in the robotics programme. They are also good in creating their own blogs".[44]

But the "liberal" values and practices of the West must be avoided and rejected at all costs. Instead Muslims should continue to preserve and protect their treasured Islamic traditions. This approach to modernity is summarised by Fazlur Rahman as follows:

> [T]he acquisition of modern knowledge [is to] be limited to the practical technological sphere, since at the level of pure thought Muslims need not need Western intellectual products—indeed, that these should be avoided, since they might create doubt and disruption in the Muslim mind, for which the traditional Islamic system of belief already provides satisfactory answers to ultimate questions of world view.[45]

This approach explains why epistemological but not religious pluralism is accepted by most Islamic schools in Indonesia. Abdullah Saeed maintains that Islamic institutions have historically remained "a close community, averse to any non-Islamic, or even Islamic works seen to be 'deviant' in the view of the teachers and directors" such as the Mu'tazilite theology.[46] In the same spirit, many Muslims have dismissed the works by Western Orientalist scholars such as Ignaz Goldziher on the basis that these non-Muslims "do not have any positive value for Muslims" and are part of a "Western supported, Judeo-Christian attempt to destroy Islam".[47] It is also this thinking that has led some Indonesian Muslims to chastise the State Islamic Universities in Indonesia for adopting the methodology used in Western universities in studying Islamic sciences. According to Azyumardi Azra, who is the director of the graduate school of Syarif Hidayatullah State Islamic University, Jakarta:

> They [some Muslims] question, for instance, how Islam can be studied from the West since Western countries do not have an Islamic tradition comparable to that of Middle Eastern countries. Furthermore, some Muslims also argue that what Muslims can learn from Western universities is only an "Orientalist approach" which will in the end harm Islam and Muslims.[48]

In short, the Islamic educational community leaders in Indonesia predominantly believe that they should accept only the practical technological knowledge from other traditions and reject their cultural and religious beliefs, values, and practices. And this is their *control belief* that shapes their educational philosophy, practices, and relationship with the West. Influenced by this control belief, it is not surprising that, with reference to the survey results cited earlier, 94.1 percent of the Islamic leaders, teachers, and students support the adoption of Western knowledge, science, and technology. Yet paradoxically, 87.3 percent agree that Western culture has a potential negative impact on Indonesian Muslims, and 79.7 percent believe that Westerners who travel to Indonesia bring with them negative behaviour that may eradicate the Islamic elements of Indonesian culture.

Two comments can be made about the stand of accepting epistemological pluralism yet rejecting religious (and cultural) pluralism. First, such a belief contributes to and reinforces a negative attitude towards American/ Western cultures and values. In particular, it stereotypes the United States and other Western countries as the originators of immorality and countries responsible for the perceived moral degradation in Indonesian society. Clearly, such a view commits the fallacy of over-generalisation and ad hominem argument. Besides, the tables could easily be turned and unfairly applied to Indonesia too, such as caricaturing Indonesia as "a country of terrorists". Interestingly, when I told people about my research work in Indonesia, I was often greeted by surprised looks and "praised" for my "courage" to visit Indonesia or step into an Islamic school. It is as if I could be hit by a bomb anytime (actually that was what a colleague told me), or that I would be kidnapped or killed by terrorists hiding in the Islamic schools. The truth is I felt safe throughout my stay in Indonesia and was warmly received by many Indonesian Muslims. This mindset of othering those who do not share our religious and cultural traditions is a stumbling block for human beings to transcend their own tradition and engage in meaningful inter-religious dialogues.

Second, the control belief of rejecting religious pluralism results in the students of the Islamic schools holding to a small number of control beliefs—those of their own Muslim tradition. Besides depriving the students the learning opportunity to grow and be educated about other traditions, the greater danger is indoctrination in ideological totalism. Even if the danger of indoctrination is low in many Islamic schools, the rejection of alternative worldviews to the Islamic traditions makes it difficult for the students to develop strong rationality and strong autonomy.

Which Religious Pluralism?

Many Muslims are cautious about or feel negatively towards religious pluralism because of their understanding of this term. I have noted earlier that the Council of Islamic Scholars (MUI) has interpreted religious pluralism as promoting the position that all religions are similar and that the truth of each religion is relative. Din Syamsuddin who was the Chairman of Muhammadiyah echoes such a view:

> If you look at what the idea of religious pluralism is, it's the idea that you embrace all religions as the same. It says there's no absolute truth

in one religion. The ulama in the MUI see this as a contradiction to Islam, which is the absolute truth.[49]

That is why MUI and many Muslims reject religious pluralism, as it entails giving up their belief that Islam is the perfect and best religion; it also has the consequence of promoting syncretism and the assimilation of all religions.[50] Such a view of religious pluralism—that all religions are true or contain truth—has also been advocated by other religious scholars. A well-known example is Christian theologian John Hicks who argues that all religious traditions are paths of salvation; every religious figure such as the Prophet Muhammad and Jesus Christ is a contact point with the "Ultimate Reality".[51] However, this is not and *should not be* the only definition of pluralism. An alternative and more acceptable interpretation of religious pluralism is not to focus on truth claims but on the *right* of everyone—Muslims and non-Muslims—to choose their religion and subscribe to what they believe to be true about their religion. As a recent report by the Islamic Centre of the University of Cambridge puts it, religious pluralism "does not mean that Muslims are required to regard other faiths and belief systems as equally true in the theological sense". Rather,

> Pluralism in this sense means that Muslims should accept that holders of other faiths or of no faith have a right to assert the validity and truth of their basic beliefs and values, and even claim it as the only true way, just as Muslims can. It means that no faith community should be forced in any way to compromise the integrity of its belief system in order to be part of this admirable code of co-existence and mutual respect for the choices of fellow human beings.[52]

The two meanings of pluralism (truth claims and religious freedom) also apply to the concept of religious harmony. It could refer to a harmony of *religions* with the view that all religions are the same or a harmony of *adherents* of different religions co-existing peacefully. This distinction was pointed out by the president of the National Council of Churches of Singapore. He rejects a harmony of religions, as he claims that "that route is very theoretical and doctrinal and has a lot of problems anyway" and favours "a harmony among people of different faiths living in a multi-religious society".[53]

Of course, it will greatly accelerate religious harmony if Muslims (or adherents of other religions) are able to accept the truth claims of other faiths. Such a position argues that salvation is possible outside one's religion. For example, according to Jane Idleman Smith, Muslim scholar Abdulaziz Sachedina endorses "the salvific efficacy of the other religions of the Book".[54] Similarly, Nurcholish Madjid maintains that salvation is not confined to the Muslims and God will reward all believers, including

Jews and Christians. Expectedly, Nurcholish's views are not condoned by conservative Muslims and he has been condemned as *kafir* (unbeliever).[55] But I do not think that we need to go down that path in promoting religious pluralism. What is advocated is simply an acknowledgement that different religions assert different truth claims, that all of us have a right to choose our own religion, and that it is desirable for adherents of different faiths to co-exist and appreciate one another. This does not mean that a Muslim should cave in and accept syncretism and polytheism. She could still assert, if she wishes, that her religion is superior, the best, or contains the only truth. She may even proselytise to others as long as it is within the confines of the law and does not cause inter-religious conflicts. She may do all of the above as long as she respects the right of non-Muslims to *do the same.*

CONCLUSION

That religious pluralism is not ubiquitous among the Islamic schools in Indonesia is not confined to Islamic educational institutions. Such a phenomenon also exists in the public schools in Indonesia. Policy wise, religious harmony is taught through the subject Religious Education that is offered in all public schools. The addendum of article 39 of the Education Act of 1989 highlights the necessity to respect the followers of other religions and promote inter-religious harmony in order to sustain national unity. The textbooks produced by the state and used in the public schools also emphasise the importance of respecting other religions and fostering inter-religious harmony and national unity.[56] However, these educational goals do not appear to be translated into action on a wide scale. Commenting on the current religious education in the public schools in Indonesia, Zakiyuddin Baidhawy describes it as leaning heavily towards "dogmatic indoctrination" where religious teachers teach "their own systems of religion or belief as the truth and the only path to salvation and regarding other religions as inferior".[57] Echoing his observation is the finding of a research project conducted by an inter-faith organisation Interfidei on the teaching of religion in public schools. It concludes that the curriculum leaves the students ignorant of and uninterested in other people's religions, does not dispel the misunderstandings and mutual suspicion of other religions, and fails to prevent existing religious conflict and violence.[58]

We can conclude from our discussion that most Islamic schools in Indonesia are not like Ngruki in reflecting an indoctrinatory tradition. But their environments also do not generally express the conditions of an educative tradition—one that is underpinned by religious pluralism, strong rationality, and strong autonomy. This of course does not mean that educative traditions do not exist in all Islamic educational institutions in Indonesia. Progressive, innovative, and ground-breaking educational practices have been carried out by some higher institutions of Islamic learning in Indonesia. These institutions blaze the trail for other Islamic institutions in creating and strengthening Muslim educative traditions. We shall look at these exciting examples in the next chapter.

8 Beyond Indoctrination
Towards Educative Muslim Traditions

"I learned they [the Westerners] were nice, normal human beings."[1]

The above statement was uttered by a graduate of Ngruki who had been warned many times of the "evils" of Westerners and their "conspiracy" to destroy Muslims. But his views of them changed after he graduated and met some of them while working as a tour guide. His experience is a good example of how his control beliefs that were implanted at Ngruki were challenged and revised subsequently when he was confronted with a reality that he has hitherto been shielded from. His story reminds us that a cure for and antidote to indoctrination is an educative tradition where we live in an open tradition that thrives on a plurality of beliefs, values and world views. This chapter discusses how indoctrination can be countered and avoided primarily through the creation, sustenance, and propagation of educative traditions. I shall outline how the control beliefs of religious pluralism, strong rationality, and strong autonomy can be introduced in formal, non-formal, and informal education.

TOWARDS RELIGIOUS PLURALISM

For religious pluralism to be acceptable to most Muslims, there is a need to situate and justify it within an Islamic context. Sohail H. Hashmi asserts that "if modern Muslims are to build tolerant and pluralistic societies based on Qur'anic teachings, they must also be prepared to chart a new exegetical course".[2] Muslim scholars such as Nurcholish Madjid have proposed a methodological system grounded in rational hermeneutic in determining the validity of a prescription that is particular to a time and place.[3]

A good example of an approach that promotes religious pluralism from an Islamic perspective is a programme "Muslim Tolerance and Appreciation for Multiculturalism" implemented at the Muhammadiyah University of Surakarta. According to an Indonesian lecturer who was involved in this programme, it aims to "develop arguments for multicultural Islam based on theological, philosophical and Islamic jurisprudential precepts, using these to legitimate the concept of multicultural Islam, and to promote religious tolerance towards the multicultural society".[4] What is noteworthy about this programme is that it anchors its theological arguments on an Islamic premise of respecting the diversity among human beings. The programme has identified the core values that correspond to their implementation and goals. These core values function as control beliefs for the recipients of the programme. Let me elaborate with an example of the goal of promoting a non-violent culture.[5] I have presented some of the core values taken from the programme in the following format:

Theory: Muslims should promote a non-violent culture (*lyn*) in their attitude, behaviour, structures, and systems.

Data beliefs: beliefs on the concept, attitude, behaviour, structures, and systems of *lyn*.

Data-background beliefs: *Tasamuh* (tolerance), *Tafahum* (mutual understanding), *Sulh* (reconciliation), etc.

Control beliefs: *Tawhid* (the unity of Godhead), *Ummah* (living together), *Rahmah* (love), and *Al-musawah, taqwa* (egalitarianism)

A non-violent culture is created and sustained through understanding the data beliefs on the concept, attitude, behaviour, structures, and systems of *lyn* that preserve and protect physical, mental, social, and environmental security and safety. The data beliefs are in turn influenced by the data-background beliefs, particularly *Tasamuh* (tolerance) on the desire to accept and respect the plurality of religious and cultural differences, *Tafahum* (mutual understanding) on the need to understand and empathise with those who are different from us, and *Sulh* (reconciliation) on the means to make peace after violence has taken place.

These data-background beliefs are further conditioned by four control beliefs. First, *Tawhid* (the unity of Godhead) emphasises the need to maintain the unity of humankind as brothers (*ukhuwwah basyariyyah*) based on God as the primary source of all humankind. The second control belief is *Ummah* (living together) where all human beings, regardless of religion, can co-exist peacefully. The third control belief is *Rahmah* (love) which refers to a spirit of love and care in human interaction based on the attributes of God the Merciful and Benevolence. Finally the control belief of *Al-musawah, taqwa* (egalitarianism) reminds all of our equal status before God despite our differences. In short, Muslims who subscribe to the control beliefs as spelt out above will be shaped by these control beliefs in forming and accepting theories that contribute towards the creation and perpetuation of an educative Islamic tradition. At the same time, these control beliefs serve as the filter for them to assess and reject theories that contradict or are inconsistent with the control beliefs. A case in point is the theory on violence against and hatred towards non-Muslims as propounded by some Muslim militant groups.

How then can we further inculcate and entrench the control belief of religious pluralism to all and sundry in society? I propose promoting religious pluralism through a *dialogical education* that aims to balance openness and rootedness.[6] A dialogical education can take place at three related and overlapping levels between Muslims and non-Muslims: preliminary dialogue, practical dialogue, and critical dialogue.

First, preliminary dialogue refers to minimal inter-religious engagement through symbolic acts of interest and support towards another religion. Examples include visiting a place of worship of another faith and attending an exhibition showcasing the religious artefacts from different faiths. Any encounter with believers of another faith is spontaneous and sporadic. As it does not require direct interaction among adherents of different faiths, it is the easiest to achieve but is limited in building bridges. The next two types of inter-religious dialogues foster greater exchanges through planned face-to-face encounters. A practical dialogue focuses on cooperation among adherents of different faiths through a community or humanitarian project that is not explicitly religious in nature. The objective, as Heid Leganger-Krogstad puts it, is to make common celebrations and ethical practice possible, understandable, and transparent, thereby motivating participants to discover common values and essential differences for harmonious living.[7] The last type is critical dialogue that involves dialogues planned for participants to discuss religious issues based on theological similarities and differences. The commonalities are the shared values that transcend religions, such as love, truth, respect for human dignity, and good works. An Islamic research in Britain suggests how a "civic morality" can be established through such interactions:

> In practice, this means articulating a kind of civic morality that identifies how to treat others well: affirming mutual respect, and not discriminating against others. Muslims should treat non-Muslim individuals as equal in the domain of social interaction, regardless of religious or doctrinal disagreements. The starting point for building this framework, from the Islamic point of view, is the body of principles outlined in the Qur'an and Islamic traditions, including good neighbourliness, charity, hospitality, non-aggression, honouring of commitments and competing in doing good.[8]

The "body of principles outlined in the Qur'an and Islamic traditions" brings to mind the "transcendental principles of reason" that were discussed in Chapter 5.

Critical dialogue should also focus on the differences within a religious tradition as well as between religious traditions. Though difficult to achieve, it is necessary to engage in controversial and contested issues between the various faiths at an appropriate time and place for mature participants. The objective is not to win the argument or even to reach a consensus (although this is desirable) but to empathise and understand. Examples are competing truth claims, salvation of those outside one's faith, and religious conversion. Without dialogues on the fundamental differences, interfaith dialogues may remain superficial without an understanding of the deep commitments, suspicions, and grievances of other religious traditions. The discussion should take place within a framework of all parties stating and justifying their views rationally while respecting the right of others to hold to their views and agree to disagree.

In the context of the Islamic traditions, Farish A. Noor argues that "there is a desperate need for Muslims to re-learn the norms and rules of dialogue and communication", including the "right and duty to communicate its anger, pain, frustration, and fears to the rest of the world" in a spirit of intelligence, honesty, and compassion.[9] He adds that a pluralist mindset is essential for Muslims. Addressing fellow Muslims, he writes:

> Recognising the multiplicity within ourselves opens the way for us to recognise the multiplicity of the other as well. It would mean that we would be able to look at the West (and the rest) for what it truly is: a complex assembly of actors and agents, interests, beliefs, values, and ideas that may not be completely in harmony with each other. It may also help us realise that in the midst of that confusing and complex heterogeneity that is the other are also values, beliefs, and ideas that are common to ours. . . . We need to remind ourselves continually of the fact that the Western world is far from uniform and that there exists a vast array of Western thinkers, leaders, activists, and citizens who care for Muslims as much as they do for their own. These are our real allies and friends, and we must never abandon or disregard them in our pursuit of justice and equity.[10]

The three types of dialogues can be implemented sequentially, progressively, or concurrently, depending on the specific needs. What is important is to encourage dialogues in all contexts, that is, not just in formal but also non-formal and informal education. It should also involve the key stakeholders from all segments of society such as the schools, religious institutions, social groups, and of course the state. To illustrate dialogical education, I would like to highlight some international examples of initiatives to foster inter-religious harmony between Muslims and non-Muslims.

The first example is the initiative of an Islamic school in Singapore to strengthen its curriculum on inter-religious understanding and harmony. This is achieved by introducing a new compulsory subject known as "Islamic Social Studies" for its students. A content analysis of the textbooks used at the primary level shows that the value of religious pluralism is emphasised through the messages that a good Muslim appreciates the richness of other civilisations, is inclusive and practises pluralism, and is a blessing to other communities.[11] For example, in the lesson "Let's meet our neighbours", the primary 2 textbook states:

> We help and care for one another. We even visit each other during our different celebrations. We treat our neighbours with respect and kindness. Rasulullah s.a.w [Messenger of Allah, peace be upon him] respected and took care of his neighbours. As Muslims, we should follow Rasulullah's footsteps.[12]

Qur'anic verses are judiciously included to provide the religious justification for religious pluralism. For example, this verse is cited in the primary 4 textbook: "O mankind! We created you from a single (pair) of a male and a female, and made you into nations and tribes, that you may know each other (not that you may despise each other)".[13] In a classroom lesson that I have observed on Islamic social studies, the topic was on a Chinese celebratory event known as the *lantern festival*. It was an engaging lesson where the madrasah students learned about the meaning and significance of the event for the Chinese, the need for Muslims to respect the beliefs of non-Muslims, and practical ways to join the Chinese in the celebrations. The lesson ended with an arts and craft session where the children made their own colourful lanterns. Besides classroom lessons, the students also carried out project work such as creating a photo album of their multi-religious neighbourhood and profiling their non-Muslim neighbours.[14] The Islamic school also organises sports events and educational meetings between its students and non-Muslim students from the public schools.

The second example is a specific programme known as "(Re)embracing Diversity in New York City Public Schools: Educational Outreach for Muslim Sensitivity".[15] Aimed at addressing and preventing intolerance towards Arab American and Muslim American students in the wake of the 9/11 attack, the programme incorporates activities such as problem solving, critical thinking, and collaborative learning. Examples of topics include "Towards Understanding Islam and Muslims," "A Common Language for Discussing Bias and Hatred," "Reflections on Prejudice," and "Field Trip to an Islamic Institution." Initial research conducted by Seyfi Kenan shows that the programme has succeeded in promoting and restoring the values of tolerance, peace, and diversity in public school communities.[16]

Another example of a Christian-Muslim endeavour in the United States is "THE ISLAM PROJECT" in the United States. This initiative provides the platform for interfaith and community organisations to collaborate with Muslim groups to understand the issues facing Muslims in the United States and elsewhere through multimedia resources and group discussions.[17] Other multi-faith initiatives led by Muslims include the "Amman Message" (2004–2005) and "A Common Word Between Us and You" (2007) to counter religious extremism and mobilise religious leaders and others to build ties.[18]

Another commendable inter-religious dialogue where informed, empathetic, and critical comments were exchanged was a Christian-Muslim dialogue entitled "Building Bridges" held at Lambeth Palace in Britain in 2002. Bridges were built when the participants examined contemporary and controversial issues such as monotheism, the figure of Jesus, assimilation of Muslim minorities, and toleration.[19] Research centres that foster inter-religious understanding and engagement also play an important role. An example is the Centre for Muslim-Christian Studies in Oxford that aims to promote the study of Islam among Christians, the study of Christianity among Muslims, and rigorous academic teaching and research on the Muslim-Christian interface.[20]

TOWARDS STRONG RATIONALITY AND STRONG AUTONOMY

I have already discussed strong rationality and strong autonomy in Chapter 5. "Strong rationality" essentially means that Muslims are willing and able to ask both internal and external questions about their own tradition and those of others. The learners are open to and engaged with other Islamic and non-Islamic traditions. "Strong autonomy" implies that Muslims are encouraged to reflectively and critically apply Islamic teachings to their lives by making their own decisions and adapting to changing times and places. The educational goal, as noted by Tariq Ramadan, is to help "all Muslims to enter into personal growth and, consequently to become autonomous in their lives, their choices, and, more generally, in the management of their freedom".[21] To encourage the children's development of strong rationality and strong autonomy, educators and parents could provide the following conducive conditions: preparing and inviting the children to ask questions; teaching them that religious doctrines are not universally and publicly agreed-on beliefs but are primarily grounded in and derivative of religious faith; being willing to respond to the questioning honestly and in a way that is compatible with their developing cognitive and emotional maturity; and nurturing their attitudes of tolerance and understanding regarding religious differences.[22]

Two points of clarifications are needed here. First, my recommendation of strong rationality and strong autonomy does not imply that I am recommending the adoption of "liberal approaches". This point was raised by Kathleen Taylor who suggests that the antidote to avoiding brainwashing is to adopt "liberal approaches". Such approaches include minimising state and group control, maximising individual freedom, and empowering people to possess "the rights and pleasures we in the West enjoy".[23] However, I do not think that "liberal approaches" that originate from and that are widely practised in Western liberal democratic societies are appropriate for all societies. As explained earlier, I advocate a culturally and contextually sensitive account of "normal rationality" and "normal autonomy" where they arise from and interact with contingent historical factors. Besides, "liberal approaches" are unlikely to be embraced by Indonesian Muslims who do not view the "pleasures we in the West enjoy" favourably. Instead, what is proposed is for Muslims to possess strong rationality and strong autonomy grounded in Islamic principles and compatible with the cultural context of Indonesia.

That leads us to the second clarification. In supporting the creation of educative Muslim traditions, we need to recognise that they are not monolithic and homogeneous. There is a spectrum of educative traditions that hold to different views on the proper relationship between *reason* and *revelation*. Muslim traditions that are described as "modernist" or "rationalist" tend to subscribe to the view that revelation is not the only source for Muslims, and that human beings can use reason as a yardstick of morality. Such a position has historical precedents. Back in the period between the ninth and eleventh centuries, Muslim philosophers such as al-Kindi, al Farabi, and Ibn Sina argued that values were objective and could be understood through reason alone.[24] The Mu'tazili theologians (from the eighth to eleventh centuries) went as far as positing that reason, *not* revelation, was the starting point for human beings to know about God's existence, salvation, and their moral responsibility. They held that "speculative reason (*nazar*) was theoretically prior to faith—a tool for bringing rational human beings to Islamic faith, from which they could discover the benefits of accepting God's revealed religious duties".[25] However, there are other Muslim traditions that do not go that far and instead assert the primacy of revelation over reason. Despite their divergence of views, all educative Islamic traditions share a common vision of the good that seeks to educate rather than indoctrinate.

Having outlined the salient characteristics of religious pluralism, strong rationality, and strong autonomy, let us see how educative Muslim traditions can be introduced, strengthened, and propagated in formal, informal, and non-formal education in Indonesia.

EDUCATIVE TRADITIONS IN A FORMAL CONTEXT

A good example of Islamic educational institutions that consciously and systematically develop their students' pluralism, strong rationality, and strong autonomy within an educative tradition are the State Islamic Universities (UINs) such as the UIN Syarif Hidayatullah Jakarta. UINs are part of the Islamic higher education institutions in Indonesia; the others include the State Institute for Islamic Studies (Institut Agama Islam Negeri/IAIN) and State Islamic Colleges (Sekolah Tinggi Agama Islam Negeri/STAIN). UIN Jakarta came into existence in 2002 when IAIN Jakarta was converted to a full-fledged university that offers not just Islamic subjects but the humanities, social sciences, and natural sciences.

UIN has been described as a "major centre of educational innovation".[26] Fuad Jabali and Jamhari note that the Islamic culture in IAIN (the predecessor of UIN) is modern, contextual, and rational with the educational goal for Muslim Indonesians to understand the important meaning of modernity, progress, societal pluralism, and tolerance toward people who profess other religions.[27] According to Azyumardi Azra, the former rector of UIN Jakarta and current director of its graduate school, UIN Jakarta is able to play a major role in promoting a form of Islam that is tolerant and inclusive because of its fundamental approach towards the study of Islam. Islam is treated not only as a religion but also as a historical phenomenon that has evolved and adapted to many societies and cultures; this makes it possible to critically analyse Islam as an observable phenomenon.[28] UIN fosters strong rationality and strong autonomy through three main ways: its curriculum, methodology in the study of Islam, and learning environment. Let us look at them accordingly.

The curriculum for Islamic subjects at UIN encourages its students to engage in critical thinking by considering and comparing a variety of traditions, both within and outside the Islam faith. This is achieved in two ways. First, the students' horizon is not limited to one Islamic school of thought but covers a wide canvass of Islamic discourses. The UIN curriculum goes beyond the confines of the Shafi'i law to study other legal schools of thought such as the Hanafi, Hanbali, Maliki, and Ja'fari law.[29] That is not all: UIN moves beyond the usual staple of *Sunnite* literature grounded in the Ash'ari theology to include non-mainstream Islamic literature such as the theological school of Maturidis, Sufism, Shi'i, and Mu'tazila schools of thought.[30] These are subjects that many other Muslims have denounced as syncretistic, impure, or heretical. The students are also exposed to the works of contemporary Muslim scholars known for their progressive views such as Fazlur Rahman, Muhammed Arkoun, Muhammed al-Jabiri, Hassan Hanafi, and even Western Orientalists such as Ignaz Goldziher.[31] The focus of the study transcends identifying the differences or critiquing other schools of thought. The educational objective is for the students to be more open, tolerant, and pluralist by appreciating different religious interpretations and new thoughts on religion.[32]

The students do not just learn about other Islamic traditions: they are also introduced to ideas and thoughts from non-Islamic sources and systems. Rather than seeing the West as an enemy, UIN welcomes intellectual, social, and cultural interactions with the West in order to broaden the intellectual vistas of its students. Works by modern non-Muslim philosophers such as Kant, Husserl, Heidegger, and Gadamer are consulted. Students study other religions such as Christianity and Judaism from the perspective of their adherents and are free to debate on the essential validity of these religions.[33] Further exposure to and interaction with non-Muslim scholars and their ideas are achieved through attending lectures by visiting non-Muslim theologians and educators—something I have personally experienced during my sojourn in UIN Jakarta.

In terms of the methodology used in the study of Islam, UIN does not just rely on the textual approach that is commonly used in most universities in the Middle East; it also uses the contextual approach that is popularly used in many universities in Western countries.[34] This means situating Islam within a social-historical context and using modern approaches such as social analysis in approaching Islamic studies. It adopts "a comprehensive, holistic study of Islam and the Prophet Muhammad tradition (hadith) and respect for the humanistic, tolerant, egalitarian and open tradition of classical Islam".[35] Such a historical, sociological, and empirical methodology, rather than a pure normative approach, recognises the human socio-historical realities facing Muslims and thereby assists them to adapt to changing times and circumstances. Its accent on objective inquiry also facilitates the students' endeavours in comparative study without being influenced by their personal preferences and biases.

Complementing the inclusive and progressive curriculum and methodology are a conducive learning environment and ethos. Motivated by the freedom of thought and opinion, the students are not obliged to hold to any particular Islamic ideology and are instead encouraged to make up their own minds and substantiate their stand based on relevant texts and reasoning.[36] Abdullah Saeed points out that the methods of teaching value "a degree of critical thinking, teach analytical skills and problem solving", and display the importance of ijtihad (individual interpretation).[37] Rather than learning passively from lectures given by a teacher who is viewed as the dispenser of knowledge, UIN students engage in student-directed activities such as independent study through fieldwork and dissertation writing. The teacher's key role is to facilitate critical discussions and guide the students to explore possible aspects of a problem. Azyumardi Azra explains that

> a participatory, democratic, and inclusive approach is encouraged. Critical thought is no longer the exclusive preserve of an entrenched hierarchy of Muslim ulama and scholars. Self-criticism promotes self-reliance, coexistence, and tolerance, and a readiness to accept, analytically, critically, and unemotionally, the positions of others.[38]

Overall, UIN Jakarta is an exemplary model of a forward-looking Islamic educational institution that is firmly rooted in an educative Muslim tradition. However, the modernist and pluralist educational efforts of UIN Jakarta and other UINs have not gone unopposed. Muslim individuals and organisations from more traditionalist and conservative traditions have objected to UIN's rational and contextual approaches to Islamic knowledge.[39] They argue that UINs and other Islamic schools that follow suit have departed from the "authentic" Islamic traditions. Some Muslims scholars such as Hartono Ahmad Jaiz have even published works to refute what they perceive to be inaccurate and unIslamic teachings of Muslim intellectuals associated with UIN, such as Harun Nasution (professor of theology and rector of IAIN Jakarta in the 1970s) and Nurcholish Madjid.[40] They further allege that UIN Jakarta has been influenced by "Zionist" and "Orientalist" agenda.[41]

Religious pluralism should take place not only in Islamic educational institutions but in non-Islamic schools as well. A good example is Madania, a national school that follows the national curriculum from the elementary to the senior high school levels. The founder of Madania School was Nurcholish Madjid, a well-known inclusive Islamic intellectual who advocated pluralism, religious harmony, and tolerance for the students to develop religious maturity and be respectful towards other religious communities. As implied by its name "madani" (civil), the school's vision is to be "a true Indonesian school for the next generation of leaders" in a global world. That is achieved through the development of the students' strong autonomy to "participate actively, study independently, develop creativity, and own the chance to solve their own problems".[42] Another interesting and unique feature of Madania is its promotion of religious pluralism and tolerance. Noting that religious pluralism is a feature of the global community, the school provides religious instruction based on the students' choice in the school curriculum: Islam, Christianity, Catholicism, Jehovah Witnesses, Buddhism, and Hinduism. A premium is placed on the students' understanding and demonstration of religious tolerance towards those of different religious backgrounds as progressive Indonesians with a global outlook. Unsurprisingly, Madania, like UINs, has been criticised by conservative Muslims for its religiously pluralist belief and practices.

EDUCATIVE TRADITIONS IN AN INFORMAL CONTEXT

Beyond Islamic educational institutions, the larger socio-political context plays a significant role in shaping the worldview of the Muslims. That is why I have consistently emphasised the role of the Muslim tradition in (re)constructing and transmitting the text. As Milton Viorst succinctly puts it, "[T]he texts speak through those who command them"; Khaled Abou El Fadl adds that interpretive communities that are formed around the text "hold the moral insights of the text hostage".[43] How then can informal education—the teaching and learning that takes place naturally through one's interactions and experiences as a member of society—counter indoctrinatory traditions and contribute to educative traditions?

First, there is a need to weaken the socio-political conditions that contribute to the entrenched control beliefs of ideological totalism. This can be achieved by exposing Muslims in closed traditions to new and alternative ideas, people, and influences in society. Such was the experience of the Ngruki graduate cited at the start of the chapter. Like him, other graduates of Ngruki may be confronted with new and contrary beliefs when they are enrolled in a higher educational institution that does not share Ngruki's totalistic ideology. Others who join the workforce may meet Muslims of different religious orientations as well as non-Muslims with their own religious traditions. That appears to be the case as Ismail points out that the vast majority of the Ngruki's graduates change their views when they make contact with the wider world.[44] They may realise that non-Muslims including the Westerners can be "nice, normal human beings". Such an awareness is the first step towards religious pluralism. More of such opportunities should be created between Muslims and non-Muslims through a dialogical education, as expounded earlier.

Another major factor is the role of the indoctrinated person's family and community. The psychologist Robert Jay Lifton concludes from his study of brainwashing that emotional support and confirmation from peers are effective in resisting indoctrination.[45] This means that a lack of support or the presence of resistance from the family and community serves to weaken the control beliefs of the Muslim militants and their networks. A real-life example is the refusal of the villagers of a convicted militant in Indonesia to allow his body to be buried in the village. They objected to his militant activities and did not wish the village to have the reputation of a "terrorist village".[46] Such a move sends out a powerful message to the whole community that militancy and ideological totalism are unacceptable. The community also plays a decisive role in discrediting Islamic schools that promote ideological totalism. This is illustrated in the rejection of an Al-Islam pesantren by the Tenggulun community in Lamongan. The pesantren was believed to be advocating militancy and three of its graduates were involved in the Bali bombing (Ali Ghufron, Amrozi, and Ali Imron).[47] The community openly rejected the ideology of the Islamic school, thus making it more challenging for the school to enroll students and obtain the community support.

Third, we need to acknowledge and address the concerns and frustrations of many Indonesian Muslims about the perceived social problems of rampant corruption, moral decline especially among the young (as evidenced in access to pornography and premarital sex), widespread unemployment, general poverty, and distrust of the state. These triggers are likely to incline and push the masses to support an ideology of violence and implementation of Islamic governance in their search for a solution.[48] These are pressing issues the policymakers in Indonesia need to address urgently. Noting that Abu Bakar Ba'asyir is a charismatic figure with many followers, an Indonesian university lecturer contends that strong evidence and transparency should be put forward by the police in prosecuting Ba'asyir; otherwise, his arrest may be seen as unjust and inadvertently encourage more militant sympathisers and participants.[49]

There is also a corresponding need for the international community to confront the political developments affecting Muslims worldwide that have caused or added to deep and sustained Muslim grievances. Examples, according to Muhammad Haniff Hassan, are "the uneven foreign policy of the United States in the Middle East, especially vis-à-vis Israel and Palestine, the occupation of Iraq and the continued American 'support' for undemocratic regimes in the region".[50] Khaled Abou El Fadl maintains that "Western hostility, suspicion, and dismissiveness" have "doomed Muslims to ages of despair, distrust, degradation, and extremism".[51] Hassan explains the link between Muslim grievances and Muslim militancy:

> Terrorist leaders may be so committed to their ideas that nothing can change their minds. But they will be less successful in gaining support from the people if there is no context for their ideas to blossom. . . . If the international community continues to be ineffective in addressing these grievances, people will empower themselves. The answer therefore requires the political will of governments to address the root causes of the grievances that terrorist groups seize upon and exploit in the name of avenging Islam.[52]

Without resolving or alleviating these internal and external problems, quiescent Muslims who hitherto have rejected Islamist political parties or relied on democratic means to establish an Islamic state may be tempted to become active militants.[53]

EDUCATIVE TRADITIONS IN A NON-FORMAL CONTEXT

Besides formal and informal education, non-formal education is the third piece in the jigsaw. The religious leadership of mainstream and respectable Muslim organisations is influential in undermining indoctrinatory traditions and promoting educative traditions. In particular, Nahdlatul Ulama (NU) and Muhammadiyah, the two Muslim organisations that enjoy the support of almost half of the Muslim population in Indonesia, play a major role in countering ideological totalism and fostering religious pluralism.

It is well-known that NU and Muhammadiyah do not support the ideology of armed jihad and the establishment of an Islamic state propagated by Ngruki and Jemaah Islamiyah (JI). It has been noted that a JI cell in Central Java had tried to establish contacts with pesantrens affiliated with the NU and Muhammadiyah but found them "inaccessible".[54] It is helpful to note that a fatwa was released by NU ulama of East Java stating that the implementation of *khilafa* (caliphate system of governance) is not compulsory in Islam since there is no clear text (*nas*) in Islam on that point.[55] That NU does not endorse terrorism is also alluded to in my interview with a NU pesantren. What makes this pesantren different from other NU pesantrens is that the kyai requires all its female staff and students to don a *niqab* (the headgear that covers the whole face except the eyes). This is an unusual practice that is more commonly associated with Salafi/Wahhabi pesantrens that advocate armed jihad. The kyai frankly said:

> Some [visitors] would be candid with us and asked as to why our wives and female students look like the wives of the terrorists. . . . We found hadiths that support this ruling. The ruling may be similar to Wahhabi's teaching. . . . But we do not subscribe to terrorism. We are a NU pesantren.[56]

Given that the Muslim leaders from NU and Muhammadiyah are knowledgeable and respectable public figures, their words, actions, and activities to counter an indoctrinatory tradition and strengthen educative traditions are likely to be accepted by most Muslims. It is worthwhile recalling that the control beliefs of an indoctrinated person are based on thought-terminating and ultimate terms that are extremely difficult to be replaced. To counter or weaken ideological totalism in indoctrinatory traditions, the strategy is not to reject ultimate terms such as "God" and "jihad", but to *redefine* them in ways that are compatible with educative traditions. An example would be to affirm the centrality of jihad for Muslims but reject the interpretation by Ngruki and JI in favour of one that is more mainstream and moderate. Doing so is more acceptable to the Muslim militants or aspiring militants than persuading them to jettison their religious beliefs. Scott Atran's research with militants who have rejected suicide bombings shows that they remain very committed to Salafi principles. The best way, according to him, is to "turn altruistic suicide bombers who believe that what they are doing is sacred away from violence by religiously promoting competing sacred values, such as spreading the faith and promoting equal economic opportunity, as well as social and political advancement through educational achievement and personal piety".[57]

Admittedly, those who have already been indoctrinated and are active in Ngruki, JI, and its network of like-minded Muslims may not be receptive to the admonition and educational activities of NU and Muhammadiyah. However, NU and Muhammadiyah could influence the mindset of the majority of Muslims who are potential victims of indoctrination and quietly supportive of the militants. The target audience should also include the Islamic educational community, especially the kyais, teachers, and students of the Islamic schools interviewed in the national surveys. These people may not be militants but are ostensibly intolerant and anti-pluralist towards non-Muslims. According to NU's executive leader Hafidz Usman, NU is already working with the government to support its "deradicalisation programme" of convicted militants.[58] Though that is a good start, more can be done to de-indoctrinate the Muslim militants and their families, and create and proliferate educative traditions in Indonesia.

Besides NU and Muhammadiyah, other social organisations could play a significant part too in promoting religious pluralism among the adherents of different faiths. A good example is Interfidei (The Institute for Interfaith Dialogue in Indonesia), founded by Th. Sumartana and his colleagues in 1991.[59] Its vision is to establish a civilised and plural civic society that is rooted in the values of humanity, democracy, justice, and integrity. Comprising both Muslim and Christian members in the organising committee, Interfidei aims to promote religious pluralism and interfaith dialogue where members of a religious community can interact with and listen to one another. Such opportunities are created through various platforms such as short courses, exchange programmes, conferences, workshops, publications, community-service learning, and visits to religious centres. Its strategies are to create an awareness of religious pluralism; encourage honest, open, and critical networking groups; and uphold interfaith groups as peaceful, non-violent, and democratic social movements. The participants include activists of non-governmental organisations (NGOs), university students, and other Indonesians. In underlining "interfaith" rather than "inter-religious", Interfidei aims to go beyond the institutional baggage of religion to focus on the faith of the individuals. What is worthy of mention about the interfaith dialogues is the friendship that is built in the course of the interaction. Achmad Munjid who is a key figure in Interfidei observes that the initial interactions among participants of different religions are often marked by mutual suspicion and misunderstanding. But these give way to mutual understanding and affection as the participants begin to see one another beyond the religious label. This emphasis reflects a dialogical education where bridges are built through intellectual and emotional connections.

In conclusion, more educational activities initiated and endorsed by NU, Muhammadiyah, and other organisations are needed to engender a spirit of religious pluralism among the Muslims. This point has been noted by Alwi Shihab who is a leading authority on Muslim-Christian relation in Indonesia and a former Minister of Foreign Affairs (1999–2001) of Indonesia:

> The failure to promote the spirit of tolerance and religious pluralism of the Qur'an will only strengthen the Muslim radical wing. Conversely, success in developing Islamic religious tolerance mainly depends on Muslims' ability to spread a popular understanding of the numerous quranic principles of religious pluralism in general and a positive attitude toward Christianity in particular. Individual Muslims and groups therefore have a moral responsibility to draw on the rich cultural and intellectual inheritance that was developed during the formative stage

of Islam in which harmonious interactions between Islam and Christianity were conspicuously evident.[60]

CONCLUSION

This chapter proposed ways in which the control beliefs of religious pluralism, strong rationality, and strong autonomy can be introduced and promoted in formal, non-formal, and informal education. The way to recover from and avoid indoctrination is to work at one's control beliefs. The lack of attention on one's control beliefs may explain the unsuccessful attempts by the Indonesian state to rehabilitate convicted militants. Zachary Abuza, in his review of the rehabilitation programmes in Indonesia and Malaysia, asserts that the priority of these programmes is to get the militants to reject their violent means rather than their goals of living in an Islamic state governed by shari'ah. As a result, they "continue to maintain their cognitive radicalism, if not their behavioural radicalism".[61] In other words, any rehabilitation programmes that do not target "cognitive radicalism" (that springs from one's control beliefs) are bound to fail in changing one's mindset in the long term. Without revising their control beliefs, these militants are likely, upon release, to return to their former lifestyle, network, and community. In short, they will continue to be victims of indoctrination. Indeed, many militants in Indonesia who were released from jail went back to their old ways and did not give up their ideology on armed jihad. The latest were two convicted militants involved in the 2002 Bali bombing. Their life sentences have been reduced to 20 years due to "good behaviour". But one of them Adbul Ghoni told the press that he still admired the men who carried out the violent attacks as "God will still reward them"; the other militant Sawad said that he would do the same thing again if given the choice.[62] Another example is Abdullah Sunata who supposedly gave up his violent ways during his rehabilitation, only to return to militancy upon his release.[63]

Indonesia is known for a "tolerant, moderate, and 'middle way' (*Ummah wasat*) Islam", with mainstream Muslim organisations open to religious dialogues with Christian and other non-Muslim organisations at the local, national, and international levels.[64] However, we need to acknowledge that there are Muslims who reject religious pluralism in favour of a totalistic ideology that results in armed jihad and war between Muslims and non-Muslims. The case in Indonesia demonstrates the diversity and dynamism of Muslim traditions in (re)constructing and influencing the masses on the "correct" interpretations of religious issues that impinge on the Muslims. The next chapter draws our study of Islamic education and indoctrination to a close by discussing their international significance and implications.

Conclusion

"[A]s Americans we are not and will never be at war with Islam. It was not a religion that attacked us that September day. It was Al-Qaeda, a sorry band of men which perverts religion."

—President Barack Obama[1]

The events preceding the recent anniversary of 9/11 attack in 2010 were troubling. The world was fixated with a controversial plan announced by Imam Feisal Abdul Rauf to build an Islamic community centre and mosque near Ground Zero. It triggered violent protests from non-Muslim Americans who called the plan insensitive and provocative. Adding fuel to the fire was a Christian pastor who proclaimed that "Islam is of the devil" and threatened to burn copies of the Qur'an on the anniversary of the 9/11 attack.[2] In trying to mediate the rift between Muslims and non-Muslims in the United States, President Barack Obama reminded the Americans that they should not be at war with Islam but with people who have "perverted Islam."

It has been close to a decade since the 9/11 attack. But it appears that we are still living in the shadows of that fateful day. Every anniversary of the 9/11 attack, far from healing the wounds, reopens them and threatens to worsen the relationship between Muslims and others. Many people are keen to have a say on what Islam is or is not, and what Muslims do or do not. But what *is* Islam? And what *do* Muslims do?

Answers to the above questions often run the risk of misrepresenting, essentialising, and homogenising Islam and Muslims. Such a tendency is not new, but it has become more prevalent after the 9/11 attack. This point was noted by the Muslim academic Omid Safi who found himself repeating statements such as "Islam is a religion of peace" whenever he was asked by non-Muslims this question: "So, what does Islam really say about violence?" He reflectively asks:

And yet, for some reason, this simplistic response has left a not altogether satisfactory feeling behind—at least in my own mind. Had I not spent the better part of my own training and teaching trying to avoid grand generalisations? Had we not worked so hard to critique orientalist assumptions and essentialisations that described Islam as a religion of law, of unity of the "Semitic mind," of the "Arab mind," of every other "single-key" explanation? Have we not strived to emphasise the historical, cultural, and intellectual diversity of the Islamic experience? While it is understandable that at such a time of crisis we would find refuge in "Islam is a religion of peace," I yearned to rise above that nicety and find a framework for deeper, more honest, more difficult, and perhaps more truthful conversations.[3]

This book represents an attempt to base our discussion of Islamic education and indoctrination on Safi's "framework for deeper, more honest, more difficult, and perhaps more truthful conversations". The caution against essentialising and homogenising Islam takes us back to our introductory chapter. I have stated at the start that my focus is not to define *what Islam is* at the abstract level. Rather, it is to study how Islam is interpreted and translated into practice by Muslims in their various and competing traditions. To avoid over-generalising Islamic education, I have contextualised our study by using Indonesia as an illustrative case study. I have highlighted the diversity of Muslim traditions within Indonesia by drawing our attention to indoctrinatory and educative traditions in Islamic education. I have explained how indoctrination occurs when a person holds to control beliefs that result in ideological totalism. I have also expounded on the conditions for indoctrinatory traditions to exist and thrive. I further suggested ways to counter and avoid indoctrination in formal, non-formal, and informal education, highlighting the need to create and promote educative traditions. In short, we need a good fishing net that is weaved from the control beliefs of religious pluralism, strong rationality, and strong autonomy. But our horizon needs to go beyond the ocean of Indonesia. This concluding chapter draws out the key international significance and implications of our study.

INTERNATIONAL SIGNIFICANCE AND IMPLICATIONS

Our case study of Indonesia offers international significance and implications primarily in three ways. As noted at the start of this chapter, there remains a propensity for people—Muslims and non-Muslims—to speak of Islam as a monolithic and undifferentiated religion for the 1.3 billion believers in the world. This assumption may have prompted some Muslims themselves to deny that Osama bin Laden is a Muslim or to object to using "Islamist" or "jihadist" to describe the actions of Osama and other militant Muslims. Such an endeavour to define what Islam is and is not, or what Muslims do and do not, is underpinned by a desire to stress the unity of Islam and the Muslim ummah (community). Concomitantly, there is an apologist motivation by some Muslims to present Muslim groups as united and homogenous. Ed Husain who joined militant Muslim groups as a college student in Britain shares his experiences and conclusion:

> Although there were other Islamist groups at the college with whom we were in conflict (such as the despised Dawatul Islam group), we were keen to present a united front, particularly to the detested kuffar [unbelievers].

> To a large extent we achieved that objective; indeed, the presentation of a united Islamist front to the outside world continues today.[4]

Such a response fundamentally relies on what Aaron W. Hughes aptly describes as an amorphous, essentialist, and ahistorical methodology to study Islam and the sacred texts.[5] I propose that we move beyond a study of "what is Islam?" in terms of the ontological status and the foundations of the Islamic faith, to focus on the question of "what does Islam mean to its adherents?" in terms of the disparate interpretations, articulations, and manifestations of Islam found among the Muslims.[6] This means underscoring Islam as a cultural system comprising various and competing Muslim traditions. Each tradition has its inherited conceptions expressed in symbolic forms for people to communicate, perpetuate, and develop their knowledge about and attitudes towards life. The plurality of and contestations among the Muslim traditions is a recurring theme in our study of Islamic education in Indonesia. From this pluralist point of view, it is (more) acceptable for us to describe Osama bin Laden as a Muslim or apply the terms "Islamist" or "jihadist" to militant Muslims who belong to a particular tradition. Through topics such as jihad and pluralism, I have highlighted the varied and irreconcilable views among Muslims on these issues. I have argued that their differences are due to their different control beliefs that shape not only their individual perspectives, but those of their communities and traditions. In emphasising the diversity within Islam, I reiterate the need to approach Islam as "a broad canopy that covers diverse and often contradictory sets of commitments, expressions, and ideologies".[7] Zakiyuddin Baidhawy makes the same point when he reminds us that "Islam is in and by itself a great tradition, but it also fosters plurality through the Islamisation of the extant culture it encounters and the way in which it absorbs aspects of that culture into itself, creating distinct sub-traditions of Islam".[8] Given that there is no Islamic monolith, Mohammed Ayoob asserts that no single individual, group, or institution can rightfully claim to speak for Muslims or on behalf of Islam.[9]

Second, this study has extended the topic of terrorism beyond security issues and anti-terrorism measures to the realm of ideological struggle. I have highlighted the active role of control beliefs in shaping the cognitive landscapes of individuals and their communities. I have maintained that the strategy to counter and avoid indoctrination is not to simply focus on the phenomenon of indoctrination but on the *conditions* that contribute to it. These conditions, encompassing formal, non-formal, and informal education, are the result of the interplay between internal and external socio-political factors. Additionally, I have gone beyond the discourse on indoctrinatory traditions to propose the strong presence and propagation of *educative traditions* as a long-term measure to weaken indoctrinatory traditions and influences in a society.

Third, this study has contributed to philosophy of education on the topic of indoctrination. Since the middle of the twentieth century, philosophers have prodominantly relied on the *conceptual analytical approach* to define indoctrination. This approach basically seeks to identify indoctrination based on one or a combination of the following criteria: intention, content, method, and outcome.[10] I have chosen not to continue with this tradition in exploring the concept of indoctrination. The obvious reason is that this approach has not resolved the fundamental disagreements among philosophers or brought us closer to understanding indoctrination. The failure of this approach is largely due to the fallacy of explanatory reductionism where a phenomenon or behaviour is explained purely by measuring it based on a set of common features or group membership.[11] That is why I have not conceptualised indoctrination in terms of a neat set of necessary and sufficient conditions that are quantifiable. I have also not confined indoctrination to a specific criterion such as the intention, content, method, or result. Instead, I have linked indoctrination to the phenomenon of ideological totalism that is characterised and expressed by broad conditions. My conception of indoctrination allows us to bypass the criteria of intention, content, process, and outcome. At the same time, my conception enables us to link indoctrination to a specific criterion when the situation calls for it. For example, if the question is on the process of indoctrination, we could examine how ideological totalism is introduced using various strategies. On another occasion, our interest of study may be on the content or specific teachings that promote ideological totalism.

I have also attempted to bridge the gap between theory and practice by referring to actual cases of indoctrination and indoctrinary traditions. It is now timely for us to return to the cases of alleged indoctrination mentioned in the introductory chapter. In instances where Muslims have joined militant groups such as the Jemaah Islamiyah (JI) and participated in violent actions against non-Muslims, we could ascertain if an indoctrinatory tradition exists based on the conditions of ideological totalism. However, the charge of indoctrination for students in American public schools is a different story. The mere exposure of the students to courses, textbooks, and activities on Islam does not entail that indoctrination has taken place. *Even if* the courses, textbooks, and activities are indeed biased, dangerous, and propagandistic (this is debatable), it takes more than these for indoctrination to exist and thrive. As I have argued, indoctrination involves a closed tradition that seeks to implant and entrench a select number of control beliefs that result in ideological totalism. It requires the joint and sustained efforts of active agents to create and sustain an indoctrinatory environment and imperil the students' development of strong rationality and strong autonomy.

CONCLUDING REMARKS

Indoctrinatory traditions are not confined to Indonesia, of course. It has been noted that the totalistic ideology of JI in Indonesia parallels those of Al-Qaeda, Hizb ut-Tahrir, and other militant Muslim movements in other countries. Given the pervasiveness of transnational networks of Muslims, it is easy for individual Muslims to be influenced and indoctrinated by an ideology of hostility and armed jihad against non-Muslims. A recent case in point is American Muslim Faisal Shahzad, a financial analyst, who was convicted of attempting violent attacks at Times Square, New York, in May 2010. When asked by the judge whether he thought that it was right of him to target innocent civilians, including children, he replied:

> Well, the people select the government. We consider them all the same. Well, the drone hits in Afghanistan and Iraq, they don't see children, they don't see anybody. They kill women, children, they kill everybody. It's a war, and in war, they kill people. They're killing all Muslims. . . . I am part of the answer to the US terrorising the Muslim nations and the Muslim people. And on behalf of that, I'm avenging the attack.[12]

Shahzad's words are disturbingly similar to those of Iman Samudra, Mukhlas, and other Muslim militants who attempted to justify their militancy and armed jihad. What is evident is their simplistic binary worldview of "Us versus Them", and evidences of being mystically manipulated and controlled by ideological totalism. Clearly, what is happening in Indonesia finds resonance worldwide. John L. Esposito and Dalia Mogahed note that "those with extremist views are a potential source for recruitment or support for terrorist groups" as they are "so committed to changing political conditions that they are more likely to view other civilian attacks as justifiable".[13]

Against a backdrop of global terrorist threats, many countries from Asia to Europe are scrutinising the Islamic schools and endeavouring to implement curricular changes in these institutions.[14] These reforms include introducing non-religious subjects and more student-centred teaching methods in the curriculum. At the same time, a number of Islamic schools have reciprocated by welcoming these additions into their religious curricula to allay the non-Muslims' fears and meet the changing needs of a globalised world.[15] While these changes in terms of modernising the curricula, pedagogy, and assessment in the Islamic schools are commendable, what is still being overlooked is the need to change the underlying ideology. In other words, there is a need to address the *control beliefs* from which a person's worldview and actions are shaped. I have argued in this book that the main strategy to weaken and avoid indoctrinatory traditions is to create and promote educative traditions that are underpinned by religious pluralism, strong rationality and strong autonomy. The aspiration and effort to foster religious pluralism between Muslims and non-Muslims cannot be one-sided, of course. Both Muslims and non-Muslims need to engage in a dialogical education to connect and clarify any misconceptions they may have of each other. It is telling that a 2007 Gallup Poll of Americans informs us that while the majority (8 in 10 Americans) believe that people in Muslim countries have an unfavourable opinion of them, more than half (57 percent) say it is because of "misinformation" about American actions.[16] A misinformation about American culture, values and actions also explains the prevailing negative perceptions of the United States by the Indonesian Muslims. This shows that inter-religious engagement at all levels (formal, informal, and non-formal) is urgently needed to foster mutual understanding, respect, and trust in the world.

One of my most memorable experiences in Indonesia was my conversation with a kyai of a pesantren. Friendly, knowledgeable, and humble, he shared freely about his vision and burden for his Islamic school that was founded by his grandfather. A devout Muslim, he was at the same time self-critical of his tradition. Lamenting that many Muslims are not open to learning from non-religious sources, he said:

> Qur'anic verses are brought down in different types. First is written, second is nature, third is in man. For us Muslims, we only learn the written one, we do not learn about nature and man. Maybe we do but very limited. And in the end the non-Muslims are the ones who master the knowledge about man, in terms of physical and spiritual components. So we're also *kuffar* [unbelieving] in this aspect.[17]

As I enjoyed the Javanese food served by him and listened to him dispensing words of wisdom, I was reminded of my former Muslim neighbour, my dear Nyonya. To me, both of them epitomise the type of Muslims— the *only* type I know of in my childhood days—whose devotion to their faith does not stop them from being affable and kind to non-Muslims like myself. Towards the end of our interview, he added this parting shot:

> A good Muslim is a good person. We should have an understanding of the religion that is moderate, not extreme, appreciates other people's opinions, befriend anybody. But how difficult it is to produce this.[18]

I left Indonesia with these words percolating in my mind. He has summed up the thesis of this book—and my personal hope—that the net of educative Muslim traditions may be cast far and wide in Indonesia and other parts of the world.

Notes

NOTES TO PREFACE

1. I.A. Snook, *Indoctrination and Education* (London and Boston: Routledge & Kegan Paul, 1972), 1–2.
2. Another philosopher Thomas F. Green makes a similar point on the disagreement on facts, although he was referring to a different topic on the difference between "indoctrinating" and "instructing". He points out that while instructing and indoctrinating can be defined and distinguished based on clear criteria, the respects in which they differ *in practice* may be exemplified in varying degrees, and hence are not clearly manifested in reality. But the practical difficulty in separating indoctrination from instructing does not mean that the two terms are conceptually the same. See Thomas F. Green, "Indoctrination and Beliefs," in *Concepts of Indoctrination*, ed. I.A. Snook (London and Boston: Routledge & Kegan Paul, 1972), 26.
3. Pew Forum on Religion and Public Life, *Mapping the Global Muslim Population: A Report on the Size and Distribution of the World's Muslim Population* (Washington, DC: Pew Research Centre, 2009), 5, 13.
4. Ibid., 5.
5. This is quoted in Richard Allen Greene, "Nearly 1 in 4 people worldwide is Muslim, Report Says," *CNN World,* October 7, 2009, available at: http://articles.cnn.com/2009–10–07/world/muslim.world.population_1_god-but-god-middle-east-distant?_s=PM:WORLD (accessed September 2, 2010).

NOTES TO INTRODUCTION

1. This is cited in Saied R. Ameli, Aliya Azam, and Arzu Merali, *British Muslims' Expectations of the Government* (Wembley: Islamic Human Rights Commission, 2005), 68.
2. The articles cited are Ron Synovitz, "Afghanistan: Would-Be Suicide Bomber Speaks of Indoctrination, Fear," *GlobalSecurity.org,* October 2, 2007, available at: http://www.globalsecurity.org/security/library/news/2007/10/sec-071002-rferl02.htm (accessed February 2, 2009); Geeta Anand, Matthew Rosenberg, Siobhan Gorman, and Susan Schmidt, "Alleged Terrorist Group Steers Young Men to Fight," *Wall Street Journal*, December 8, 2008, available at: http://online.wsj.com/article/SB122869042642886443.html (accessed February 2, 2009); Cinnamon Stillwell, "Islam in America's Public Schools: Education or Indoctrination?" *San Francisco Chronicle*, June 11, 2008, available at: http://www.sfgate.com/cgi-bin/article.cgi?f=/g/a/2008/06/11/cstillwell.DTL (accessed February 2, 2009); "'Islamic

Indoctrination' taken to Supreme Court," *WorldNewDaily*, June 9, 2006, available at: http://www.worldnetdaily.com/news/article.asp?ARTICLE_ID=50562 (accessed February 2, 2009).

3. The "public schools" refer to state schools in the United States. They should not be confused with the public schools in Britain that are actually exclusive private schools.

4. William J. Bennetta, "How a Public School in Scottsdale, Arizona Subjected Students to Islamic Indoctrination," *The Textbook League*, n.d., available at: http://www.textbookleague.org/tci-az.htm (accessed February 2, 2009). For more discussion on such "indoctrinatory" Islamic textbooks, see Robert Spencer's chapter on "Readin', writin', and subjugatin' the infidel: the stealth jihad in American schools" in his *Stealth Jihad: How Radical Islam is Subverting America without Guns or Bombs* (Washington, DC: Regnery Publishing, Inc., 2008), 189–226.

5. Spencer, *Stealth Jihad*, 228 and passim.

6. This point is noted by Jacob Høigilt in his *Raiding Extremists? Islamism and Education in the Palestinian Territories*, Fafo report, 2010, 9. The recent studies cited by Høigilt are J.M. Burr and R.O. Collins, *Alms for Jihad: Charity and Terrorism in the Islamic World* (Cambridge: Cambridge University Press, 2006); M. Levitt, *Hamas: Politics, Charity, and Terrorism in the Service of Jihad* (New Haven: Yale University Press, 2006); B. Rougier, *Everyday Jihad: The Rise of Militant Islam among Palestinians in Lebanon* (Cambridge: Harvard University Press, 2007).

7. See National Commission on Terrorist Attacks. *The 9/11 Commission Report: The Final Report of the National Commission on Terrorist Attacks Upon the United States* (New York: W.W. Norton, 2004), as cited in Justin Magouirk, "Connecting a Thousand Points of Hatred," *Studies in Conflict & Terrorism* 31/4 (2008): 343; Farish A. Noor, Yoginder Sikand, and Martin van Bruinessen, "Introduction," in *The Madrasa in Asia: Political Activism and Transnational Linkages*, ed. Farish A. Noor, Yoginder Sikand, and Martin van Bruinessen (Amsterdam: Amsterdam University Press, 2008), 11. The plural of "madrasa" or "madrasah" is actually "madaris", but I have chosen to follow the convention in international literature and spell it as "madrasahs".

8. Andrew Coulson, "Education and Indoctrination in the Muslim World: Is There a Problem? What Can We Do About It?" *Policy Analysis* 511 (2004): 1, 3.

9. Suzanne Goldenberg, "The Men behind the Suicide Bombers," *The Guardian*, June 12, 2002, available at: http://www.guardian.co.uk/world/2002/jun/12/israel1 (accessed February 2, 2009); Daphne Burdman, "Education, Indoctrination, and Incitement: Palestinian Children on their Way to Martyrdom," *Terrorism and Political Violence* 15/1 (2003): 96–123.

10. Scott Atran, "The Moral Logic and Growth of Suicide Terrorism," *The Washington Quarterly* 29/2 (2006): 127.

11. I.A. Snook, *Indoctrination and Education*, 28.

12. Richard H. Gratchel, "The Evolution of the Concept," in *Concepts of Indoctrination: Philosophical Essays*, ed. I.A. Snook (London and Boston: Routledge & Kegan Paul, 1972), 11.

13. William Heard Kilpatrick, "Indoctrination and Respect for Persons," in *Concepts of Indoctrination: Philosophical Essays*, ed. I.A. Snook (London and Boston: Routledge & Kegan Paul, 1972), 47. Eamonn Callan and Dylan Arena point out that the philosopher John Stuart Mill, back in 1852, already used the word "indoctrination" pejoratively when he wrote: "What the poor as well as the rich require is not to be indoctrinated, is not to be taught other people's opinions, but to be induced and enabled to think for themselves." See

Eamonn Callan and Dylan Arena, "Indoctrination," in *The Oxford Handbook of Philosophy of Education*, ed. by Harvey Siegel (Oxford: Oxford University Press, 2009), 120. While Callan and Arena are right about Mill, this pejorative usage was confined to scholarly treatises and was not widely used until the middle of the twentieth century through the influence of American Progressivists.

14. Even so, as Terence Copley points out, the word "indoctrination" was used in the U.S. Navy as recent as World War II to refer positively to "the fundamentals of military discipline, naval customs and usage". See his *Indoctrination, Education and God: The Struggle for the Mind* (London: SPCK, 2005), 3; also see Christopher S. DeRosa, *Political Indoctrination in the U.S. Army from World War II to the Vietnam War* (Lincoln and London: University of Nebraska Press, 2006). That shows that indoctrination has evolved over the years and remains contested today.

15. For a useful reading of the challenges of indoctrination in the European context, see Copley, *Indoctrination, Education and God*.

16. Snook, *Indoctrination and Education*, 17.

17. See the collection of essays in I.A. Snook, ed., *Concepts of Indoctrination: Philosophical Essays* (London and Boston: Routledge & Kegan Paul, 1972); and a continuation of the debate in Ben Spiecker and Roger Straughan, eds., *Freedom and Indoctrination in Education* (London: Cassell Educational Ltd., 1991).

18. For example, Denise Winn contends that English public schools foster indoctrination in a closed environment because individuals only mingle with others who share a similar upbringing. See Denise Winn, *The Manipulated Mind: Brainwashing, Conditioning and Indoctrination* (Cambridge, Massachusetts: Malor Books, 2000), 198. The science educator Wolff-Michael Rolf asserts that unless science, as well as other subjects such as mathematics and history, includes a reflexive component that allows students to critically evaluate the knowledge claims of a particular field, students "will always be subject to some form of indoctrination". See Wolff-Michael Roth, "'Enculturation': Acquisition of Conceptual Blind Spots and Epistemological Prejudices," *British Educational Research Journal* 27/1 (2001): 7; on the indoctrination of secular education, see Warren A. Nord, "Rethinking Indoctrination," *Education Week*, May 24, 1995, 44, 36; Terence Copley, "Non-Indoctrinatory Religious Education in Secular Cultures," *Religious Education* 103/1 (2008): 22–31 and passim; Warren A. Nord, *Does God Make a Difference? Taking Religion Seriously in our Schools and Universities* (Oxford University Press, New York: 2010); on the indoctrination of teacher education, see Bernard F. Bull, "Constructivist Crap in Christian Colleges: The Indoctrination of Teacher Education," *The Educational Forum* 66/2 (2002): 162–4. On the indoctrination of secular education, Nord asserts that state schools "come close—perilously close—to indoctrinating students by socialising them to accept, uncritically, secular over religious ways of making sense of the world". See Nord, "Rethinking Indoctrination," 1. Likewise, Copley maintains that a secular indoctrination process is occurring in some Western democracies as "[p]eople who are products of a secular worldview have real difficulty understanding the claims of religions, which appear to them either as harmless private hobbies on the one hand, or dangerous fanaticism on the other". See Copley, "Non-Indoctrinatory Religious Education in Secular Cultures," 25.

19. Syed Farid Alatas, "Islam and Modernisation," in *Islam in Southeast Asia: Political, Social and Strategic Challenges for the 21st Century*, eds. K.S. Nathan and Mohammad Hashim Kamali (Singapore: Institute of Southeast Asian Studies, 2005), 223.

20. Bassam Tibi, *Islam's Predicament with Modernity* (Oxon: Routledge, 2009), 7.
21. Hanan A. Alexander, "Education in Ideology," *Journal of Moral Education* 34/1 (2005): 3.
22. On not seeing Islam as "Islams", see Ebrahim Moosa, "The Debts and Burdens of Critical Islam," in *Progressive Muslims: On Justice, Gender, and Pluralism*, ed. Omid Safi (Oxford: Oneworld Publications, 2003), 114; Tariq Ramadan, *Western Muslims and the Future of Islam* (New York: Oxford University Press, 2004), 23.
23. Azyumardi Azra, "Teaching Tolerance through Education in Indonesia," paper presented at RoundTable Discussion 'Religion in Indonesia: An Overview' Indonesian Ministry of Foreign Affairs and Ma'arif Institute Jakarta, February 19, 2008, 6. It is interesting to note that this approach of treating Islam not only as a religion but a historical phenomenon that has evolved and been adapted to many societies and cultures is a foundational principle that guides the teaching of Islamic studies in the State Institute for Islamic Studies and State Islamic Universities in Indonesia. See Azra, "Teaching Tolerance," 10. For more discussion on the State Islamic Universities in Indonesia, see Chapter 8 of this book.
24. For further discussion on the differences among formal, informal, and non-formal education, see Philip H. Combs, Roy C. Prosser, and Manzoor Ahmed, *New Paths to Learning for Rural Children and Youth* (New York: International Council for Educational Development, 1973).
25. Under Indonesian law, formal education refers to structured and organised education under the purview of the state from elementary to higher education. Any structured and organised education outside the formal school system is considered non-formal education. Informal education, on the other hand, refers to non-structured education held within a family or a community. See Muhammad Zuhdi, "Political and Social Influences on Religious School: A Historical Perspective on Indonesian Islamic School Curricula," PhD thesis, McGill University, 2006, 181.
26. Ameli, Azam, and Merali, *British Muslims' Expectations of the Government*, 12.
27. Susan L. Douglass and Munir A. Shaikh, "Defining Islamic Education: Differentiation and Applications," *Current Issues in Comparative Education* 7/1 (2004): 5–18.
28. For instance, see the collection of essays in Robert W. Hefner and Muhammad Qasim Zaman, eds., *Schooling Islam: The Culture and Politics of Modern Muslim Education* (Princeton: Princeton University Press, 2007); Robert W. Hefner, ed., *Making Modern Muslims: The Politics of Islamic Education in Southeast Asia* (Honolulu: University of Hawai'i Press, 2009).
29. Azyumardi Azra, Dina Afrianty, and Robert W. Hefner, "Pesantren and Madrasa: Muslim Schools and National Ideals in Indonesia," in *Schooling Islam: The Culture and Politics of Modern Muslim Education*, ed. Robert W. Hefner and Muhammad Qasim Zaman (Princeton: Princeton University Press, 2007), 172–98.
30. This is taken from Robert W. Hefner, "Islamic Schools, Social Movements, and Democracy in Indonesia," in *Making Modern Muslims: The Politics of Islamic Education in Southeast Asia.*, ed. Robert W. Hefner (Hawai'i: University of Hawai'i Press, 2009), 90.
31. Ronald Lukens-Bull, "Between Text and Practice: Considerations in the Anthropological Study of Islam," in *Defining Islam: A Reader*, ed. Andrew Rippin (London: Equinox Publishing Ltd., 2007), 46.
32. Talal Asad, *The Idea of an Anthropology of Islam* (Washington, DC: Centre for Contemporary Arab Studies, Georgetown University, 1986), 14, as cited in Muhammad Qasim Zaman, *The Ulama in Contemporary Islam*

(Princeton: Princeton University Press, 2002), 6. My understanding of "tradition" is informed by Asad and Zaman, but I do not necessarily agree with all their views on the essence of Islamic traditions.

33. Lukens-Bull, "Between Text and Practice," 50.
34. Seyyed Hossein Nasr, *Knowledge and the Sacred* (Albany: State University of New York Press, 1989), 67. While I refer to Nasr's etymological study of the term "tradition", I do not adopt his definition of tradition. He has defined it as "truths or principles of a divine origin revealed or unveiled to mankind and, in fact, a whole cosmic sector through various figures envisaged as messengers, prophets, *avataras*, the Logos or other transmitting agencies, along with all the ramifications and applications of these principles in different realms including law and social structure, art, symbolism, the sciences, and embracing of course Supreme Knowledge along with the means for its attainment". See ibid., 68. In my conception of tradition, the divine origin of truths or principles may be present, but it is not necessary; my focus is on how shared meaning is constructed and transmitted in a social process that is historically situated.
35. I am aware that some readers may confuse the "Muslim tradition" here with *sunnah* and *hadith*. According to Abdullah Saeed, sunnah refers to the "normative practice, primarily of the Prophet Muhammad; his sayings, deeds and tacit approvals" while hadith refers to "a report containing information about the sayings, practices and descriptions of the Prophet Muhammad". See Abdullah Saeed, *Islamic Thought: An Introduction* (Oxford: Routledge, 2006), 156, 162. Another Islamic scholar Abdulaziz Sachedina defines sunnah as "Tradition" (with capitalised *T*) to refer to "all that is reported as having been said (*aqwal al-rasul*), done (*a'mal al-rasul*), and silently confirmed (*taqrirat al-rasul*) by the Prophet" and hadith as "tradition" (with lower case *t*) to refer to the vehicle of the sunnah through which it is related. See Abdulaziz Sachedina, *The Islamic Roots of Democratic Pluralism* (New York: Oxford University Press, 2001), 146. My use of the word "tradition" in this book goes beyond the sunnah and hadith to include the discourses or social processes of constructing and transmitting the shared beliefs and practices of Muslims in a community.
36. Zaman, *The Ulama in Contemporary Islam*, 6.
37. Ameli, Azam, and Merali, *British Muslims' Expectations of the Government*, 10.
38. Mark J. Halstead, *The Case for Muslim Voluntary-Aided Schools: Some Philosophical Reflections* (Cambridge: The Islamic Academy, 1986), 50–1, as cited in Elmer John Thiessen, *Teaching for Commitment: Liberal Education, Indoctrination and Christian Nurture* (Gracewing, Leominster: McGill-Queen's University Press, 1993), 130–1.
39. Asad, *The Idea of an Anthropology of Islam*, 14, as cited in Zaman, *The Ulama in Contemporary Islam*, 6.
40. Zaman, *The Ulama in Contemporary Islam*, 4. Zaman also refers to the views of Alasdair MacIntyre on the external and internal conflicts of a tradition. See Alasdair MacIntyre, *Whose Justice? Which Rationality?* (Notre Dame: University of Notre Dame, 1988).
41. Jessica Stern, *Terror in the Name of God: Why Religious Militants Kill* (New York: ECC, HarperCollins Publishers, 2003), xx.
42. See Greg Fealy and Virginia Hooker, eds., *Voices of Islam in Southeast Asia: A Contemporary Sourcebook* (Singapore: Institute of Southeast Asian Studies, 2006), 362.
43. This is cited in Fealy and Hooker, eds., *Voices of Islam in Southeast Asia*, 377. The underlined words and capitalised "tremble" are in the original text.

44. This is cited in Huala Noor, "Pride within Stigma: The Case of Indonesian Terrorists' Families," Master's dissertation, Syarif Hidayatullah State Islamic University, Jakarta, 2009, 109.

45. This is based on the interview conducted by Huala Noor with him in April 2007. See ibid., 109.

46. This definition by Saad Eddin Ibrahim is cited in Martin van Bruinessen in "Muslim Fundamentalism: Something to be Understood or to be Explained Away?" *Islam and Muslim Christian Relations* 6/2 (1995): 157–71, available at: http://www.let.uu.nl/~martin.vanbruinessen/personal/publications/muslim_fundamentalism.htm (accessed May 28, 2010). Also see Saad Eddin Ibrahim, "Anatomy of Egypt's Militant Islamic Groups: Methodological Note and Preliminary Findings," *International Journal of Middle East Studies* 12 (1980): 423–53; Saad Eddin Ibrahim, "Islamic Militancy as a Social Movement: The Case of Two Groups in Egypt," in *Islamic Resurgence in the Arab World*, ed. Ali E. Hillal Dessouki (New York: Praeger, 1982), 117–37.

47. See John L. Esposito and Dalia Mogahed, *Who Speaks for Islam? What a Billion Muslims Really Think* (New York: Gallup Press, 2007), 76.

48. See "Armed and Radical," *Today*, March 31, 2010, 10.

49. Other variants include "radical Islam" and "fundamentalism". Vedi R. Hadiz notes that "radical Islam" can "variably refer to those who seek the establishment of an Islamic state or caliphate or the promulgation of the *Syaria* as the source of all laws, with or without outright violence". See Vedi R. Hadiz, "Towards a Sociological Understanding of Islamic Radicalism in Indonesia," *Journal of Contemporary Asia* 38/4 (2008): 638–9. Similarly, the term "fundamentalism", as noted by Martin van Bruinessen, is ambiguous and is commonly employed in a disapprovingly manner; calling a person a fundamentalist is akin to calling him a "fanatic". He adds that he prefers to employ the term as neutral a way as possible, to denote "all movements and ideologies that place a literal interpretation of the Islamic revelation and norms believed to be directly derived from it (Islamic values, Islamic economics, the Islamic state) above all other possible sources of legitimacy (such as local tradition, mystical experience, humanism, rationalism, secular law, and international conventions)". See Martin van Bruinessen, "Muslim Fundamentalism: Something to be Understood or to be Explained Away?" available at: http://www.let.uu.nl/~martin.vanbruinessen/personal/publications/muslim_fundamentalism.htm_ (accessed May 28, 2010).

50. Jajat Burhanudin and Jamhari, "Assessment of Social and Political Attitudes in Indonesia Islamic Education Institution," *Studia Islamika: Indonesian Journal for Islamic Studies* 13/3 (2006): 416.

51. John T. Sidel, *The Islamist Threat in Southeast Asia: A Reassessment* (Washington, DC: East-West Centre Washington, 2007), 2.

52. Daniel Pipes, *Militant Islam Reaches America* (New York and London: W.W. Norton, 2003), 8, as cited in Kumar Ramakrishna, "'Constructing' the Jemaah Islamiyah Terrorist: A Preliminary Inquiry," Working Paper, Institute of Defence and Strategic Studies, October 2004, Singapore, 11.

53. For example, see Atran, "The Moral Logic and Growth of Suicide Terrorism"; Brynjar Lia, "Doctrines for Jihadi Terrorist Training," *Terrorism and Political Violence* 20/4 (2008): 518–42.

54. Syed Farid Alatas, "A Critical Approach to Studying Muslim Revival Movements," *The Straits Times*, August 12, 2010, A28.

55. See Muchammad Tholchah, "The Impact of Terrorism Issue on Parents' Trust (A Study of Ngruki Pesantren, Surakarta, Central Java)," Master's dissertation, Syarif Hidayatullah State Islamic University, Jakarta, 2007, 58

and passim; Noor, "Pride within Stigma: The Case of Indonesian Terrorists' Families," 124 and passim.

NOTES TO CHAPTER 1

1. An example of an inquiry into the content of beliefs has been offered by Reformed Epistemologists such as Alvin Plantinga. He has published widely on the epistemology of religious belief, especially Christian theistic belief. Plantinga is primarily concerned with the actual objective status of beliefs, not the assigned logical status of beliefs. He focuses on "epistemic warrant": what turns true belief into knowledge. He argues that the belief in God is "properly basic"—a belief that is not accepted on the basis of any other beliefs, is capable of functioning foundationally in a rational noetic structure, and is grounded in justification-conferring conditions. For more details, see Alvin Plantinga, "Reason and Belief in God," *Faith and Rationality: Reason and Belief in God*, eds. Alvin Plantinga and Nicholas Wolterstorff (Notre Dame: University of Notre Dame Press, 1983); Alvin Plantinga, *Warranted Christian Belief* (Oxford: Oxford University Press, 2000). For a good discussion on the epistemic nature of religious beliefs from various faith systems including Islam, see Eleonore Stump and Michael J. Murray, eds., *Philosophy of Religion: The Big Questions* (Malden and Oxford: Blackwell Publishers, 1999); Philip L. Quinn and Charles Taliaferro, eds., *A Companion to Philosophy of Religion* (Malden and Oxford: Blackwell Publishers, 1999).
2. All references to these three writers are taken from Thomas F. Green, "Indoctrination and Beliefs," in *Concepts of Indoctrination*, ed. I.A. Snook (London and Boston: Routledge & Kegan Paul, 1972), 25–46; Nicholas Wolterstorff, *Reason within the Bounds of Religion*, 2nd ed. (Grand Rapids: Wm B. Eerdmans Publishing Co, 1984); Kathleen Taylor, *Brainwashing: The Science of Thought Control* (Oxford: Oxford University Press, 2004).
3. I borrow the term "control beliefs" from Nicholas Wolterstorff. Although Wolterstorff's book is written from a Christian perspective, he clarifies that the structure of his ideas is applicable to readers of all religions. He writes: "To the convinced Buddhist I would say that integrity requires that he use his religious beliefs as control within his devising and weighing of theories—an obvious counterpart of what I say to Christians". See Wolterstorff, *Reason within the Bounds of Religion*, 11–2.
4. Scott David Foutz, "On Establishing an Evangelical Historiography for the 21st Century," *Quodlibet Journal*, n.d., available at: http://www.quodlibet. net/foutz-histfinl.shtml (accessed April 2, 2010).
5. The idea of primitive beliefs is borrowed from Green, "Indoctrination and Beliefs," 30–1.
6. Wolterstorff, *Reason within the Bounds of Religion*, 18–9, 68.
7. The materials in this section on control beliefs, data beliefs, and data-background beliefs are taken from Wolterstorff, 65–9 and passim. Wolterstorff is mainly interested in scientific theories, but I have expanded the scope to include all theories about ourselves, others, and the world.
8. This example is adapted from ibid., 65–8.
9. Ibid., 69.
10. Ibid., 29.
11. These examples are taken from Plantinga, "Reason and Belief in God," 55.
12. Wolterstorff, *Reason within the Bounds of Religion*, 88–9.

13. Timothy Tow, *The Law of Moses & of Jesus* (Singapore: Christian Life Publishers, 1982), 15–6, 21, 23.
14. Green, "Indoctrination and Beliefs," 31–3.
15. On the point of a person making a judgement, Ludwig Wittgenstein asserts that "We do not learn the practice of making empirical judgments by learning rules: we are taught judgments and their connection with other judgments. A *totality* of judgments is made plausible to us." See Ludwig Wittgenstein, *On Certainty*, eds. G.E.M. Anscombe and G.H. von Wright, trans. G.E.M. Anscombe and D. Paul (Oxford: Basil Blackwell, 1969), 140, as cited in Charlene Tan, *Teaching without Indoctrination: Implications for Values Education* (Rotterdam: Sense Publishers, 2008), 29.
16. Taylor, *Brainwashing*, 129 and passim.
17. Ibid., 210.
18. Ibid., 138.
19. Wolterstorff, *Reason within the Bounds of Religion*, 95–6.
20. Taylor, *Brainwashing: The Science of Thought Control*, 211.
21. Francis Collins, *The Language of God: A Scientist Presents Evidence for Belief* (London: Pocket Books, 2007); Denis Alexander, *Creation or Evolution: Do We have to Choose?* (Oxford: Monarch Books, 2008).
22. Green, "Indoctrination and Beliefs," 33.
23. Frank D. Jerome, *Persuasion and Healing* (New York: Schocken Books, 1963), as cited in Winn, *The Manipulated Mind: Brainwashing, Conditioning and Indoctrination*, 44–5.
24. Wolterstorff, *Reason within the Bounds of Religion*, 15–7, 94.
25. By identifying indoctrination with ideological totalism, I am not thereby arguing that indoctrination is only about the result or outcome, regardless of the intention, content, or process involved. This question of whether indoctrination is necessarily linked to the criterion of intention, content, process, or outcome is part of the conceptual analytical approach used by philosophers since the 1970s. Despite many years of debate, no consensus has been reached on the definition of indoctrination. For further readings, see Snook, *Concepts of Indoctrination: Philosophical Essays*; Spiecker and Straughan, *Freedom and Indoctrination in Education*.
26. Robert Jay Lifton, *Thought Reform and the Psychology of Totalism: A Study of 'Brainwashing' in China* (Chapel Hill and London: The University of North Carolina Press, 1989), 419.
27. This definition is adapted from Lifton, 419; Alexander, "Education in Ideology," 3. It is important to note that "ideology" is not used pejoratively here; it can be indoctrinatory or educative.
28. Lifton, *Thought Reform and the Psychology of Totalism*, 419.
29. Taylor, *Brainwashing: The Science of Thought Control*, 222.
30. Muhammad Haniff Hassan, *Unlicensed to Kill: Countering Iman Samudra's Justification for the Bali Bombing* (Singapore: Nature Media Pte Ltd., 2006), 15–6.
31. Interview with a director of a pesantren, May 15, 2010.
32. Hassan, *Unlicensed to Kill*. Also see Muhammad Haniff Bin Hassan, "Iman Samudra's Justification for Bali Bombing," in *Islam in Southeast Asia: Critical Concepts in Islamic Studies*, eds. Joseph Chinyong Liow and Nadirsyah Hosen, Vol. 4 (London and New York: Routledge, 2010), 340–68. For an extract of the book written by Iman Samudra, *Aku Melawan Teroris* [I Fight Terrorists], see Greg Fealy and Virginia Hooker, eds., *Voices of Islam in Southeast Asia*, 373–7.
33. This is cited in Hassan, *Unlicensed to Kill*, 16.

34. All the verses from the Qur'an and hadiths mentioned in this chapter are taken from Hassan, passim.
35. Ibid., 27.
36. Mark Juergensmeyer, *Terror in the Mind of God: The Global Rise of Religious Violence* (Berkeley and Los Angeles: University of California Press, 2000), 81, as cited in Kumar Ramakrishna, "'Constructing' the Jemaah Islamiyah Terrorist: A Preliminary Inquiry," Working Paper, Institute of Defence and Strategic Studies, October 2004, Singapore, 16. Ramakrishna, citing Marc Sageman, adds that Osama bin Laden accepted Faraj's argument in attacking Muslim leaders who are judged as apostate. See ibid., 17; also see Marc Sageman, *Understanding Terror Networks* (Philadelphia: University of Pennsylvania Press, 2004), 18.
37. Examples of Muslims who reject the interpretation of jihad as armed struggle and militancy against noncombatants include a group of Muslim leaders who issued a statement condemning the London bombing in 2005. They asserted that there is "absolutely no sanction in Islam, nor is there any justification whatsoever in our noble religion for such evil actions". See "Joint Statement of Muslim Leaders Condemning London Bombing on 7th July 2005," as cited in Hassan, *Unlicensed to Kill*, 155. Other supporters of this tradition include the Fiqh Council of North America and the Islamic Religious Council of Singapore (Muis); they have publicly condemned the Bali bombing and other violent attacks such as the London bombing in 2005 and the Sharm El-Sheikh bombing in Egypt in 2005. See their statements of condemnation of the Bali bombing in ibid., 149–70. An Islamic scholar states that the militant group Jemaah Islamiyah's teaching contains "misinterpretation and misunderstanding of certain religious concepts" while another Islamic scholar bluntly describes the teaching of Muslim terrorists as "their twisted ideology of hate and terror". See Hj Ali Hj Mohamed, "The Peaceful Message of Islam," in *Fighting Terrorism: The Singapore Perspective*, ed. Abdul Halim Bin Kader (Singapore: Taman Bacaan Pemuda Pemudi Melayu Singapura, 2007), 114; Mohamed Bin Ali, "Coping with the Threat of Jemaah Islamiyah—The Singapore Experience," in ibid., 123.
38. For a good discussion of the contested meanings of jihad in Muslim history, see Patricia Martinez, "Deconstructing Jihad: Southeast Asian Contexts," IDSS Working Paper, Institute of Defence and Strategic Studies, Nanyang Technological University, Singapore, 2003. For further readings on various and competing interpretations of jihad, see John J. Donohue and John L. Esposito, eds., *Islam in Transition: Muslim Perspectives*, 2nd ed. (Oxford: Oxford University Press, 2007), 393–472. For useful readings on views that reject jihad as war and hostility against all non-Muslims, see Sachedina, *The Islamic Roots of Democratic Pluralism*, 112–31; Reza Shah-Kazemi, "Recollecting the Spirit of Jihad," in *Islam, Fundamentalism, and the Betrayal of Tradition: Essays by Western Muslim Scholars*, ed. Joseph E.B. Lumbard (Bloomington: World Wisdom, 2004), 121–42; Khaled Abou El Fadl, *The Great Theft: Wrestling Islam from the Extremists* (New York: HarperOne, 2005), 220–49; M. Fethullah Gulen, *Towards a Global Civilisation of Love and Tolerance* (New Jersey: The Light, 2004), 169–90. For further readings on the different interpretations of jihad, see the chapter on jihad in Fealy and Hooker, ed., *Voices of Islam in Southeast Asia*, 353–410. The chapter classifies the writings of various Muslim activists, scholars, and groups into "Salafi Jihadism", "Regionalist Jihad", and "Moderate and liberal interpretations of Jihad".
39. The term "brainwashing" was first used by an American journalist Edward Hunter when he quoted Chinese informants claiming that the Communists

were "washing the brains" (*xi nao*) of the masses. See Lifton, *Thought Reform and the Psychology of Totalism*, 3. When 21 U.S. soldiers who were imprisoned in China refused to be repatriated back to the United States after World War II, the American public was shocked and suspected that these soldiers had fallen prey to a "fearsome and mysterious practice: purported Chinese 'brainwashing'". See Christopher S. DeRosa, *Political Indoctrination in the U.S. Army: From World War II to the Vietnam War*, 124. It is interesting to note that the official term used and preferred by the Chinese Communists was *si xiang gai zao*, which literally means "thought redevelopment". Thought redevelopment, unlike "brainwashing", has no coercive and derogatory connotation. It merely implies that there is something lacking or wanting in the original condition that warrants a change in thought. Hence "thought redevelopment" is technically compatible with citizenship and moral education—a salutary nation-building endeavour carried out by many governments today. What *is* objectionable about the Communists' thought redevelopment, in my view, is not the intention but the method used: it was forced upon the prisoners who were subjected to immense and prolonged physical, mental, and emotional abuse.

40. For example, see John White, "The Justification of Autonomy as an Educational Aim," in *Freedom and Indoctrination in Education*, eds. Ben Spiecker and Roger Straughan (London: Cassell Educational Ltd., 1991), 126–7; Snook, *Indoctrination and Education*, 107–8; R.S. Peters, *Psychology and Ethical Development* (London: Allen & Unwin, 1974), 346, 47, 56, as cited in Ben Spiecker, "Indoctrination: The Suppression of Critical Dispositions," in *Freedom and Indoctrination in Education*, eds. Ben Spiecker and Roger Straughan (London: Cassell Educational Ltd., 1991), 26; Burdman, "Education, Indoctrination, and Incitement," 112.

41. Robert S. Baron, "Arousal, Capacity, and Intense Indoctrination," *Personality and Social Psychology Review* 4/3 (2000), 240.

42. Spiecker, "Indoctrination: The Suppression of Critical Dispositions," 25; also see White, "The Justification of Autonomy as an Educational Aim," 126–7.

43. Taylor, *Brainwashing*, 253.

NOTES TO CHAPTER 2

1. The intention should be distinguished from the motive. According to I.A. Snook, intention specifies *what* a person is doing, while motive explains *why* he is doing it. In our context of an indoctrinatory tradition, the intention of indoctrinator is to implant control beliefs that result in ideological totalism, such as the control belief of armed jihad against all non-Muslims. His motive may be his sincere belief and firm conviction that jihad is the sixth pillar and that armed jihad is the only way to get to heaven. Two persons or traditions may have the same intention but different motives. In this book, I am interested in the intention and not the motive of the indoctrinator. See Snook, *Indoctrination and Education*, 62.

2. Alexander, "Education in Ideology," 4. Alexander distinguishes between what he calls "moral or ethical ideologies" and "amoral or non-ethical ideologies". Corresponding to these two ideologies are "open societies" and "closed societies". He writes that "[o]pen societies tend to rely on moral ideologies infused with concepts of the good, whereas closed societies prefer more uniform, amoral ideologies". See ibid., 5. In line with the key terms used in this book, I have adapted his ideas to distinguish between

"educative tradition" and "indoctrinatory tradition", with the former corresponding to (but not identical with) an open society that relies on moral ideologies, whereas the latter corresponds to a closed society that prefers amoral ideologies.

3. John Wilson, "Religious (Moral, Political, etc.) Commitment, Education and Indoctrination," in *Freedom and Indoctrination in Education*, eds. Ben Spiecker and Roger Straughan (London: Cassell Educational Ltd., 1991), 44. Wilson's "closed" and "open" traditions are in tandem with Alexander's and Karl Popper's distinction between "closed" and "open" societies. See Alexander "Education in Ideology," 3; Karl Popper, *The Open Society and its Enemies* (London: Routledge and Kegan Paul, 1945).

4. Lifton, *Thought Reform and the Psychology of Totalism*, 419–37. It is noteworthy that Edward Schils, based on his analysis of Nazi and Russian ideologies, identifies similar features of indoctrination: in-group exclusiveness and hostility to all outside it; the categorisation of people according to selected characteristics and making overall judgements on the basis of these; the view that any tenderness for family bonds or toleration of enemies serves only to weaken the in-group in its struggle and dilute commitment; belief in a wholly harmonious society which can only be created by the in-group; demand for total submissiveness to the in-group which alone can bring about good; promotion of the idea that the world is a scene of unceasing conflict; belief in hostile conspiratorial forces whose aim is to destroy the in-group; and the justification of violence. See Edward Schils, "Authoritarianism Right and Left," in *Studies in the Scope and Method of Authoritarian Personality*, eds. Richard Christie and Marie Jajoda (Glencoe, Illinois: The Free Press, 1954), as cited in Winn, *The Manipulated Mind*, 2000, 157.

5. Lifton, *Thought Reform and the Psychology of Totalism*, 430.

6. Farish A. Noor, "What is the Victory of Islam? Towards a Different Understanding of the Ummah and Political Success in the Contemporary World," in *Progressive Muslims: On Justice, Gender, and Pluralism*, ed. Omid Safi (Oxford: Oneworld Publications, 2003), 323.

7. Gabriel A. Almond, R. Scott Appleby, and Emmanuel Sivan, *Strong Religion: The Rise of Fundamentalism around the World* (Chicago and London: University of Chicago Press, 2003), 33–7, as cited in Noorhaidi Hassan, "The Salafi Madrasas of Indonesia," in *The Madrasa in Asia: Political Activism and Transnational Linkages*, eds. Farish A. Noor, Yoginder Sikand, and Martin van Bruinessen (Amsterdam: Amsterdam University Press, 2008), 259.

8. Quintan Wiktqrqwicz and Karl Kaltenthaler, "The Rationality of Radical Islam," *Political Science Quarterly* 121/2 (2006): 312.

9. Syed Qutb, "A Muslim's Nationality and His Belief," available at: http://www.witness-pioneer.org/vil/Articles/politics/nationalism.htm (accessed August 12, 2010). It is important to note that not all Muslims agree with Syed Qutb's arguments. For an example of a robust refutation of his views, see Hassan, *Unlicensed to Kill*, 28–39.

10. Ibid.

11. Lifton, *Thought Reform and the Psychology of Totalism*, 428.

12. Ibid., 312.

13. Wahyudi Soeriaatmadja, "Indonesia Arrests Cleric over Terror Ties," *The Straits Times*, August 10, 2010, A6.

14. Roderick Hindery, "The Anatomy of Propaganda within Religious Terrorism," *The Humanist* March/April 2003: 17.

15. Hafez, "Rationality, Culture, and Structure in the Making of Suicide Bombers," 169.

16. Taylor, *Brainwashing*, 231 and passim.
17. Winn, *The Manipulated Mind*, 156.
18. This is cited in Lifton, *Thought Reform and the Psychology of Totalism*, 48.
19. Hafez, "Rationality, Culture, and Structure in the Making of Suicide Bombers," 170–1.
20. Ibid., 169.
21. Ibid., 170.
22. For a detailed discussion of the stages and strategies of indoctrination, see Baron, "Arousal, Capacity, and Intense Indoctrination," 238–54; also see Carol Dyer, Ryan McCoy, Joel Rodriguez, and Donald N. Van Duyn, "Countering Violent Islamic Extremism: A Community Responsibility," *FBI Law Enforcement Bulletin* December 2007: 3–9.
23. Dyer, McCoy, Rodriguez, and Van Duyn, "Countering Violent Islamic Extremism," 6.
24. These are cited in Wiktqrqwicz and Kaltenthaler, "The Rationality of Radical Islam," 303; Lia, "Doctrines for Jihadi Terrorist Training," 530. Natasha Hamilton-Hart argues against focusing on religious brainwashing as the source of militancy or terrorism. Her reason is that "this focus makes it almost impossible to take seriously the values and grievances of the supposedly brainwashed", as "it is all too easy to confound extreme anger or uncongenial goals with acts of terrorism." See Natasha Hamilton-Hart, "Terrorism in Southeast Asia: Expert Analysis, Myopia and Fantasy," in *Islam in Southeast Asia: Critical Concepts in Islamic Studies*, eds. Joseph Chinyong Liow and Nadirsyah Hosen, Vol. 4 (London and New York: Routledge, 2010), 329. However, her argument mistakenly assumes that brainwashing is primarily about extreme anger or uncongenial goals and is therefore irrational. I have argued that brainwashing is an extreme form of indoctrination that has its own strategic logic and rationality, albeit in a limited way.
25. Spencer, J. Maxcy, "The Democratic 'Myth' and the Search for a Rational Concept of Education," *Educational Philosophy and Theory* 17/1 (1985): 22–37; Mark Weinstein, "Reason and the Child," *Philosophy of Education: Proceedings of the forty-sixth annual meeting of the Philosophy of Education Society in Normal, IL., 1990*, by the Philosophy of Education Society, 159–71; David Carr, "Towards a Distinctive Conception of Spiritual Education," *Oxford Review of Education* 21/1 (1995): 83–98.
26. Tapio Puolimatka, *Democracy and Education: The Critical Citizen as an Educational Aim* (Helsinki: The Finnish Academy of Science and Letters, 1995); Tan, *Teaching without Indoctrination*.
27. Ronald S. Laura and Michael Leahy, "Religious Upbringing and Rational Autonomy," *Journal of Philosophy of Education* 23/1 (1989): 263.
28. Thiessen, *Teaching for Commitment*, 237.
29. Joseph Runzo, "Worldviews and the Epistemic Foundations of Theism," *Religious Studies* 25 (1989): 31–51.
30. Lawrence Haworth, *Autonomy: An Essay in Philosophy Psychology and Ethics* (New Haven and London: Yale University Press, 1986), 3–4, as cited in Thiessen, *Teaching for Commitment*, 130.
31. Green, "Indoctrination and Beliefs," 34, italics mine.
32. Snook, *Indoctrination and Education*, 38, 55–6.
33. Harvey Siegel, "Indoctrination and Education," in *Freedom and Indoctrination in Education*, eds. Ben Spiecker and Roger Straughan (London: Cassell Educational Ltd., 1991), 31.
34. Callan and Arena, "Indoctrination," 104–21.

35. For example, see Ehud Sprinzak, "Rational Fanatics," *Foreign Policy* 120 (2000): 66–74; Atran, "The Moral Logic and Growth of Suicide Terrorism," 127–47; Robert Pape, "The Strategic Logic of Suicide Terrorism," *American Political Science Review* 97/August (2003): 343–62; Robert Pape, *Dying to Win: The Strategic Logic of Suicide Terrorism* (New York: Random House, 2005); Wiktqrqwicz and Kaltenthaler, "The Rationality of Radical Islam," 295–319; K.M. Fierke, "Agents of Death: The Structural Logic of Suicide Terrorism and Martyrdom, *International Theory* 1 (2009): 155–84.

36. Hafez, "Rationality, Culture, and Structure in the Making of Suicide Bombers," 167.

37. Tom McCawley, "Indonesia Hotel Bomber: A Graduate of Jihad 'Ivy League,' *Christian Science Monitor*, July 20, 2009, available at: http://www.csmonitor.com/World/Asia-Pacific/2009/0720/p06s10-woap.html (accessed June 12, 2010).

38. Ed Husain, *The Islamist* (London: Penguin Books, 2007).

39. Ibid., 156.

40. Ibid., 86.

41. Ibid., 86.

42. Fealy and Hooker, *Voices of Islam in Southeast Asia*, 371.

43. The excerpts are taken from Aly Ghufron bin Nurhasyim (Mukhlas), "Jihad Bom Bali: Sebuah Pembelaan. Operasi Peledakan Bom Legian dan Renon. Oktober 12, 2002" [The Bali Bomb Jihad: A Defence. Operation Legian and Renon Mobb Explosions. October 12, 2002], Bali District Police Jail, Denpasar, 25 March, 35–7, 40–1, 50, 95–130, reproduced in Fealy and Hooker, *Voices of Islam in Southeast Asia*, 377–87. All page references refer to the extract in Fealy and Hooker's book.

44. Ibid., 378.

45. Ibid., 377.

46. Ibid., 380.

47. Ibid., 383.

48. Brynjar Lia has offered an excellent review of the discourses on armed jihad and militant training by analysing the writings of four leading Islamic scholars. See Lia, "Doctrines for Jihadi Terrorist Training," 518–42.

49. Thiessen, *Teaching for Commitment*, 237.

50. White, "The Justification of Autonomy as an Educational Aim," 85. White refers to the works of John Gray on autonomy. See John Gray, *Mill on Liberty: A Defense* (London: Routledge & Kegan Paul, 1983), 74.

51. Jan Steutel, "Discipline, Internalisation and Freedom: A Conceptual Analysis," in *Freedom and Indoctrination in Education*, eds. by Ben Spiecker and Roger Straughan (London: Cassell Educational Ltd., 1991), 65. I am not assuming that John White and Jan Steutel are in full agreement regarding their respective concepts on autonomy. But for the purpose of our discussion, it suffices to note the parallels between their views.

52. Gratchel, "The Evolution of the Concept," 15. Terence Copley refers to the close association between indoctrination and enculturation in his example of Slovakia. As a country with a majority of Roman Catholics, it passed a controversial law in 2004 requiring all students between the ages of six and 18 in public schools to take Christian religious education. By replacing the former atheistic curriculum propaganda of the old communist regime with religious education, Copley poses this question: "In this situation, has one type of indoctrination, atheistic, been replaced by another, Christian? . . . Perhaps in a staunchly Catholic culture, defenders of the current arrangement would argue that this is inculturation (sic), rather than

indoctrination". See Copley, "Non-Indoctrinatory Religious Education in Secular Cultures," 23.

53. Pierre Bourdieu, *Meditation Pascalienne* [Pascalian meditations], (Paris: Seuil, 1997), as cited in Roth, "'Enculturation': Acquisition of Conceptual Blind Spots and Epistemological Prejudices," 6.

54. Gratchel, "The Evolution of the Concept," 15.

55. Roth, "'Enculturation': Acquisition of Conceptual Blind Spots and Episte-mological Prejudices," 6.

56. Hans Toch, *The Social Psychology of Social Movements* (London: Methuen, 1966), as cited in Winn, *The Manipulated Mind*, 38. Both Hans Toch and Denise Winn equate socialisation with indoctrination. That is why Winn claims that "most of us are indoctrinated throughout our lives, often without even knowing it". See Winn, *The Manipulated Mind*, 38. However I think the *mere* uncritical acceptance of a particular belief system or set of views does not constitute indoctrination. That is why that is a need to differentiate enculturation (including socialisation) from indoctrination.

57. Aziz Esmail, "Introduction," in *Intellectual Traditions in Islam*, ed. Farhad Daftary (London and New York: I.B. Tauris Publishers, 2001), 7.

NOTES TO CHAPTER 3

1. This is cited in Noor Huda Ismail, "Schooled For Jihad," *The Washington Post*, June 26, 2005, available at: http://www.washingtonpost.com/wpdyn/content/article/2005/06/25/AR2005062500083.html (accessed September 6, 2010).

2. Azra, Afrianty, and Hefner, "Pesantren and Madrasa: Muslim Schools and National Ideals in Indonesia," 172; also see International Crisis Group (ICG), *Al-Qaeda in Southeast Asia: The Case of the 'Ngruki Network' in Indone-sia*, August 8 (Jakarta and Brussels: ICG, 2002).

3. For example, see Marwann Macan-Markar, "My Roommate, the Terror-ist," *IPS News*, November 25, 2008, available at: http://ipsnews.net/news.asp?idnews=44841 (accessed May 26, 2010); Tom McCawley, "Indonesia Hotel Bomber: A Graduate of Jihad 'Ivy League'," *Christian Science Moni-tor*, July 20, 2009, available at: http://www.csmonitor.com/World/Asia-Pacific/2009/0720/p06s10-woap.html (accessed May 28, 2010).

4. Azyumardi Azra, "Islamic Radical Movements in Indonesia," a paper pre-sented at the conference on 'Islamic Radicalism, Securities Issues and Economic Activities in Indonesia', Syarif Hidayatullah State Islamic University, Decem-ber 7, 2005, as cited in Tholchah, "The Impact of Terrorism Issue on Parents' Trust," 4.

5. It may appear incongruous to some readers that I am referring to formal, non-formal, and informal *education* as contributing towards indoctrination. This is because the word "education" is often regarded as a positive term and antithetical to indoctrination. This is a question about values (see my com-ments in the Preface). In this context, I am using the word "education" in a neutral sense to refer to the process of teaching and learning that may or may not be salutary.

6. Azra, Afrianty, and Hefner, "Pesantren and Madrasa: Muslim Schools and National Ideals in Indonesia," 192.

7. Greg Barton claims that there are only five *pesantrens* known to be closely linked to JI and teaching a jihadi interpretation of Islam. See Greg Barton, *Jemaah Islamiyah* (Singapore: Ridge Books, 2005), 57. Zachary Abuza estimates that there are "some one dozen" Islamic schools that have clear

ties to JI. See Zachary Abuza, *Political Islam and Violence in Indonesia* (London and New York: Routledge, 2007), 64. Sidney Jones avers that there are fewer than 20 Islamic schools across Indonesia in the network of JI schools. See Sidney Jones, "Terrorism and 'Radical Islam' in Indonesia," in *Islamic Terrorism in Indonesia: Myths and Realities*, eds. Marika Vicziany and David Wright-Neville (Victoria: Monash University Press, 2005), 11.

8. Burhanudin and Jamhari, "Assessment of Social and Political Attitudes in Indonesia Islamic Education Institution," 404. The research materials for this chapter are based on literature review, content analysis of documents obtained from the school's website and school personnel (visit on May 9, 2010), and discussions with Indonesians who are acquainted with the school.

9. "Profile of Pesantren," August 2008, available at: http://almukmin-ngruki. com/index.php?option=com_content&view=article&id=46&Itemid=56 (accessed August 23, 2010).

10. See van Bruinessen, "Traditionalist and Islamist Pesantrens in Contemporary Indonesia," 222. We should note that the reference to Salafism does not imply that Salafism is a monolithic ideology. Nor am I assuming that key Salafi figures and Muslim militant groups such as Jemaah Islamiyah and Al-Qaeda share identical beliefs and practices. For a useful reading of how Al-Qaeda differs from Jemaah Islamiyah and Egypt's Muslim Brotherhood, see Faisal Devji, *Landscapes of the Jihad: Militancy, Morality, Modernity* (Ithaca: Cornell University Press, 2005). For an historical overview of the causes and diversity of "Islamic fundamentalism" since World War II, see Beverly Milton-Edwards, *Islamic Fundamentalism Since 1945* (Oxon: Routledge, 2005).

11. Jajat Burhanudin and Jamhari, "Assessment of Social and Political Attitudes in Indonesia Islamic Education Institution," 411.

12. van Bruinessen, "Traditionalist and Islamist Pesantrens in Contemporary Indonesia," 232; also see van Bruinessen, "Divergent Paths from Gontor: Muslim Educational Reform and the Travails of Pluralism in Indonesia," n.d., available at: http://www.let.uu.nl/~martin.vanbruinessen/personal/ publications/Bruinessen_Divergent_paths_from_Gontor.pdf (accessed May 28, 2010), 197.

13. "Profile of Pesantren," August 2008, available at: http://almukmin-ngruki. com/index.php?option=com_content&view=article&id=46&Itemid=56 (accessed August 23, 2010).

14. See Pondok Pesantren Islam Al Mukmin. "Pendaftaran Santri Baru 2010– 2011/1431 H.," [Registration for New Students 2010–2011], School Brochure.

15. Kulliyatul Mu'allimin (KMI) is for boys only. Although this was not mentioned in the school brochure and website, it appears that there is another course Kulliyat al-Mu'allimat (KMA) for girls that is similar to KMI. See Hassan, "The Salafi Madrasas of Indonesia," 261.

16. van Bruinessen, "Traditionalist and Islamist Pesantrens in Contemporary Indonesia," 243.

17. Jamhari and Jajang Jahroni, eds., *Gerakan Salafi Radikal di Indonesia* [Radical Salafiyyah movements in Indonesia] (Jakarta: Raja Grafindo Persada, 2004), 61–2, as cited in Azra, Afrianty, and Hefner, "Pesantren and Madrasa: Muslim Schools and National Ideals in Indonesia," 192.

18. Aqidah 1b, 17, as cited in Hefner, "Islamic Schools, Social Movements, and Democracy in Indonesia," 85.

19. Ibid., 85–6.

20. This is cited in Tholchah, "The Impact of Terrorism Issue on Parents' Trust," 33.

21. Hefner, "Islamic Schools, Social Movements, and Democracy in Indonesia," 86.
22. Imam Tirmidzi, *Al-Jami'u As-Shohihu Sunan Tirmidzi*, juz 5, (Beirut: Darul Kutub Al-Ilmiyah), 13, as cited in Tholchah, "The Impact of Terrorism Issue on Parents' Trust," 64.
23. Noorhaidi Hassan, "The Salafi Madrasas of Indonesia," in *The Madrasa in Asia: Political Activism and Transnational Linkages*, eds. Farish A. Noor, Yoginder Sikand, and Martin van Bruinessen (Amsterdam: Amsterdam University Press, 2008), 247–74.
24. van Bruinessen, "Traditionalist and Islamist Pesantrens in Contemporary Indonesia," 243.
25. This is cited in McCawley, "Indonesia Hotel Bomber: A Graduate of Jihad 'Ivy League,'" avaliable at: http://www.csmonitor.com/world/Asia-Pacific/2009/0720/p06510-woap.html (accessed June 12, 2010).
26. van Bruinessen, "Traditionalist and Islamist Pesantrens in Contemporary Indonesia," 243.
27. Aqidah 1a, 38, as cited in Hefner, "Islamic Schools, Social Movements, and Democracy in Indonesia," 85–6.
28. McCawley, "Indonesia Hotel Bomber: A Graduate of Jihad 'Ivy League'."
29. Tholchah, "The Impact of Terrorism Issue on Parents' Trust," 63–4; also see Salim Osman, "Jakarta Arrests Rekindle Fears of Terrorism," *The Straits Times*, November 5, 2010, available at: http://www.asianewsnet.net/news.php?id=11841&sec=1 (accessed May 28, 2010).
30. Brek Batley, *The Complexities of Dealing with Radical Islam in Southeast Asia: A Case Study of Jemaah Islamiyah* (Canberra: Strategic and Defence Studies Centre, Australian National University, 2003), 85. This dichotomy of "good versus evil" is also discernible in Al Qaeda's ideology. For a discussion of its ideology and channels of dissemination, see Elena Pavlova, "An Ideological Response to Islamist Terrorism: Theoretical and Operational Overview," in *Terrorism in the Asia-Pacific: Threat and Response*, ed. Rohan Gunaratna (Singapore: Eastern Universities Press, 2003), 30–45.
31. Ibid., 64.
32. Tholchah, "The Impact of Terrorism Issue on Parents' Trust," 70.
33. Macan-Markar, "My Roommate, the Terrorist," available at: http://ipsnews.net/news.asp?idnews=44841 (accessed May 26, 2010).
34. Hassan, "The Salafi Madrasas of Indonesia," 261.
35. A.V. Kelly, *The Curriculum: Theory and Practice*, 5th ed. (London: Sage Publications, 2004), 5. For more information on the different conceptions, aspects, and levels of curriculum, see Charlene Tan, "Curriculum," in *Critical Perspectives on Education: An Introduction*, eds. Charlene Tan, Benjamin Wong, Jude Soo Meng Chua, and Trivina Kang (Singapore: Prentice Hall, 2006), 96–111.
36. Macan-Markar, "My Roommate, the Terrorist."
37. Zalman Mohamed Yusof and Mohammad Ishak, "Inside a JI School," *The New Paper*, January 4, 2004; as cited in Ramakrishna, "'Constructing' the Jemaah Islamiyah Terrorist: A Preliminary Inquiry," 26.
38. Yusof and Ishak, "Inside a JI School"; Timothy Mapes, "Indonesian School Gives High Marks to Students Embracing Intolerance," *Asian Wall Street Journal*, September 2, 2003, both cited in Ramakrishna, "'Constructing' the Jemaah Islamiyah Terrorist: A Preliminary Inquiry," 26.
39. Macan-Markar, "My Roommate, the Terrorist," available at: http://ipsnews.net/news.asp?idnews=44841 (accessed May 26, 2010). Here I should qualify that I am not assuming that all the school leaders and teachers hold the same totalistic ideology or militant mindset. There are certainly those who do not

share the same convictions but are associated with the school because of its high academic standard or other personal reasons. On the academic reputation of Ngruki, see my concluding remarks in this chapter.

40. Ismail, "Schooled For Jihad"; Noor Huda Ismail, "Ngruki: Is it a Terrorism School?" *The Jakarta Post*, March 14, 2005, available at: http://www.the-jakartapost.com/news/2005/03/14/part-1–2-ngruki-it-terrorism-school.html (accessed September 6, 2010).
41. Hassan, "The Salafi Madrasas of Indonesia," 260.
42. Zamakhsyari Dhofier, *The Pesantren Tradition: The Role of the Kyai in the Maintenance of Traditional Islam in Java* (Arizona: Programme for Southeast Asian Studies, Arizona State University, 1999), 135.
43. This is cited in ibid., 62. Interestingly, the teaching to regard and respect one's teacher as one's father is also found in Chinese societies. A popular proverb is "A person who is your teacher for one day becomes your father for life" [*yi tian wei shi, zhong shen wei fu*]. The similarity between the high regard for one's teacher in Indonesian and Chinese societies may be explained by the fact that they are both collectivist societies. Kumar Ramakrishna, citing Olufemi A. Lawal, maintains that individuals in collectivist societies are expected to be loyal to the in-group, subordinate personal goals to those of the collective, and accept the concentration of authority and power in the hands of a leader. See Ramakrishna, "'Constructing' the Jemaah Islamiyah Terrorist: A Preliminary Inquiry," 20. On the collective nature of Asian societies, see Charlene Tan, "Creating "Good Citizens" and Maintaining Religious Harmony in Singapore," *British Journal of Religious Education* 30/2 (2008): 133–42.
44. Dhofier, *The Pesantren Tradition*, 61.
45. Interview with senior religious leaders of a pesantren, May 6, 2010.
46. Zuhdi, "Political and Social Influences on Religious School," 40.
47. Lukens-Bull, *A Peaceful Jihad*, 85.
48. See H. Imron Arifin and Muhammad Slamet, *Kepimimpin Kyai: Dalam Perubahan Manajemen Pondok Pesantren: Kasus Ponpes Tebuireng Jombang* [Kyai Leadership: Change Management in Boarding School: The Case of Tebuireng Jombang] (Yogyakarta: CV. Aditya Media, 2010), 106.
49. Martin van Bruinessen, "Pesantren and Kitab Kuning: Maintenance and Continuation of a Tradition of Religious Learning," in *Texts from the Islands. Oral and Written Traditions of Indonesia and the Malay World* [*Ethnologica Bernica*, 4], ed. Wolfgang Marschall (Berne: University of Berne, 1994), 121–45, available at: http://www.let.uu.nl/~martin.vanbruinessen/personal/publications/pesantren_and_kitab_kuning.htm (accessed May 28, 2010).
50. Dhofier, *The Pesantren Tradition*, 61.
51. It should be qualified that a kyai's influence is dependent on the steadfast and continual support of his followers; after all, the title of a kyai is not conferred by oneself or one's peers but by the masses. This means that there exists a dynamic relationship in the relationship between the kyai and his followers, a dialectic process of claim, evaluation, and counterclaim that points to the evolving nature of Islamic traditions. See Lukens-Bull, *A Peaceful Jihad*, 91.
52. Dhofier, *The Pesantren Tradition*, 62.
53. Tholchah, "The Impact of Terrorism Issue on Parents' Trust," 48.
54. Ibid., 64.
55. Ibid., 94.
56. Hefner, "Islamic Schools, Social Movements, and Democracy in Indonesia," 85.
57. Azra, Afrianty, and Hefner, "Pesantren and Madrasa: Muslim Schools and National Ideals in Indonesia," 192.

58. Hefner, "Islamic Schools, Social Movements, and Democracy in Indonesia," 68.
59. Ibid., 86.
60. "Profile of Pesantren," August 2008, available at: http://almukmin-ngruki.com/index.php?option=com_content&view=article&id=46&Itemid=56 (accessed August 23, 2010).

NOTES TO CHAPTER 4

1. This is cited in Chairul Fahmy Hussaini, "Suicide Bombings: A Threat to Homeland Security," in *Fighting Terrorism: The Singapore Perspective*, ed. Abdul Halim Bin Kader (Singapore: Taman Bacaan Pemuda Pemudi Melayu Singapura, 2007), 157.
2. Bilveer Singh points out that the actual name of the organisation, according to a key document of the organisation that was obtained by Indonesian security forces, is Al-Jama'ah Al-Islamiyyah, which means "The (or An) Organisation of Muslims", but the organisation is popularly known as Jemaah Islamiyah (with slight variations in spelling). See Bilveer Singh, *The Talibanisation of Southeast Asia: Losing the War on Terror to Islamist Extremists* (Westport: Praeger Security International, 2007), 51.
3. Abuza, *Political Islam and Violence in Indonesia*, 65.
4. Ramakrishna, "'Constructing' the Jemaah Islamiyah Terrorist: A Preliminary Inquiry," ii and passim.
5. Rohan Gunaratna, "Ideology in Terrorism and Counter Terrorism: Lessons from Combating Al Qaeda and Al Jemaah Al Islamiyah in Southeast Asia," in *Fighting Terrorism: The Singapore Perspective*, ed. Abdul Halim Bin Kader (Singapore: Taman Bacaan Pemuda Pemudi Melayu Singapura, 2007), 86. Also see "The Jemaah Islamiyah Arrests and the Threat of Terrorism," White Paper published by the Ministry of Home Affairs, Republic of Singapore, 2003, 17. Justin Magouirk's research on JI shows that a key ingredient of indoctrination is "halaqahs" or external study groups that take place outside the usual madrasah curriculum; there are small-group dynamics with "ongoing student interaction and sometimes mutual radicalisation outside of the classroom". See Magouirk, "Connecting a Thousand Points of Hatred," 339. Elena Pavlova concurs that the structural model of a jama'ah (group) is instrumental to "recruit, indoctrinate, and train its followers into obedience". Elena Pavlova, "From Counter-Society to Counter-State: Jemaah Islamiyah according to PUPJI," IDSS Working Paper, Institute of Defence and Strategic Studies (Singapore: Nanyang Technological University, 2006), 13.
6. Noor, "Pride within Stigma: The Case of Indonesian Terrorists' Families," 127.
7. This is taken from *The Straits Times*, October 10, 2005, as cited in Mohamed Khairunan Bin Ali. "Islamic Religious Education in Singapore: Making it Relevant to Global Demand," Master's dissertation, S. Rajaratnam School of International Studies, Nanyang Technological University, 2007, 43.
8. See Noor Huda Ismail and Carl Ungerer, "Jemaah Islamiyah: A Renewed Struggle?" *Policy Analysis*, by Australian Strategic Policy Institute, July 16, 2009, 2.
9. See Kumar Ramakrishna and See Seng Tan, eds., "Is Southeast Asia a 'Terrorist Haven'?" in *After Bali: The Threat of Terrorism in Southeast Asia* (Singapore: Institute of Defence and Strategic Studies and World Scientific, 2003), 27–8.
10. See Martin van Bruinessen, "Divergent Paths from Gontor: Muslim Educational Reform and the Travails of Pluralism in Indonesia," available at: http://

www.let.uu.nl/~martin.vanbruinessen/personal/publications/Bruinessen_Divergent_paths_from_Gontor.pdf (accessed May 28, 2010); van Bruinessen, "Traditionalist and Islamist Pesantrens in Contemporary Indonesia," 244.

11. John T. Sidel critiques what he calls "an alarmist picture" of the "Islamist threat" in Southeast Asia propagated by academics such as Zachary Abuza. He counters that the turn to terrorist violence by small numbers of Muslim militants should be understood as "a symptom of and reaction to the decline, domestication, and disengagement from state power of Islamist forces in the region". See Sidel, *The Islamist Threat in Southeast Asia*, 54. This debate of the extent to which Southeast Asia, including Indonesia, is experiencing an Islamist threat is tangential to our discussion on indoctrination. While there is an overlap between indoctrination, terrorism, and Islamism (for example, some Muslim militants or Islamists have indeed been indoctrinated), my focus is not so much on militancy but on whether their beliefs are held in an ideological totalistic manner.

12. This is cited in Harold Crouch, "Radical Islam in Indonesia: Some Misperceptions," in *Islamic Terrorism in Indonesia: Myths and Realities*, eds. Marika Vicziany and David Wright-Neville (Victoria: Monash University Press, 2005), 45.

13. Gunaratna, "Ideology in Terrorism and Counter Terrorism," 79–81.

14. For a useful discussion on the origin, growth, ideology, structure, and strategy of JI, see Singh, *The Talibanisation of Southeast Asia: Losing the War on Terror to Islamist Extremists*, 50–99; Barton, *Jemaah Islamiyah*; Batley, *The Complexities of Dealing with Radical Islam in Southeast Asia: A Case Study of Jemaah Islamiyah*; Ken Conboy, *The Second Front: Inside Asia's Most Dangerous Terrorist Network* (Jakarta: Equinox Publishing, 2006); International Crisis Group (ICG), *Indonesia Backgrounder: How the Jemaah Islamiyah Terrorist Network Operates* (Jakarta and Brussels: ICG, December 11, 2002). The history and ideology of Muslim militancy in Indonesia Muslim political movements can be traced to the Masyumi party in the 1940s and the Darul Islam movement that rebelled against the central Indonesian government during the 1950s and early 1960s. For a good discussion, see Martin van Bruinessen, "Genealogies of Islamic Radicalism in Post-Suharto Indonesia," in *Islam in Southeast Asia: Critical Concepts in Islamic Studies*, eds. Joseph Chinyong Liow and Nadirsyah Hosen, Vol. 4 (London and New York: Routledge, 2010), 35–66; Greg Fealy, "Half a Century of Violent Jihad in Indonesia: A Historical and Ideological Comparison of Darul Islam and Jema'ah Islamiyah," in *Islamic Terrorism in Indonesia: Myths and Realities*, eds. Marika Vicziany and David Wright-Neville (Victoria: Monash University Press, 2005), 14–32.

15. Pavlova, "From Counter-Society to Counter-State," 11. For excerpts of PUPJI, see Singh, *The Talibanisation of Southeast Asia: Losing the War on Terror to Islamist Extremists*, 159–82. The status of PUPJI as the official constitution of JI has been disputed as Abu Bakar Ba'asyir claims to be unaware of it. See ibid., 200. It is nevertheless a useful document to inform us about the ideology and strategies of JI.

16. See Saeed, *Islamic Thought: An Introduction*, 3.

17. Atran, "The Moral Logic and Growth of Suicide Terrorism," 138–9.

18. This is taken from Batley, *The Complexities of Dealing with Radical Islam in Southeast Asia*, 84, 86.

19. Tim Behrend, "Reading Past the Myth: Public Teachings of Abu Bakara Ba'asyir," February 19, 2003, available at: http://www.arts.auckland.ac.nz/asia/tbehrend/abb-myth.htm (accessed April 30, 2004); John L. Esposito, *Unholy War: Terror in the Name of Islam* (New York: Oxford University

Press, 2002), 52–3, both cited in Ramakrishna, "'Constructing' the Jemaah Islamiyah Terrorist: A Preliminary Inquiry,"14.

20. This is cited in Fealy and Hooker, *Voices of Islam in Southeast Asia*, 372, 375.
21. This was based on Huala Noor's interview with him. See Noor, "Pride within Stigma," 105.
22. This is taken from Hassan, *Unlicensed to Kill*, 94–5. Hassan notes that *al-fai* as a basis for committing robbery against corporations run by non-Muslims was also espoused by another militant group Darul Islam in Indonesia. See ibid., 96. For an excellent refutation of Iman Samudra's interpretation of *al-fai*, see ibid., 95–101.
23. Ibid.
24. Iman Samudra, *Aku Melawan Teroris* [I Fight Terrorists] (Indonesia: Solo Jazeera, 2004), 67–70, 93–118, reproduced in Fealy and Hooker, *Voices of Islam in Southeast Asia*, 373–7. All page references refer to the extract in Fealy and Hooker's book.
25. Ibid., 373, 374.
26. Gunaratna, "Ideology in Terrorism and Counter Terrorism," 84.
27. Ministry of Home Affairs, "The Jemaah Islamiyah Arrests and the Threat of Terrorism," 15.
28. Ibid., 16.
29. Abuza, *Political Islam and Violence in Indonesia*, 40.
30. Ismail and Ungerer, "Jemaah Islamiyah: A Renewed Struggle?" 3.
31. See Batley, *The Complexities of Dealing with Radical Islam in Southeast Asia*, 11.
32. van Bruinessen, "Traditionalist and Islamist Pesantrens in Contemporary Indonesia," 232; also see van Bruinessen, "Divergent Paths from Gontor: Muslim Educational Reform and the Travails of Pluralism in Indonesia," 197; Ramakrishna, "'Constructing' the Jemaah Islamiyah Terrorist," 8–9.
33. See Singh, *The Talibanisation of Southeast Asia*, 84. For excerpts of PUPJI, see ibid., 159–80.
34. van Bruinessen, "Divergent Paths from Gontor: Muslim Educational Reform and the Travails of Pluralism in Indonesia," 198; Martin van Bruinessen, "The Violent Fringes of Indonesia's Radical Islam", available at: http://www.let.uu.nl/~martin.vanbruinessen/personal/publications/violent_fringe.htm (accessed July 29, 2010).
35. Hefner, "Islamic Schools, Social Movements, and Democracy in Indonesia," 72; John T. Sidel, *Riots, Pogroms, Jihad: Religious Violence in Indonesia* (Ithaca: Cornell University Press, 2006), 38.
36. See van Bruinessen, "Genealogies of Islamic Radicalism in Post-Suharto Indonesia," 45.
37. Abuza, *Political Islam and Violence in Indonesia*, 124.
38. Ramakrishna, "'Constructing' the Jemaah Islamiyah Terrorist: A Preliminary Inquiry," 38.
39. Noor, "Pride within Stigma: The Case of Indonesian Terrorists' Families," 126.
40. "Indonesia: Fathers Pass Jihad Ideas to Sons," *The Straits Times*, June 26, 2010, C2.
41. Wahyudi Soeriaatmadja, "Prison for Woman who Hid Terrorist," *The Straits Times*, July 30, 2010, B4.
42. Interview with the director of a pesantren, May 14, 2010.
43. The following information is drawn from recent interviews conducted by Huala Noor with some of the family members of convicted militants. For details see Noor, "Pride within Stigma: The Case of Indonesian Terrorists' Families," 68.
44. Ibid., 124.

45. Ibid., 56–9; personal communication with Huala Noor, May 15, 2010.
46. Ibid., 139.
47. Ibid., 105–6.
48. See Azyumardi Azra, "Bali and Southeast Asian Islam: Debunking the Myths," in *After Bali: The Threat of Terrorism in Southeast Asia*, eds. Kumar Ramakrishna and See Seng Tan (Singapore: Institute of Defence and Strategic Studies and World Scientific, 2003), 50.
49. Azra, "Bali and Southeast Asian Islam: Debunking the Myths," 48.
50. Vedi R. Hadiz, "Towards a Sociological Understanding of Islamic Radicalism in Indonesia," *Journal of Contemporary Asia* 38/4 (2008): 645; Sidel, *Riots, Pogroms and Jihad: Religious Violence in Indonesia*.
51. Hafez, "Rationality, Culture, and Structure in the Making of Suicide Bombers," 170–1.
52. Hassan, *Unlicensed to Kill*, 147.
53. Zakiyuddin Baidhawy, "Building Harmony and Peace through Multiculturalist Theology-based Religious Education: An Alternative for Contemporary Indonesia," *British Journal of Religious Education* 29/1 (2007): 16.
54. Interview with the director of a pesantren, May 15, 2010.
55. Interview with the director of a pesantren, May 6, 2010.
56. Interview with the director of a pesantren, May 15, 2010.
57. Interview with the director of a pesantren, May 14, 2010; also see Tim JSIT, *Sekolah Islam Terpadu, Konsep dan Aplikasinya* [Integrated Islamic School, Concept and Application] (Bandung: Syaamil Cipta Media, 2006).
58. Tholchah, "The Impact of Terrorism Issue on Parents' Trust," 116.
59. The details are available in Jajat Burhanudin and Jamhari, "Assessment of Social and Political Attitudes in Indonesia Islamic Education Institution," *Studia Islamika: Indonesian Journal for Islamic Studies* 13/3 (2006): 399–433.
60. See Saeed, *Islamic Thought: An Introduction*, 45.
61. See Esposito and Mogahed, *Who Speaks for Islam?* 6, 35.
62. HRH Prince Alwaleed Bin Talal Centre of Islamic Studies, "Contextualising Islam in Britain: Exploratory Perspectives," a project by the University of Cambridge in association with the Universities of Exeter and Westminster, October 2009. Cambridge: Centre of Islamic Studies, 12.
63. Ishtiaq Ahmed, "The Pakistan Islamic State Project: A Secular Critique," in *State and Secularism: Perspectives from Asia*, eds. Michael Siam-Heng Heng and Chin Liew Ten (Singapore: World Scientific, 2010), 208–9.

NOTES TO CHAPTER 5

1. This is taken from Nord, "Rethinking Indoctrination," 2. In the article, Nord critiques the "conceptual net" provided by public schools that is constructed from the scientific method.
2. I am using "educated person" and "educative tradition" here in a positive sense. This praiseworthy meaning should be contrasted with the neutral term "education" used in the context of formal, non-formal, and informal education.
3. Wolterstorff, *Reason within the Bounds of Religion*, 95–6.
4. Amir Hussain, "Muslims, Pluralism, and Interfaith Dialogue," in *Progressive Muslims: On Justice, Gender, and Pluralism*, ed. Omid Safi (Oxford: Oneworld Publications, 2003), 252.
5. Nicholas Rescher, *Pluralism: Against the Demand of Consensus* (Oxford: Clarendon Press, 1993), 88–9, as cited in Fathi Osman, "Islam and Human Rights: The Challenge to Muslims and the World," *Rethinking Islam and*

Modernity: Essays in Honour of Fathi Osman, ed. Abdelwahab El-Affendi (London: The Islamic Foundation, 2001), 52; also see Fathi Osman, *Children of Adam: An Islamic Perspective on Pluralism* (Washington, DC: Georgetown University Press, 1996).

6. Jane Idleman Smith, *Muslim, Christians, and the Challenge of Interfaith Dialogue* (Oxford: Oxford University Press, 2007), 123.

7. Some readers may question whether an educative tradition should contain any ideology at all. Some liberal thinkers may insist that education, in its true philosophical, pure sense, should have nothing at all to do with ideology. However, this objection assumes a pejorative understanding of ideology. As stated earlier, I have defined ideology in a neutral way to refer to a framework of beliefs that informs us about ourselves and our relationship to the natural or supernatural world, and governs our individual or collective lives. An ideology may be indoctrinatory or educative.

8. Alexander, "Education in Ideology," 5.

9. Ibid., "Education in Ideology," 6–7.

10. See Terence H. McLaughlin, "Beyond the Reflective Teacher," *Educational Philosophy and Theory* 31/1 (1999): 14–15, as cited in Charlene Tan, "Improving Schools through Reflection for Teachers: Lessons from Singapore," *School Effectiveness and School Improvement* 19/2 (2008): 226. Also see Donald Schon, *Educating the Reflective Practitioner* (San Francisco: Jossey-Bass, 1987).

11. Wilson, "Religious (Moral, Political, etc.) Commitment, Education and Indoctrination," 44.

12. Ibid. Arguing along the same line is Harvey Siegel. See his *Educating Reason* (New York: Routledge, 1988); Harvey Siegel, *Rationality Redeemed?* (London: Routledge, 1997). For a critique of the Enlightenment notion of rationality, see Tan, *Teaching without Indoctrination*.

13. James M. Jasper, *The Art of Moral Protest: Culture, Biography and Creativity in Social Movements* (Chicago: University of Chicago Press, 1997), 83.

14. Hassan explains that *Usul Fiqh* is the science of source methodology of Islamic jurisprudence and refers to the aggregate of legal proofs and evidence that will lead either to certain knowledge of a shari'ah ruling. *Usul Tafsir*, also known as *Ulum Al-Quran*, is the science of interpretation of Al-Quran. *Usul Hadits*, also known as *Mustalah Al-Hadits*, is the science in the study of hadiths and seeks to determine the authenticity of a hadith and how rulings can be deduced from it. See Muhammad Haniff Bin Hassan, "Key Considerations in Counterideological Work against Terrorist Ideology," *Studies in Conflict & Terrorism* 29/6 (2006): 554.

15. For a useful reading on the history and characteristics of Islamic education and the typology of Islamic institutions of learning, see George Makdisi, *The Rise of Colleges: Institutions of Learning in Islam and the West* (Edinburgh: Edinburgh University Press, 1981); Ahmad Shalaby, *History of Muslim Education* (Karachi: Indus Publications, 1979); Mohamed El-Mokhtar Ould Bah, *Islamic Education between Tradition and Modernity* (Morocco: Islamic Educational, Scientific and Cultural Organisation, 1998), available at: http://www.isesco.org.ma/english/publications/ISLAMIC%20EDUCATION/Menu.php (accessed August 31, 2010); Hunt Janin, *The Pursuit of Learning in the Islamic World 610–2003* (Jefferson: McFarland & Co, 2005).

16. For further readings on political pluralism from Islamic perspectives, see Khaled Abou E. Fadl, *Islam and the Challenge of Democracy* (Princeton and Oxford: Princeton University Press, 2004); Sayed Khatab and Gary D. Bouma, *Democracy in Islam* (Oxon: Routledge, 2007); Muhammad Salim Al-Awa, "Political Pluralism from an Islamic Perspective," in *Islam in Tran-*

sition: Muslim Perspectives, eds. John J. Donohue and John L. Esposito, 2nd ed. (Oxford: Oxford University Press, 2007), 279–87; Bassam Tibi, "Islam and Cultural Modernity: In Pursuit of Democratic Pluralism in Asia," in *Islamic Legitimacy in a Plural Asia*, eds. Anthony Reid and Michael Gilsenan (London and New York: Routledge, 2007), 28–52.

17. Khaled Abou El Fadl, *The Place of Tolerance in Islam* (Boston: Beacon Press, 2002), 23.

18. Amir Hussain, "Muslims, Pluralism, and Interfaith Dialogue," in *Progressive Muslims: On Justice, Gender, and Pluralism*, ed. Omid Safi (Oxford: Oneworld Publications, 2003), 257. These historical examples, though commendable, are not perfect examples. Bassam Tibi claims that the coexistence of Muslims with non-Muslims in Islamic Spain (al-Andalus) and the Ottoman southeast Europe did not take place based on equality of religions but occurred under the rule of Islam and its claim for supremacy. See Tibi, "Islam and Cultural Modernity: In Pursuit of Democratic Pluralism in Asia," 28.

19. Sachedina, *The Islamic Roots of Democratic Pluralism*, 35.

20. Moosa, "The Debts and Burdens of Critical Islam," 116.

21. This is cited in Abubakar, "Negotiating Reform and Social Changes in Indonesia," 56.

22. Ibid.

23. This is cited in Fealy and Hooker, *Voices of Islam in Southeast Asia*, 358.

24. This is cited in Kemal Ataman, "Religion, Culture and the Shaping of Religious Attitudes: The Case of Islam," *Islam and Christian–Muslim Relations* 18/4 (2007): 500.

25. This is cited in HRH Prince Alwaleed Bin Talal Centre of Islamic Studies, "Contextualising Islam in Britain: Exploratory Perspectives," 40. The report adds that it is a misinterpretation of the Qur'an for Muslims to avoid friendly contact with non-Muslims based on the Qur'anic teaching warning Muslims against colluding or associating with enemies (see Qur'an 3:28); this injunction only applies to times of war and does not apply to "those who fight you not for (your) Faith nor drive you out of your homes" (Qur'an 60:8). See ibid., 11.

26. Nurcholish Madjid, "The Necessity of Renewing Islamic Thought and Reinvigorating Religious Understanding," in *Liberal Islam: A Sourcebook*, ed. Charles Kurzman (Oxford: Oxford University Press, 1998), 287, italics mine.

27. van Bruinessen, "Divergent Paths from Gontor: Muslim Educational Reform and the Travails of Pluralism in Indonesia," 192–3.

28. Ataman, "Religion, Culture and the Shaping of Religious Attitudes: The Case of Islam," 502–3.

29. This does not mean that there are only two views on jihad held by Muslims. Instead, there exists a variety of jihad traditions on the Islamic landscape, each with its preferred interpretations and applications of jihad. Their existence illustrates my point that a tradition is necessarily marked by internal and external conflicts. See Chapter 1 Note 38 for useful references on the evolving and contested meanings of jihad.

30. All subsequent references to the views of Iman Samudra and Muhammad Haniff Hassan are taken from Hassan, *Unlicensed to Kill*. For more information on Iman Samudra including extracts of his writings, see Fealy and Hooker, *Voices of Islam in Southeast Asia*, 370–7. I have tried to present Hassan's views as accurately as possible, but I do not claim that he has endorsed my interpretation of his views. In any case, my focus is not on him but on how views such as his exist within a jihad tradition that is different from Iman Samudra's.

31. Hassan, *Unlicensed to Kill*, 28.

32. This is cited in Fealy and Hooker, *Voices of Islam in Southeast Asia*, 358.
33. Zafar Alam, *Islamic Education: Theory & Practice* (New Delhi: Adam Publishers & Distributors, 2003), 23.
34. Niaz Erfan & Zahid A. Valie, *Education and the Muslim World: Challenges & Responses* (Leicestre & Islamabad: The Islamic Foundation and Institute of Policy Studies, 1995), 35.
35. Syed Muhammad Naquib al-Attas, *The Concept of Education in Islam* (Kuala Lumpur: International Institute of Islamic Thought and Civilisation (ISTAC), 1999), 15.
36. Ramadan, *Western Muslims and the Future of Islam*, 80.
37. al An'am: 165, as cited in Abd al Majid al Najjar, *The Vicegerency of Man: Between Revelation and Reason*, trans. Aref T. Atari (Herndon, Virginia: International Institute of Islamic Thought, 2000), 21.
38. al Najjar, *The Vicegerency of Man: Between Revelation and Reason*, 24.
39. Ramadan, *Western Muslims and the Future of Islam*, 129.
40. On how Muslim scholars disagree with one another on the final stage of jihad, see Hassan, *Unlicensed to Kill*, 142 and passim; on their disagreements on *amaliyat istisyhadiyah* (martyrdom operation), see ibid, 102 and passim; on their disagreements on *harbis* (non-Muslims at war), see ibid., 120 and passim.
41. Lukens-Bull, "Between Text and Practice," 47.
42. Saeed, *Islamic Thought*, 52–6.
43. Ramadan, *Western Muslims and the Future of Islam*, 43–8.
44. Saeed, *Islamic Thought*, 52–3.
45. Ibid., 54.
46. For a good discussion on the different views held by Muslims on ijtihad, see Richard C. Martin and Mark R. Woodward with Dwi S. Atmaja, *Defenders of Reason in Islam: Mu'tazilism from Medieval School to Modern Symbol* (Oxford: Oneworld, 1997).

NOTES TO CHAPTER 6

1. This is taken from Azra, "Teaching Tolerance through Education in Indonesia," 7–8.
2. Charlene Tan and Diwi Binti Abbas, "The 'Teach Less, Learn More' Initiative in Singapore: New Pedagogies for Islamic Religious Schools?" *KEDI Journal of Education Policy* 6/1 (2009): 28.
3. Azyumardi Azra, Dina Afrianty, and Robert W. Hefner, in an essay published in 2007, report that there are 10000 pesantrens and 37000 madrasahs, adding to a total of 47000. See Azra, Afrianty, and Hefner, "Pesantren and Madrasa: Muslim Schools and National Ideals in Indonesia," 173; Hefner, "Islamic Schools, Social Movements, and Democracy in Indonesia," 59. However, I would put the total figure closer to 50000 based on a higher calculation of pesantrens. Rather than 10000 pesantrens, H. Imron Arifin and Muhammad Slamet note that there are 16015 pesantrens based on the statistics obtained from the Department of Religious Affairs in 2006, as cited in H. Imron Arifin and Muhammad Slamet, *Kepimimpin Kyai: Dalam Perubahan Manajemen Pondok Pesantren: Kasus Ponpes Tebuireng Jombang* [Kyai Leadership: Change Management in Boarding School: The Case of Tebuireng Jombang] (Yogyakarta: CV. Aditya Media, 2010), 38.
4. Azra, Afrianty, and Hefner, "Pesantren and Madrasa: Muslim Schools and National Ideals in Indonesia," 173. It should be noted that enrolment statistics do not reflect the actual number of Islamic schools due to the problem of

double counting. According to Azra, Afrianty, and Hefner, many pesantrens have madrasahs or public schools (known as general schools in Indonesia) in their compounds, but these institutions are counted as separate entities. The same applies to the number of students; students who attend a public school in the morning and an Islamic school after school hours are counted twice. Nevertheless, it is fair to say that there are about 50000 Islamic schools in Indonesia. See ibid., 177.

5. The oldest form of Islamic education is actually *pengajian Qur'an.* According to Hefner, it refers to basic instruction in learning to read and recite the Qur'an, and usually takes place in village mosques, prayer houses, and private homes of religious teachers. Given its informal nature, I have chosen not to focus on this form of Islamic education. For more details, see Hefner, "Islamic Schools, Social Movements, and Democracy in Indonesia," 59.

6. Azra, Afrianty, and Hefner, "Pesantren and Madrasa: Muslim Schools and National Ideals in Indonesia," 175.

7. For more details on the religious curriculum in pesantrens, see van Bruin-essen, "Pesantren and Kitab Kuning: Maintenance and Continuation of a Tradition of Religious Learning," available at: http://www.let.uu.nl/~martin.vanbruinessen/personal/publications/pesantren_and_kitab_kuning.htm (accessed May 28, 2010).

8. Azra, Afrianty, and Hefner, "Pesantren and Madrasa: Muslim Schools and National Ideals in Indonesia," 176; also see Jamhari and Jahroni, eds., *Gerakan Salafi Radikal di Indonesia,* 124–6.

9. This typology of pesantrens is taken from Burhanudin and Jamhari, "Assessment of Social and Political Attitudes in Indonesia Islamic Education Institution," 404.

10. Dhofier, *The Pesantren Tradition,* 34. Dhofier adds that strictly speaking, only ulama (Islamic scholars) who lead pesantrens in Central and East Java are called kyai; in West Java, they are "ajengan". However, the term "kyai" has transcended territorial boundaries and is generally used to refer to traditionalist ulama in Indonesia. See ibid.

11. See van Bruinessen, "Pesantren and Kitab Kuning: Maintenance and Continuity of a Tradition of Religious Learning," 124; van Bruinessen, "Traditionalist and Islamist Pesantrens in Contemporary Indonesia," 218; Lukens-Bull, *A Peaceful Jihad,* 18; Clifford Geertz, *Islam Observed: Religious Development in Morocco and Indonesia* (Chicago: The University of Chicago Press, 1968), 49.

12. Burhanudin and Jamhari, "Assessment of Social and Political Attitudes in Indonesia Islamic Education Institution," 409.

13. van Bruinessen, "Traditionalist and Islamist Pesantrens in Contemporary Indonesia," 218. The mass support for these two organisations is seen in a nation-wide survey where 42 percent of the respondents identified themselves with NU and 12 percent identified themselves with Muhammadiyah. See ibid., 219.

14. For an excellent reading of the historical evolution of madrasahs as Muslim higher institutions of learning, see Makdisi, *The Rise of Colleges: Institutions of Learning in Islam and the West,* 27–32, and passim.

15. Abdullah Saeed, "Towards Religious Tolerance through Reform in Islamic Education: The Case of the State Institute of Islamic Studies of Indonesia," *Indonesia and the Malay World* 27/79 (1999): 181.

16. Azra, Afrianty, and Hefner, "Pesantren and Madrasa: Muslim Schools and National Ideals in Indonesia," 180.

17. Burhanudin and Jamhari, "Assessment of Social and Political Attitudes in Indonesia Islamic Education Institution," 409.

18. Interview with the director of a madrasah, May 12, 2010.

19. Burhanudin and Jamhari, "Assessment of Social and Political Attitudes in Indonesia Islamic Education Institution," 412.
20. Although Madrasah Aliyah Negeri Insan Cendikia Serpong and Pesantren Ibnu Salam Nurul Fikri Boarding School are officially a madrasah and a pesantren respectively, they are classified by Indonesian academics as Sekolah Islam rather than madrasahs or pesantrens. For example, see Noorhaidi Hasan, "Islamising Formal Education: Integrated Islamic School and a New Trend in Formal Education Institution in Indonesia," Working Paper, February 11, 2009, S. Rajaratnam School of International Studies, Singapore, 5; Nurlena Rifai, "The Emergence of Elite Islamic Schools in Contemporary Indonesia: A Case Study of Al Azhar Islamic School," PhD dissertation, McGill University, 2006, 58; Zuhdi, "Political and Social Influences on Religious School: A Historical Perspective on Indonesian Islamic School Curricula," 10. My visits to and interviews with the school leaders of Madrasah Aliyah Negeri Insan Cendikia Serpong and Pesantren Ibnu Salam Nurul Fikri Boarding School, also confirm that these two schools fit the description of a Sekolah Islam the best. This is because unlike most pesantrens and madrasahs, these two schools are operated along the lines of a Sekolah Islam with their strong emphasis on and success in science and technology, modern and comprehensive facilities, highly qualified teachers, and students who are mostly from middle-class and urban home backgrounds. It is also noteworthy that Madrasah Aliyah Negeri Insan Cendikia Serpong was founded in 1996 as a private Islamic school and only became a madrasah in 2001 due to political factors. As for Pesantren Ibnu Salam Nurul Fikri Boarding School, it is not a typical pesantren, as it does not have a kyai and is instead run by the school management; its students also do not study the classical commentaries (kitab kuning) used in traditional pesantrens.
21. Interview with a senior staff member of a Sekolah Islam, May 10, 2010.
22. Azra, Afrianty, and Hefner, "Pesantren and Madrasa: Muslim Schools and National Ideals in Indonesia," 173–4.
23. Lukens-Bull, *A Peaceful Jihad*, 6.
24. Burhanudin and Jamhari, "Assessment of Social and Political Attitudes in Indonesia Islamic Education Institution," 407–8.
25. Ibid., 408.
26. See Rifai, "The Emergence of Elite Islamic Schools in Contemporary Indonesia: A Case Study of Al Azhar Islamic School," 45; also see Achmad Zaini, "Kyai Haji Abdul Wahid Hasyim: His Contribution to Muslim Educational Reform and to Indonesian Nationalism during the Twentieth Century," Master's thesis, McGill University, 1998.
27. Interview with senior staff members of Pondok Pesantren Tebuireng, May 6, 2010.
28. This is taken from the pesantren's website: http://www.tebuireng.net/.
29. Burhanudin and Jamhari, "Assessment of Social and Political Attitudes in Indonesia Islamic Education Institution," 404.
30. Interview with the director of a madrasah, May 12, 2010.
31. Interview with a senior staff member of a Sekolah Islam, May 10, 2010.
32. Interview with a senior staff member of a Sekolah Islam, May 11, 2010.
33. Hasan, "Islamising Formal Education: Integrated Islamic School and a New Trend in Formal Education Institution in Indonesia," 26.
34. Hefner, "Islamic Schools, Social Movements, and Democracy in Indonesia," 77, 80.
35. Interview with a senior staff member of a Sekolah Islam, May 10, 2010.
36. Interview with the senior staff members of a pesantren, May 6, 2010.
37. Dhofier, *The Pesantren Tradition*, 104.
38. Interview with the director of a pesantren, May 15, 2010.

39. Burhanudin and Jamhari, "Assessment of Social and Political Attitudes in Indonesia Islamic Education Institution," 410; Hefner, "Islamic Schools, Social Movements, and Democracy in Indonesia," 101; van Bruinessen, "Divergent Paths from Gontor: Muslim Educational Reform and the Travails of Pluralism in Indonesia," n.d., available at: http://www.let.uu.nl/~martin.vanbruinessen/personal/publications/Bruinessen_Divergent_paths_from_Gontor.pdf (accessed May 28, 2010).
40. Interview with a senior staff member of Gontor, May 7, 2010. The school also offers a post-secondary programme (*Institute Islam Darussalam*) to train teachers in Islamic studies.
41. This is taken from the school's website: http://www.gontor.ac.id/.
42. Burhanudin and Jamhari, "Assessment of Social and Political Attitudes in Indonesia Islamic Education Institution," 410.
43. Interview with a senior staff member of Gontor, May 7, 2010.
44. van Bruinessen, "Traditionalist and Islamist Pesantrens in Contemporary Indonesia," 223.
45. Interview with a senior staff member of Gontor, May 7, 2010.
46. Ibid.
47. Robert Pringle, *Understanding Islam in Indonesia: Politics and Diversity* (Singapore: Editions Didier Millet, 2010), 126.
48. Syed Farid Alatas, "Knowledge and Education in Islam," in *Secularism and Spirituality: Seeking Integrated Knowledge and Success in Madrasah Education in Singapore*, eds. Noor Aisha Abdul Rahman and Ah Eng Lai (Singapore: Marshall Cavendish, 2006), 169.
49. Mesut Idriz Al-Attas and Syed Ali Tawfik, *The Ihazah of Abdullah Fahim: A Unique Document from Islamic Education* (Selangor: MPH Publishing, 2007), 7–8. For a useful historical survey of the evolving relationship between Islam and the enterprise of science from the eighth century to the present time, see Muzaffar Iqbal, *The Making of Islamic Science* (Kuala Lumpur: Islamic Book Trust, 2009).
50. For more details, see Tan and Abbas, "The 'Teach Less, Learn More' Initiative in Singapore: New Pedagogies for Islamic Religious Schools?" 25–39.
51. Interview with the director of a pesantren, May 15, 2010.
52. Interview with the director of a pesantren, May 14, 2010.
53. Hefner, "Islamic Schools, Social Movements, and Democracy in Indonesia," 73.
54. For more examples of including Islamic principles into general subjects in an Islamic school, see Rifai, "The Emergence of Elite Islamic Schools in Contemporary Indonesia: A Case Study of Al Azhar Islamic School," 128, 151; Zuhdi, "Political and Social Influences on Religious School: A Historical Perspective on Indonesian Islamic School Curricula," 149; Hasan, "Islamising Formal Education: Integrated Islamic School and a New Trend in Formal Education Institution in Indonesia," 17.
55. Zuhdi, "Political and Social Influences on Religious School: A Historical Perspective," 151.
56. Interview with a teacher of a madrasah, May 12, 2010.
57. Azra, Afrianty, and Hefner, "Pesantren and Madrasa: Muslim Schools and National Ideals in Indonesia," 182–3.
58. Rusydy Zakaria, *Indonesian Islamic Education: A Social, Historical and Political Perspective* (Saarbrucken: VDM Verlag Dr. Muller, 2008), 9, 82.
59. I have not discussed political pluralism, as this is less relevant than epistemological and religious pluralism in the schooling context. But it should be noted that political pluralism has a strong presence in Indonesia, as seen in the active participation of political parties, the populace's positive attitude towards democracy, and general rejection of the establishment of an Islamic

178 *Notes*

state through violent means. It is beyond the scope of this book to study the political developments of Islam and its relationship with the state in Indonesia. Interested readers may refer to Robert W. Hefner, *Civil Islam: Muslims and Democratisation in Indonesia* (Princeton: Princeton University Press, 2000); Luthfi Assyaukanie, *Islam and the Secular State in Indonesia* (Singapore: Institute of Southeast Asian Studies Publications, 2009); Bernhard Platzdasch, *Islamism in Indonesia: Politics in the Emerging Democracy* (Singapore: Institute of Southeast Asian Studies Publications, 2009).

NOTES TO CHAPTER 7

1. Interview with the director of a pesantren, May 15, 2010.
2. "Indon Cleric Abu Bakar Bashir Arrested Again," *Today*, August 10, 2010, 6.
3. "Liberalism" or "liberal" should be distinguished from "liberal Islam". M.B. Hooker explains that the "liberal Islam" is understood by many Muslims to "refer to the practice of ijtihad—the creative interpretation of Islam which enables it to remain relevant to the changing needs of conditions and times, place and history". See Virginia Hooker, "Developing Islamic Arguments for Change through 'Liberal Islam'," in *Islamic Perspectives on the New Millennium*, eds. Virginia Hooker and Amin Saikal (Singapore: Institute of Southeast Asian Studies, 2004), 236. Despite this salutary meaning of "liberal", my observation in Indonesia is that many Muslims now prefer to avoid the term "liberal", given its association with the United States and the West, and opt instead for other terms such as "open" or "progressive".
4. Interview with the director of a pesantren, May 15, 2010.
5. Tholchah, "The Impact of Terrorism Issue on Parents' Trust (A Study of Ngruki Pesantren, Surakarta, Central Java)," 96.
6. van Bruinessen, "Divergent Paths from Gontor: Muslim Educational Reform and the Travails of Pluralism in Indonesia," 77.
7. Hasan, "Islamising Formal Education: Integrated Islamic School and a New Trend in Formal Education Institution in Indonesia," 7.
8. Ibid., 8; Ehud Rosen, "The Muslim Brotherhood's Concept of Education," *Current Trends in Islamist Ideology*, Vol. 5 (Washington, DC: Hudson Institute, 2008).
9. Hasan, "Islamising Formal Education: Integrated Islamic School and a New Trend in Formal Education Institution in Indonesia," 18.
10. Majelis Ulama Indonesia (MUI), *Keputusan Fatwa Majelis Utama Indonesia Nomor: 7/Munas VII/MUI/II/2005 Tentang Pluralisme, Liberalisme dan Sekularisme Agama* [The Decision of Indonesian Ulama No7/Munas VII/MUI/II/2005 on Pluralism, Liberalism and Secularism], available at: http://www.mui.or.id/ (accessed February 2, 2009), as cited in Muhammad Zuhdi, "Political and Social Influences on Religious School," 208.
11. Zuhdi, "Political and Social Influences on Religious School: A Historical Perspective on Indonesian Islamic School Curricula," 207; also see M.N. Ichwan, "Ulama, State and Politics: Majelis Ulama Indonesia after Suharto," *Islamic Law and Society* 12/1 (2005): 45–72; A. Husaini, "Pluralisme Agama: MUI terlambat [Religious Pluralism: It's late for MUI]," *Republika* (Indonesian Daily News), August 4, 2005.
12. Abuza, *Political Islam and Violence in Indonesia*, 88.
13. Hasan, "Islamising Formal Education: Integrated Islamic School and a New Trend in Formal Education Institution in Indonesia," 23.

14. The results have been published in Burhanudin and Jamhari, "Assessment of Social and Political Attitudes in Indonesia Islamic Education Institution," 399–433.
15. Ibid., 420.
16. The findings here are taken from a document provided by Dr Jajat Burhanudin, executive director of Centre for the Study of Islam and Society, State Islamic University (UIN) of Jakarta. The document is Pusat Pengkajian Islam dan Masyarakat (PPIM), *Sikap dan Perilaku Sosial-Keagamaan Guru-Guru Agama di Jawa: Temuan Survey* [Attitudes and Social Behaviour of Religious Teachers of Java: Survey Findings] (Jakarta: PPIM UIN Jakarta, 2008). I thank Dr Jajat for sharing this document with me and for a discussion on the survey findings, and Professor Azyumardi Azra, the director of Graduate School, UIN Jakarta for permission to cite the survey findings in this book.
17. Hasan, "Islamising Formal Education: Integrated Islamic School and a New Trend in Formal Education Institution in Indonesia," 3.
18. van Bruinessen, "Divergent Paths from Gontor: Muslim Educational Reform and the Travails of Pluralism in Indonesia," n.d., available at: http://www.let.uu.nl/~martin.vanbruinessen/personal/publications/Bruinessen_Divergent_paths_from_Gontor.pdf (accessed May 28, 2010).
19. Fred R. von der Mehden, "Islam in Indonesia in the Twenty-First Century," in *Asian Islam in the 21st Century*, eds. John L. Esposito, John O. Voll, and Osman Bakar (Oxford: Oxford University Press, 2008), 18.
20. Besides the bandongan and sorogan methods, there is another method known as *mushawarah*. The students are expected to study advanced texts independently in their groups, followed by a seminar where they present and justify their opinions to the kyai and fellow students. The seminar is organised according to questions and subjects set in advance. See Dhofier, *The Pesantren Tradition*, 12, 229. However, the mushawarah method is not meant for students of all levels and is reserved for post-graduate students who are training to be Islamic teachers. Furthermore, Dhofier claims that this method was discontinued in Pesantren Tebuireng upon the death of Hadratus-Shaikh in 1947, as there has been no great ulama to replace him. See ibid., 86.
21. Ibid., 11; van Bruinessen, "Traditionalist and Islamist Pesantrens in Contemporary Indonesia," 221; Zuhdi, "Political and Social Influences on Religious School: A Historical Perspective on Indonesian Islamic School Curricula," 98. Some writers have claimed that the pesantren system and its teaching methods such as the sorogan originated from Hindu traditions. See Zakaria, *Indonesian Islamic Education: A Social, Historical and Political Perspective*, 63; A. Maksum, *Madrasah: Sejarah dan Perkembangannya* [Madrasah: History and Development] (Jakarta: Logos, 1999), 63.
22. Zuhdi, "Political and Social Influences on Religious School: A Historical Perspective on Indonesian Islamic School Curricula," xvi. Zamakhsyari Dhofier claims that the sorogan is supposed to be for new students, while the bandongan is for intermediate and advanced students. See Dhofier, *The Pesantren Tradition*, 104. However, there appears to be a high level of flexibility and modification in practice. A kyai of a pesantren said that he combines both methods for his students so that the students can benefit from group teaching and individual attention at the same time. This is taken from an interview with the director on May 15, 2010.
23. van Bruinessen, "Traditionalist and Islamist Pesantrens in Contemporary Indonesia," 221; Dhofier, *The Pesantren Tradition*, 11; also see van Bruinessen, "Pesantren and Kitab Kuning: Maintenance and Continuation of a Tradition of Religious Learning," 121–45.

24. Interview with the head of the religious department of a pesantren, May 6, 2010.
25. Dhofier, *The Pesantren Tradition*, 102.
26. Lukens-Bull, *A Peaceful Jihad*, 55; also see Johannes Pederson, "Madrasa," in *Shorter Encyclopedia of Islam*, eds. H.A.R. Gibb and J.H. Kramers (Leiden, Netherlands: E.J. Brill, 1953), 306.
27. van Bruinessen, "Pesantren and Kitab Kuning: Maintenance and Continuation of a Tradition of Religious Learning," 121–45; Zuhdi, "Political and Social Influences on Religious School: A Historical Perspective on Indonesian Islamic School Curricula," xvi.
28. See Makdisi, *The Rise of Colleges*, 103.
29. van Bruinessen, "Traditionalist and Islamist Pesantrens in Contemporary Indonesia," 222.
30. Lukens-Bull, *A Peaceful Jihad*, 67; Zuhdi, "Political and Social Influences on Religious School: A Historical Perspective on Indonesian Islamic School Curricula," xvi.
31. Saeed, "Towards Religious Tolerance through Reform in Islamic Education," 187.
32. M. Amin Abdullah, *Keilmuan Umum Dan Agama Dalam Sistem Sekolah Dan Madrasah* [General and Religious Sciences in School and Madrasah System] (Jakarta: INCIS, 2004), 26, as cited in Zakaria, *Indonesian Islamic Education*, 8.
33. Interview with a senior staff member of a Sekolah Islam, May 10, 2010.
34. Interview with the director of a pesantren, May 14, 2010.
35. Interview with the director of a pesantren, May 15, 2010.
36. Zakaria, *Indonesian Islamic Education*, 60; also see Azymardi Azra, *Pendidikan Islam Tradisi dan Modernisasi Menuju Millennium Baru* [Traditional Islamic Education and Modernisation Towards the New Millennium] (Jakarta: Logos, 1999).
37. Aziz Talbani, "Pedagogy, Power and Discourse: Transformation of Islamic Education," *Comparative Education Review* 44/1 (1996): 70; also see Jaddon Park and Sarfaroz Niyozov, "Madrasa education in South Asia and Southeast Asia: Current Issues and Debates," *Asia Pacific Journal of Education* 28/4 (2008): 327.
38. Tariq Ramadan, *Radical Reform: Islamic Ethics and Liberation* (Oxford: Oxford University Press, 2009), 278.
39. Rukhsana Zia, "Islamic Education: From Ancient to Modern Times," in *Globalisation, Modernisation and Education in Muslim Countries*, ed. Rukhsana Zia (New York: Nova Science Publishers, 2006), 33, as cited in Tan and Abbas, "The 'Teach Less, Learn More' Initiative in Singapore: New Pedagogies for Islamic Religious Schools?" 33.
40. Moosa, "The Debts and Burdens of Critical Islam," 112.
41. For more details on the Islamisation of knowledge in Malaysia and Egypt, see Mona Abaza, *Debates on Islam and Knowledge in Malaysia and Egypt* (London: RoutledgeCurzon, 2002).
42. Abdul Rashid Moten, "Modernisation and the Process of Globalisation: The Muslim Experience and Responses," in *Islam in Southeast Asia: Political, Social and Strategic Challenges for the 21st Century*, eds. K.S. Nathan and Mohammad Hashim Kamali (Singapore: Institute of Southeast Asian Studies, 2005), 246. Also see International Institute of Islamic Thought (IIST), *Islamisation of Knowledge: General Principles and Work Plan* (Herndon, VA: IIST, 1987), 15, as cited in Charlene Tan, "The Reform Agenda for Madrasah Education in Singapore," *Diaspora, Indigenous, and Minority Education* 3/2 (2009): 70.

43. Interview with a senior staff member of a Sekolah Islam, May 10, 2010.
44. Interview with a senior staff member of a Sekolah Islam, May 11, 2010.
45. Fazlur Rahman, *Islam & Modernity: Transformation of an Intellectual Tradition* (Chicago, University of Chicago Press, 1982), 46.
46. Saeed, "Towards Religious Tolerance through Reform in Islamic Education," 186.
47. Ibid., 187.
48. Azyumardi Azra, "The Making and Development of Islamic Studies in Indonesia," paper presented at the Conference on 'New Horizons in the Islamic Area Studies: Islamic Studies across Cultures and Continents' National Institute of Humanities, Japan & Asia-Europe Institute, University of Malaya, Kuala Lumpur Nikko Hotel, November 22–24, 2008, 14–5. Of course, it should be acknowledged that some Orientalists have indeed adopted a scholarly approach that "has often not extended to a consideration of social and political engagement and the real-world application of the documents they are studying". See Barton, *Jemaah Islamiyah*, 26.
49. Gordon P. Means, *Political Islam in Southeast Asia* (Petaling Jaya: Strategic Information and Research Development Centre, 2009), 312.
50. Irfan Abubakar, "Negotiating Reform and Social Changes in Indonesia," in *Muslim Reform in Southeast Asia: Perspectives from Malaysia, Indonesia and Singapore*, ed. Syed Farid Alatas (Singapore: Majlis Ugama Islam Singapura, 2009), 54; Zuhdi, "Political and Social Influences on Religious School," 208.
51. Ataman, "Religion, Culture and the Shaping of Religious Attitudes: The Case of Islam," 496; John Hicks, *God Has Many Names* (Philadelphia: Westminster Press, 1982); John Hicks, *An Interpretation of Religion: Human Responses to the Transcendent* (New Haven: Yale University Press, 1989).
52. HRH Prince Alwaleed Bin Talal Centre of Islamic Studies, "Contextualising Islam in Britain: Exploratory Perspectives," 39.
53. See Xueying Li and Keith Lin, "Does God Get in the Way of Social Cohesion?" *The Straits Times*, October 21, 2006, S12.
54. Smith, *Muslim, Christians, and the Challenge of Interfaith Dialogue*, 130.
55. John L. Esposito, *The Future of Islam* (New York: Oxford University Press, 2010), 110.
56. Azra, "Teaching Tolerance through Education in Indonesia," 3.
57. Baidhawy, "Building Harmony and Peace through Multiculturalist Theology-based Religious Education: An Alternative for Contemporary Indonesia," 18. He also asserts that "the prevailing Muslim attitude of identifying Islam with Arabia has caused Indonesian Islam to have little respect for the plurality of local cultures". See ibid., 23.
58. Achmad Munjid, "Building a Shared Home for Everyone—Interreligious Dialogue at the Grass Roots in Indonesia," *Journal of Ecumenical Studies* 43/2 (2008): 109–19.

NOTES TO CHAPTER 8

1. The quote is taken from McCawley, "Indonesia Hotel Bomber: A Graduate of Jihad 'Ivy League,'" available at: http://www.csmonitor.com/World/Asia-Pacific/2009/0720/p06s10-woap.html (accessed May 28, 2010).
2. This is cited in Fadl, *The Place of Tolerance in Islam*, 36.

3. For details, see, M.B. Hooker, "Perspectives on *Shari'a* and the State," in *Islamic Perspectives on the New Millennium*, eds. Virginia Hooker and Amin Saikal (Singapore: Institute of Southeast Asian Studies, 2004), 214–7. Another well-known Islamic scholar is Mohamed Arkoun who argues for a "rethinking" of Islamic interpretation through the use of contemporary social-scientific methods. See Mohamed Arkoun, "Rethinking Islam Today," in *Liberal Islam: A Sourcebook*, ed. Charles Kurzman (Oxford: Oxford University Press, 1998), 205–21. Kurzman's book also provides useful excerpts from other Muslim scholars and leaders such as Fazlur Rahman and Muhammad Iqbal. For another book that contains a useful section on "religious interpretation" with excerpts by Muhammad 'Abduh, Muhammad Rashid Rida, Sayyid Jamal al-Din al-Afghani, and Sayyid Ahmad Khan, see Charles Kurzman, *Modernist Islam 1840–1940: A Sourcebook* (Oxford: Oxford University Press, 2002).
4. Baidhawy, "Building Harmony and Peace through Multiculturalist Theology-based Religious Education: An Alternative for Contemporary Indonesia," 22–3; also see Zakiyuddin Baidhawy and M. Thoyibi, eds., *Reinventing Multicultural Islam* (Surakarta: Center for Cultural Studies and Social Change, 2005).
5. The materials in this section are taken from Baidhawy, "Building Harmony and Peace through Multiculturalist Theology-based Religious Education: An Alternative for Contemporary Indonesia," 21–2.
6. For more details of a dialogical education and its application in the Singaporean context, see Charlene Tan, "Dialogical Education for Inter-Religious Engagement in a Plural Society," in *International Handbook of Inter-Religious Education*, eds. Kathleen Engebretson, Marian de Sousa, Gloria Durka, and Liam Gearon (Dordrecht: Springer, 2010), 361–76.
7. Heid Leganger-Krogstad, "Dialogue among Young Citizens in Pluralistic Religious Education Classroom," in *International Perspectives on Citizenship, Education and Religious Diversity*, ed. R. Jackson (London: RoutledgeFalmer, 2003), 169–190.
8. HRH Prince Alwaleed Bin Talal Centre of Islamic Studies, "Contextualising Islam in Britain: Exploratory Perspectives," 12.
9. See Farish A. Noor, "What is the Victory of Islam? Towards a Different Understanding of the Ummah and Political Success in the Contemporary World," in *Progressive Muslims: On Justice, Gender, and Pluralism*, ed. Omid Safi (Oxford: Oneworld Publications, 2003), 325.
10. Ibid., 327.
11. For more information, see Charlene Tan, "Maximising the Overlapping Area: Multiculturalism and a Muslim Identity for Madrasahs in Singapore," *Journal of Beliefs and Values* 30/1 (2009): 41–8.
12. Majlis Ugama Islam Singapura (Muis). *Our Neighbourhood, Our World.* Islamic Social Studies. Primary level 2A (Singapore: Muis, 2003), 3.
13. Al-Hujurat: 13, as cited in Majlis Ugama Islam Singapura (Muis), *Our Society, Our World.* Islamic Social Studies. Primary level 4B (Singapore: Muis, 2006), 52.
14. Interview with a teacher of Islamic social studies of a madrasah in Singapore, November 21, 2007.
15. Charlene Tan, "Taking Faith Seriously: Philosophical Thoughts on Religious Education," *Beliefs and Values* 1/2 (2009): 214. For more information of the modules, materials, and video resources, visit its website: http://www.sipa.columbia.edu/mei/research.shtml.
16. Seyfi Kenan, "Reconsidering Peace and Multicultural Education after 9/11: The Case of Educational Outreach for Muslim Sensitivity Curriculum in New York City," *Educational Sciences: Theory and Practice* 5/1 (2005): 172–80.

17. Smith, *Muslims, Christians, and the Challenge of Interfaith Dialogue*, 145.
18. For more details, see Esposito, *The Future of Islam*, 186–91.
19. For a record of the dialogue, see Michael Ipgrave, *The Road Ahead: A Christian-Muslim Dialogue* (London: Church House Publishing, 2002).
20. For more information, see its website: http://www.cmcsoxford.org.uk.
21. Ramadan, *Western Muslims and the Future of Islam*, 129, as cited in Tan, "Taking Faith Seriously: Philosophical Thoughts on Religious Education," 212.
22. For more details, see Tan, "Taking Faith Seriously," 213; also see Terence H. McLaughlin, "Parental Rights and the Religious Upbringing of Children," *Journal of Philosophy of Education* 18/1 (1984): 75–83.
23. Taylor, *Brainwashing: The Science of Thought Control*, 266.
24. George F. Hourani, *Reason and Tradition in Islamic Ethics* (Cambridge: Cambridge University Press, 1985), 2, and passim, as cited in J. Mark Halstead, "Islamic Values: A Distinctive Framework for Moral Education? *Journal of Moral Education* 36/3 (2007): 286.
25. Martin, Woodward, with Atmaja, *Defenders of Reason in Islam*, 14.
26. van Bruinessen, "Divergent Paths from Gontor: Muslim Educational Reform and the Travails of Pluralism in Indonesia," n.d., available at: http://www.let.uu.nl/~martin.vanbruinessen/personal/publications/Bruinessen_Divergent_paths_from_Gontor.pdf (accessed May 28, 2010). In that article, van Bruinessen was referring to IAIN (Institut Agama Negeri or State Islamic Institutes) Jakarta, which is the predecessor of UIN Jakarta. IAIN Jakarta was converted into a full-fledged Islamic University known as Universitas Islam Negeri (UIN; State Islamic University) Jakarta in 2002. For more information on the evolution of Islamic higher educational institutions, see Azra, Afrianty, and Hefner, "Pesantren and Madrasa: Muslim Schools and National Ideals in Indonesia," 188–91.
27. Fuad Jabali and Jamhari, *IAIN dan Modernisasi Islam di Indonesia [State Islamic Institutes and the Modernisation of Islam in Indonesia]* (Jakarta: UIN Jakarta Press, 2002), 114, as cited in Azra, Afrianty, and Hefner, "Pesantren and Madrasa: Muslim Schools and National Ideals in Indonesia," 191.
28. Azra, "Teaching Tolerance through Education in Indonesia," 10.
29. Saeed, "Towards Religious Tolerance through Reform in Islamic Education: The Case of the State Institute of Islamic Studies of Indonesia," 184. Although Saeed was commenting on IAINs, the institutions are now known as UINs. Despite the change of name, the institutions remain unchanged in terms of their progressive and pluralist educational philosophy and practices.
30. Syafiq Hasyim, "Education Reform and Modernisation in Indonesia: Critical Reflection on Role of Islamic Higher Educational Institutions and *Pesantren* in the Making of Progressive Islam," in *Muslim Reform in Southeast Asia: Perspectives from Malaysia, Indonesia and Singapore*, ed. Syed Farid Alatas (Singapore: Majlis Ugama Islam Singapura, 2009), 69.
31. Saeed, "Towards Religious Tolerance through Reform in Islamic Education," 185.
32. Azra, "The Making and Development of Islamic Studies in Indonesia," 14.
33. Saeed, "Towards Religious Tolerance through Reform in Islamic Education," 188.
34. Hasyim, "Education Reform and Modernisation in Indonesia," 69.
35. Azra, "Teaching Tolerance through Education in Indonesia," 10.
36. Hasyim, "Education Reform and Modernisation in Indonesia," 72.

37. Saeed, "Towards Religious Tolerance through Reform in Islamic Education," 179. On ijtihad, see my discussion in Chapter 5.
38. Azra, "Teaching Tolerance through Education in Indonesia," 10.
39. Azra, Afrianty, and Hefner, "Pesantren and Madrasa: Muslim Schools and National Ideals in Indonesia," 191.
40. van Bruinessen, "Divergent Paths from Gontor: Muslim Educational Reform and the Travails of Pluralism in Indonesia," 193; also see Hartono Ahmad Jaiz, *Ada pemurtadan di IAIN* [The IAIN Encourages Apostasy] (Jakarta: Pustaka Al-Kautsar, 2005).
41. See Hasyim, "Education Reform and Modernisation in Indonesia," 76. Besides UINs, these Muslim groups have also castigated other Islamic groups and centres deemed to be "liberal" or even heretical, such as Liberal Islam Network (JIL) and the International Centre for Islam and Pluralism (ICIP). See ibid., 61.
42. See the school's website: http://www.madania.net/.
43. This is cited in Fadl, *The Place of Tolerance in Islam*, 29, 105.
44. McCawley, "Indonesia Hotel Bomber: A Graduate of Jihad 'Ivy League.' available at: http://www.csmonitor.com/world/Asia-Pacific/2009/0720/p06s10-woap.html (accessed June 12, 2010).
45. Lifton, *Thought Reform and the Psychology of Totalism*, 178.
46. Noor, "Pride within Stigma: The Case of Indonesian Terrorists' Families," 61.
47. Ibid.
48. Ismail and Ungerer, "Jemaah Islamiyah: A Renewed Struggle?" 4.
49. Gun Gun Heryanto, "Label Teroris" [Terrorist Label], People's Daily Thoughts, August 11, 2010, available at: http://www.uinjkt.ac.id/ (accessed August 14, 2010).
50. Hassan, *Unlicensed to Kill*, 146.
51. Fadl, *The Place of Tolerance in Islam*, 94.
52. Ibid., 147–8.
53. Barton, *Jemaah Islamiyah* (Singapore: Ridge Books, 2005), 43.
54. van Bruinessen, "Divergent Paths from Gontor: Muslim Educational Reform and the Travails of Pluralism in Indonesia," 199.
55. Hasyim, "Education Reform and Modernisation in Indonesia," 77.
56. Interview with the director of a pesantren, May 15, 2010.
57. Atran, "The Moral Logic and Growth of Suicide Terrorism," 142.
58. See Prodita Sabarini, "An Integrated Approach to Arrested Terror Suspects in Indonesia," *The Jakarta Post*, March 26, 2010, available at: http://www.commongroundnews.org/article.php?id=27656&lan=en&sid=1&sp=0 (accessed May 28, 2010).
59. The materials on Interfidei are taken from Munjid, "Building a Shared Home for Everyone—Interreligious Dialogue at the Grass Roots in Indonesia," 109–19; and the organisation's website: http://www.interfidei.or.id.
60. Alwi Shihab, "Christian-Muslim Relations into the Twenty-first Century," in *Islam and Other Religions: Pathways to Dialogue*, ed. Irfan A. Omar (Oxon: Routledge, 2006), 63.
61. Zachary Abuza, "The Rehabilitation of Jemaah Islamiyah Detainees in South East Asia: A Preliminary Assessment," in *Leaving Terrorism Behind: Individual and Collective Disengagement*, eds. Tore Bjorgo and John Horgan (Oxon: Routledge, 2009), 211.
62. "Bali Bombmakers Could Have Life Terms Reduced for 'Good Behaviour'," *Today*, August 25, 2010, 23.
63. "Indonesia's Top Terrorist Targeted Policy, Embassy," *The Straits Times*, June 26, 2010, A18.

64. Azyumardi Azra, "Pluralism, Coexistence and Religious Harmony in Southeast Asia," in *Contemporary Islam: Dynamic, not Static*, eds. Abdul Aziz Said, Mohammed Abu-Nimer, and Meena Sharify-Funk (Oxon: Routledge, 2006), 238.

NOTES TO CONCLUSION

1. Chua Chin Hon, "Obama to Americans: Don't Turn on Each Other," *The Straits Times*, September 12, 2010, 1.
2. Cindy Swirko, "New Dove World Outreach sign again takes aim at Islam," *The Gainesville Sun*, August 1, 2009, available at: http://www.gainesville. com/article/20090708/ARTICLES/907081008 (accessed September 14, 2010.
3. Omid Safi, "Teaching Islam Through and After September 11: Towards a Progressive Muslim Agenda," in *Religion, Terror and Violence: Religious Studies Perspectives*, eds. Bryan Rennie and Philip L. Tite (New York: Routledge, 2008), 213.
4. Husain, *The Islamist*, 53.
5. For an insightful review of the study of Islam as an academic discipline, see Aaron W. Hughes, *Situating Islam: The Past and Future of an Academic Discipline* (London: Equinox, 2007).
6. The distinction between theoretical question and theological question in the study of Islam is taken from Lukens-Bull, "Between Text and Practice," 54. Applying the concept of control beliefs to myself, the belief that Islam is a cultural system functions as my control belief in my research (this does not mean that I do not see Islam in any other way all the time; for example, I regard it as a faith phenomenon when I interact with my Muslim friends). It explains why I think it is essential to recognise the diverse interpretations, articulations, and manifestations of Islam by its adherents.
7. Hughes, *Situating Islam*, 70.
8. See Baidhawy, "Building Harmony and Peace through Multiculturalist Theology-based Religious Education," 20.
9. Mohammed Ayoob, *The Many Faces of Political Islam: Religion and Politics in the Muslim World* (Singapore: NUS Press, 2008), 24.
10. For further readings on the conceptual analysis of indoctrination, see the collection of essays in Snook, *Indoctrination and Education*; Spiecker and Straughan, eds., *Freedom and Indoctrination in Education*.
11. Lukens-Bull, *A Peaceful Jihad*, 127.
12. "Times Square Bomber: I Plead Guilty 100 Times," *The Straits Times*, June 23, 2010, A10.
13. Esposito and Mogahed, *Who Speaks for Islam?* 70.
14. For example, see Erik Eckholm,, "Struggle to Control what Islamic Schools Teach," January 15, 2002, *New York Times*, A8, available at: http://www. nytimes.com/2002/01/15/world/struggle-to-control-what-islamic-schools-teach.html (accessed August 31, 2010); Michael Richardson, "Asians Take a Closer Look at Islamic Schools," *International Herald Tribune*, February 12, 2002, available at: http://www.iht.com/articles/2002/02/12/rmalay_ ed3_.php (accessed February 2, 2009).
15. For example, see Park and Niyozov, "Madrasa education in South Asia and Southeast Asia: Current Issues and Debates," 323–51; for essays on recent educational reforms in Islamic schools and the accompanying issues and challenges, see Hefner and Zaman, *Schooling Islam: The Culture and Politics of Modern Muslim Education*; Wadad Kadi and Victor Billeh, eds., *Islam*

and Education: Myths and Truths (Chicago: University of Chicago Press, 2007); Hefner, *Making Modern Muslims: The Politics of Islamic Education in Southeast Asia.*

16. Ibid., 159.
17. Interview with the director of a pesantren, May 6, 2010.
18. Ibid.

Bibliography

Abaza, Mona. *Debates on Islam and Knowledge in Malaysia and Egypt*. London: RoutledgeCurzon, 2002.

Abdullah, M. Amin. *Keilmuan Umum Dan Agama Dalam Sistem Sekolah Dan Madrasah* [General and Religious Sciences in School and Madrasah System]. Jakarta: INCIS, 2004.

Abubakar, Irfan. "Negotiating Reform and Social Changes in Indonesia." In *Muslim Reform in Southeast Asia: Perspectives from Malaysia, Indonesia and Singapore*, edited by Syed Farid Alatas, 46–59. Singapore: Majlis Ugama Islam Singapura, 2009.

Abuza, Zachary. *Political Islam and Violence in Indonesia*. London and New York: Routledge, 2007.

Abuza, Zachary. "The Rehabilitation of Jemaah Islamiyah Detainees in South East Asia: A Preliminary Assessment." In *Leaving Terrorism Behind: Individual and Collective Disengagement*, edited by Tore Bjorgo and John Horgan, 193–211. Oxon: Routledge, 2009.

Ahmed, Ishtiaq. "The Pakistan Islamic State Project: A Secular Critique." In *State and Secularism: Perspectives from Asia*, edited by Michael Siam-Heng Heng and Chin Liew Ten, 185–211. Singapore: World Scientific, 2010.

Alam, Zafar. *Islamic Education: Theory & Practice*. New Delhi: Adam Publishers & Distributors, 2003.

Alatas, Syed Farid. "A Critical Approach to Studying Muslim Revival Movements." *The Straits Times*, August 12, 2010, A28.

Alatas, Syed Farid. "Islam and Modernisation." In *Islam in Southeast Asia: Political, Social and Strategic Challenges for the 21st Century*, edited by K. S. Nathan and Mohammad Hashim Kamali, 209–30. Singapore: Institute of Southeast Asian Studies, 2005.

Alatas, Syed Farid. "Knowledge and Education in Islam." In *Secularism and Spirituality: Seeking Integrated Knowledge and Success in Madrasah Education in Singapore*, edited by Noor Aisha Abdul Rahman and Ah Eng Lai, 166–79. Singapore: Marshall Cavendish, 2006.

Al-Attas, Mesut Idriz, and Syed Ali Tawfik. *The Ihazah of Abdullah Fahim: A Unique Document from Islamic Education*. Selangor: MPH Publishing, 2007.

al-Attas, Syed Muhammad Naquib. *The Concept of Education in Islam*. Kuala Lumpur: International Institute of Islamic Thought and Civilisation (ISTAC), 1999.

Al-Awa, Muhammad Salim. "Political Pluralism from an Islamic Perspective." In *Islam in Transition: Muslim Perspectives*, 2nd edition, edited by John J. Donohue and John L. Esposito, 279–87. Oxford: Oxford University Press, 2007.

Alexander, Denis. *Creation or Evolution: Do We have to Choose?* Oxford: Monarch Books, 2008.

Alexander, Hanan A. "Education in Ideology." *Journal of Moral Education* 34/1 (2005): 1–18.

Ali, Mohamed Bin. "Coping with the Threat of Jemaah Islamiyah—The Singapore Experience." In *Fighting Terrorism: The Singapore Perspective*, edited by Abdul Halim Bin Kader, 117–28. Singapore: Taman Bacaan Pemuda Pemudi Melayu Singapura, 2007.

Ali, Mohamed Khairunan Bin. "Islamic Religious Education in Singapore: Making it Relevant to Global Demand." Master's dissertation, S. Rajaratnam School of International Studies, Nanyang Technological University, 2007.

Almond, Gabriel A., R. Scott Appleby, and Emmanuel Sivan. *Strong Religion: The Rise of Fundamentalism around the World*. Chicago and London: University of Chicago Press, 2003.

Ameli, Saied R., Aliya Azam, and Arzu Merali. *British Muslims' Expectations of the Government*. Wembley: Islamic Human Rights Commission, 2005.

Anand, Geeta, Matthew Rosenberg, Siobhan Gorman, and Susan Schmidt. "Alleged Terrorist Group Steers Young Men to Fight." *Wall Street Journal*, December 8, 2008. Available at: http://online.wsj.com/article/SB122869042642886443.html. (Accessed February 2, 2009).

Arifin, H. Imron, and Muhammad Slamet. *Kepimimpin Kyai: Dalam Perubahan Manajemen Pondok Pesantren: Kasus Ponpes Tebuireng Jombang* [Kyai Leadership: Change Management in Boarding School: The Case of Tebuireng Jombang]. Yogyakarta: CV. Aditya Media, 2010.

Arkoun, Mohamed. "Rethinking Islam Today." In *Liberal Islam: A Sourcebook*, edited by Charles Kurzman, 205–21. Oxford: Oxford University Press, 1998.

"Armed and Radical." *Today*, March 31, 2010, 10.

Asad, Talal. *The Idea of an Anthropology of Islam*. Washington, DC: Centre for Contemporary Arab Studies, Georgetown University, 1986.

Assyaukanie, Luthfi. *Islam and the Secular State in Indonesia*. Singapore: Institute of Southeast Asian Studies Publications, 2009.

Ataman, Kemal. "Islam and Christian–Muslim Relations, Religion, Culture and the Shaping of Religious Attitudes: The Case of Islam." *Islam and Christian–Muslim Relations* 18/4 (2007): 495–508.

Atran, Scott. "The Moral Logic and Growth of Suicide Terrorism." *The Washington Quarterly* 29/2 (2006): 127–43.

Ayoob, Mohammed. *The Many Faces of Political Islam: Religion and Politics in the Muslim World*. Singapore: NUS Press, 2008.

Azra, Azymardi. *Pendidikan Islam Tradisi dan Modernisasi Menuju Millennium Baru* [Traditional Islamic Education and Modernisation Towards the New Millennium]. Jakarta: Logos, 1999.

Azra, Azyumardi. "Bali and Southeast Asian Islam: Debunking the Myths." In *After Bali: The Threat of Terrorism in Southeast Asia*, edited by Kumar Ramakrishna and See Seng Tan, 39–57. Singapore: Institute of Defence and Strategic Studies and World Scientific, 2003.

Azra, Azyumordi. "Islamic Radical Movements in Indonesia." Paper presented at the conference on 'Islamic Radicalism, Securities Issues and Economic Activities in Indonesia,' Syarif Hidayatullah State Islamic University, December 7, 2005.

Azra, Azyumardi. "Pluralism, Coexistence and Religious Harmony in Southeast Asia." In *Contemporary Islam: Dynamic, not Static*, edited by Abdul Aziz Said, Mohammed Abu-Nimer, and Meena Sharify-Funk, 227–41. Oxon: Routledge, 2006.

Azra, Azyumardi. "Teaching Tolerance through Education in Indonesia." Paper presented at the roundtable discussion on 'Religion in Indonesia: An Overview', Indonesian Ministry of Foreign Affairs and Ma'arif Institute Jakarta, Indonesia, February 19, 2008.

Azra, Azyumardi. "The Making and Development of Islamic Studies in Indonesia." Paper presented at the conference on 'New Horizons in the Islamic Area Studies: Islamic Studies across Cultures and Continents', National Institute of

Humanities, Japan & Asia-Europe Institute, University of Malaya, Kuala Lumpur, Malaysia, November 22–24, 2008.

Azra, Azyumardi, Dina Afrianty, and Robert W. Hefner. "Pesantren and Madrasa: Muslim Schools and National Ideals in Indonesia." In *Schooling Islam: The Culture and Politics of Modern Muslim Education*, edited by Robert W. Hefner and Muhammad Qasim Zaman, 172–98. Princeton: Princeton University Press, 2007.

Bah, Mohamed El-Mokhtar Ould. *Islamic Education between Tradition and Modernity*. Morocco: Islamic Educational, Scientific and Cultural Organisation, 1998. Available at: http://www.isesco.org.ma/english/publications/ISLAMIC%20EDUCATION/Menu.php. (Accessed August 31, 2010).

Baidhawy, Zakiyuddin, and M. Thoyibi, eds. *Reinventing Multicultural Islam*. Surakarta: Center for Cultural Studies and Social Change, 2005.

Baidhawy, Zakiyuddin. "Building Harmony and Peace through Multiculturalist Theology-based Religious Education: An Alternative for Contemporary Indonesia." *British Journal of Religious Education* 29/1 (2007): 15–30.

"Bali Bombmakers Could Have Life Terms Reduced for 'Good Behaviour'," *Today*, August 25, 2010, 23.

Baron, Robert S. "Arousal, Capacity, and Intense Indoctrination." *Personality and Social Psychology Review* 4/3 (2000): 238–54.

Barton, Greg. *Jemaah Islamiyah: Radical Islamism in Indonesia*. Singapore: Ridge Books, 2005.

Batley, Brek. *The Complexities of Dealing with Radical Islam in Southeast Asia*. Canberra: Strategic and Defence Studies Centre, Australian National University, 2003.

Behrend, Tim. "Reading Past the Myth: Public Teachings of Abu Bakara Ba'asyir." Available at: http://www.arts.auckland.ac.nz/asia/tbehrend/abb-myth.htm. (Accessed April 30, 2004).

Bennetta, William J. "How a Public School in Scottsdale, Arizona Subjected Students to Islamic Indoctrination." *The Textbook League*. Available at: http://www.textbookleague.org/tci-az.htm. (Accessed February 2, 2009).

Bourdieu, Pierre. *Meditation Pascalienne* [Pascalian meditations]. Paris: Seuil, 1997.

Bull, Bernard F. "Constructivist Crap in Christian Colleges: The Indoctrination of Teacher Education." *The Educational Forum* 66/2 (2002): 162–4.

Burdman, Daphne. "Education, Indoctrination, and Incitement: Palestinian children on their Way to Martyrdom." *Terrorism and Political Violence* 15/1 (2003): 96–123.

Burhanudin, Jajat, and Jamhari. "Assessment of Social and Political Attitudes in Indonesia Islamic Education Institution." *Studia Islamika: Indonesian Journal for Islamic Studies* 13/3 (2006): 399–433.

Burr, J. Millard, and Robert O. Collins, *Alms for Jihad: Charity and Terrorism in the Islamic World*. Cambridge: Cambridge University Press, 2006.

Callan, Eamonn, and Dylan Arena. "Indoctrination." In *The Oxford Handbook of Philosophy of Education*, edited by Harvey Siegel, 104–21. Oxford: Oxford University Press, 2009.

Carr, David. "Towards a Distinctive Conception of Spiritual Education." *Oxford Review of Education* 21/1 (1995): 83–98.

Chua Chin Hon. "Obama to Americans: Don't Turn on Each Other." *The Straits Times*, September 12, 2010, 1.

Collins, Francis. *The Language of God: A Scientist Presents Evidence for Belief*. London: Pocket Books, 2007.

Combs, Philip H., Roy C. Prosser, and Manzoor Ahmed. *New Paths to Learning for Rural Children and Youth*. New York: International Council for Educational Development, 1973.

Conboy, Ken. *The Second Front: Inside Asia's Most Dangerous Terrorist Network*. Jakarta: Equinox Publishing, 2006.

Copley, Terence. *Indoctrination, Education and God: The Struggle for the Mind.* London: SPCK, 2005.

Copley, Terence. "Non-Indoctrinatory Religious Education in Secular Cultures." *Religious Education* 103/1 (2008): 22–31.

Coulson, Andrew. "Education and Indoctrination in the Muslim World: Is There a Problem? What Can We Do About It?" *Policy Analysis* 511 (2004): 1, 3.

Crouch, Harold. "Radical Islam in Indonesia: Some Misperceptions." In *Islamic Terrorism in Indonesia: Myths and Realities*, edited by Marika Vicziany and David Wright-Neville, 33–51. Victoria: Monash University Press, 2005.

DeRosa, Christopher S. *Political Indoctrination in the U.S. Army from World War II to the Vietnam War.* Lincoln and London: University of Nebraska Press, 2006.

Devji, Faisal. *Landscapes of the Jihad: Militancy, Morality, Modernity.* Ithaca: Cornell University Press, 2005.

Dhofier, Zamakhsyari. *The Pesantren Tradition: The Role of the Kyai in the Maintenance of Traditional Islam in Java.* Arizona: Programme for Southeast Asian Studies, Arizona State University, 1999.

Donohue, John J., and John L. Esposito, eds. *Islam in Transition: Muslim Perspectives*, 2nd edition. Oxford: Oxford University Press, 2007.

Douglass, Susan L., and Munir A. Shaikh. "Defining Islamic Education: Differentiation and Applications." *Current Issues in Comparative Education* 7/1 (2004): 5–18.

Dyer, Carol, Ryan McCoy, Joel Rodriguez, and Donald N. Van Duyn. "Countering Violent Islamic Extremism: A Community Responsibility." *FBI Law Enforcement Bulletin* December (2007): 3–9.

Eckholm, Erik. "Struggle to Control what Islamic Schools Teach." *New York Times,* January 15 2002. A8. Available at: http://www.nytimes.com/2002/01/15/world/struggle-to-control-what-islamic-schools-teach.html. (Accessed August 31, 2010).

Erfan, Niaz, and Zahid A. Valie. *Education and the Muslim World: Challenges and Responses.* Leicestre Islamabad: The Islamic Foudation and Institute of Policy Studies, 1995.

Esmail, Aziz. "Introduction." In *Intellectual Traditions in Islam*, edited by Farhad Daftary, 1–16. London and New York: I.B. Tauris Publishers, 2001.

Esposito, John L. *The Future of Islam.* New York: Oxford University Press, 2010.

Esposito, John L. *Unholy War: Terror in the Name of Islam.* New York: Oxford University Press, 2002.

Esposito, John, and Dalia Mogahed. *Who Speaks for Islam? What a Billion Muslims Really Think.* New York: Gallup Press, 2007.

Fadl, Khaled Abou El. *Islam and the Challenge of Democracy.* Princeton and Oxford: Princeton University Press, 2004.

Fadl, Khaled Abou El. *The Great Theft: Wrestling Islam from the Extremists.* New York: HarperOne, 2005.

Fadl, Khaled Abou El. *The Place of Tolerance in Islam.* Boston: Beacon Press, 2002.

Fealy, Greg. "Half a Century of Violent Jihad in Indonesia: A Historical and Ideological Comparison of Darul Islam and Jema'ah Islamiyah." In *Islamic Terrorism in Indonesia: Myths and Realities*, edited by Marika Vicziany and David Wright-Neville, 14–32. Victoria: Monash University Press, 2005.

Fealy, Greg, and Virginia Hooker, eds. *Voices of Islam in Southeast Asia: A Contemporary Sourcebook.* Singapore: Institute of Southeast Asian Studies, 2006.

Fierke, K.M. "Agents of Death: The Structural Logic of Suicide Terrorism and Martyrdom," *International Theory* 1 (2009): 155–84.

Foutz, Scott David. "On Establishing an Evangelical Historiography for the 21st Century." *Quodlibet Journal,* n.d. Available at: http://www.quodlibet.net/foutz-histfinl.shtml. (Accessed April 2, 2010).

Geertz, Clifford. *Islam Observed: Religious Development in Morocco and Indonesia*. Chicago: The University of Chicago Press, 1968.

Goldenberg, Suzanne. "The Men behind the Suicide Bombers," *The Guardian*, June 12, 2002. Available at: http://www.guardian.co.uk/world/2002/jun/12/israel1. (Accessed February 2, 2009).

Gratchel, Richard H. "The Evolution of the Concept." In *Concepts of Indoctrination: Philosophical Essays*, edited by I.A. Snook, 9–16. London and Boston: Routledge & Kegan Paul, 1972.

Gray, John. *Mill on Liberty: A Defense*. London: Routledge & Kegan Paul, 1983.

Green, Thomas F. "Indoctrination and Beliefs." In *Concepts of Indoctrination*, edited by I.A. Snook, 25–46. London and Boston: Routledge & Kegan Paul, 1972.

Greene, Richard Allen. "Nearly 1 in 4 People Worldwide is Muslim, Report Says." *CNN World*, October 7, 2009. Available at: http://articles.cnn.com/2009–10–07/world/muslim.world.population_1_god-but-god-middle-east-distant?_s=PM:WORLD. (Accessed September 2, 2010).

Gulen, M. Fethullah. *Towards a Global Civilisation of Love and Tolerance*. New Jersey: The Light, 2004.

Gunaratna, Rohan. "Ideology in Terrorism and Counter Terrorism: Lessons from Combating Al Qaeda and Al Jemaah Al Islamiyah in Southeast Asia." In *Fighting Terrorism: The Singapore Perspective*, edited by Abdul Halim Bin Kader, 60–102. Singapore: Taman Bacaan Pemuda Pemudi Melayu Singapura, 2007.

Hadiz, Vedi R. "Towards a Sociological Understanding of Islamic Radicalism in Indonesia." *Journal of Contemporary Asia* 38/4 (2008): 638–47.

Hafez, Mohammed M. "Rationality, Culture, and Structure in the Making of Suicide Bombers: A Preliminary Theoretical Synthesis and Illustrative Case Study." *Studies in Conflict & Terrorism* 29/2 (2006): 165–85.

Halstead, Mark J. "Islamic Values: A Distinctive Framework for Moral Education?" *Journal of Moral Education* 36/3 (2007): 283–96.

Halstead, Mark J. *The Case for Muslim Voluntary-Aided Schools: Some Philosophical Reflections*. Cambridge: The Islamic Academy, 1986.

Hamilton-Hart, Natasha. "Terrorism in Southeast Asia: Expert Analysis, Myopia and Fantasy." In *Islam in Southeast Asia: Critical Concepts in Islamic Studies*, Vol. 4, edited by Joseph Chinyong Liow and Nadirsyah Hosen, 314–35. London and New York: Routledge, 2010.

Hasan, Noorhaidi. "Islamising Formal Education: Integrated Islamic School and a New Trend in Formal Education Institution in Indonesia." Working Paper, February 11, 2009, S. Rajaratnam School of International Studies, Singapore.

Hassan, Muhammad Haniff Bin. "Iman Samudra's Justification for Bali Bombing." In *Islam in Southeast Asia: Critical Concepts in Islamic Studies*, Vol. 4, edited by Joseph Chinyong Liow and Nadirsyah Hosen, 340–68. London and New York: Routledge, 2010.

Hassan, Muhammad Haniff Bin. "Key Considerations in Counterideological Work against Terrorist Ideology." *Studies in Conflict & Terrorism* 29/6 (2006): 531–58.

Hassan, Muhammad Haniff. *Unlicensed to Kill: Countering Iman Samudra's Justification for the Bali Bombing*. Singapore: Nature Media Pte Ltd., 2006.

Hassan, Noorhaidi. "The Salafi Madrasas of Indonesia." In *The Madrasa in Asia: Political Activism and Transnational Linkages*, edited by Farish A. Noor, Yoginder Sikand, and Martin van Bruinessen, 247–74. Amsterdam: Amsterdam University Press, 2008.

Hasyim, Syafiq. "Education Reform and Modernisation in Indonesia: Critical Reflection on Role of Islamic Higher Educational Institutions and *Pesantren* in the Making of Progressive Islam." In *Muslim Reform in Southeast Asia: Perspectives from Malaysia, Indonesia and Singapore*, edited by Syed Farid Alatas, 60–78. Singapore, Majlis Ugama Islam Singapura, 2009.

Haworth, Lawrence. *Autonomy: An Essay in Philosophy Psychology and Ethics.* New Haven and London: Yale University Press, 1986.

Hefner, Robert W., ed. "Islamic Schools, Social Movements, and Democracy in Indonesia." In *Making Modern Muslims: The Politics of Islamic Education in Southeast Asia,* edited by Robert W. Hefner, 55–105. Hawai'i: University of Hawai'i Press, 2009.

Hefner, Robert W. *Civil Islam: Muslims and Democratisation in Indonesia.* Princeton: Princeton University Press, 2000.

Hefner, Robert W., and Muhammad Qasim Zaman, eds. *Schooling Islam: The Culture and Politics of Modern Muslim Education.* Princeton: Princeton University Press, 2007.

Hefner, Robert W., ed. *Making Modern Muslims: The Politics of Islamic Education in Southeast Asia.* Honolulu: University of Hawai'i Press, 2009.

Heryanto, Gun Gun. "Label Teroris" [Terrorist Label]. *People's Daily Thoughts,* August 11, 2010. Available at: http://www.uinjkt.ac.id/. (Accessed August 14, 2010).

Hicks, John. *An Interpretation of Religion: Human Responses to the Transcendent.* New Haven: Yale University Press, 1989.

Hicks, John. *God Has Many Names.* Philadelphia: Westminster Press, 1982.

Hindery, Roderick. "The Anatomy of Propaganda within Religious Terrorism." *The Humanist* March/April (2003): 16–9.

Høigilt, Jacob. *Raiding Extremists? Islamism and Education in the Palestinian Territories.* Oslo: FAFO, 2010.

Hooker, M.B. "Perspectives on *Shari'a* and the State." In *Islamic Perspectives on the New Millennium,* edited by Virginia Hooker and Amin Saikal, 199–20. Singapore: Institute of Southeast Asian Studies, 2004.

Hooker, Virginia. "Developing Islamic Arguments for Change through 'Liberal Islam'." In *Islamic Perspectives on the New Millennium,* edited by Virginia Hooker and Amin Saikal, 231–51. Singapore: Institute of Southeast Asian Studies, 2004.

Hourani, George F. *Reason and Tradition in Islamic Ethics.* Cambridge: Cambridge University Press, 1985.

HRH Prince Alwaleed Bin Talal Centre of Islamic Studies, "Contextualising Islam in Britain: Exploratory Perspectives." A project by the University of Cambridge in association with the Universities of Exeter and Westminster, October 2009.

Hughes, Aaron W. *Situating Islam: The Past and Future of an Academic Discipline.* London: Equinox, 2007.

Husain, Ed. *The Islamist.* London: Penguin Books, 2007.

Husaini, Adian. "Pluralisme Agama: MUI Terlambat" ["Religious Pluralism: It's Late for MUI"]. *Republika* (Indonesian Daily News), August 4, 2005.

Hussain, Amir. "Muslims, Pluralism, and Interfaith Dialogue." In *Progressive Muslims: On Justice, Gender, and Pluralism,* edited by Omid Safi, 252–69. Oxford: Oneworld Publications, 2003.

Hussaini, Chairul Fahmy. "Suicide Bombings: A Threat to Homeland Security." In *Fighting Terrorism: The Singapore Perspective,* edited by Abdul Halim Bin Kader, 154–63. Singapore: Taman Bacaan Pemuda Pemudi Melayu Singapura, 2007.

Ibrahim, Saad Eddin. "Anatomy of Egypt's Militant Islamic Groups: Methodological Note and Preliminary Findings." *International Journal of Middle East Studies* 12/4 (1980): 423–53.

Ibrahim, Saad Eddin. "Islamic Militancy as a Social Movement: The Case of Two Groups in Egypt." In *Islamic Resurgence in the Arab World,* edited by Ali E. Hillal Dessouki, 117–37. New York: Praeger, 1982.

Ichwan, M.N. "Ulama, State and Politics: Majelis Ulama Indonesia after Suharto." *Islamic Law and Society* 12/1 (2005): 45–72.

"Indon Cleric Abu Bakar Bashir Arrested Again," *Today*, August 10, 2010, 6.

"Indonesia: Fathers Pass Jihad Ideas to Sons," *The Straits Times*, June 26, 2010, C2.

"Indonesia's Top Terrorist Targeted Policy, Embassy," *The Straits Times*, June 26, 2010, A18.

International Crisis Group (ICG). *Al-Qaeda in Southeast Asia: The Case of the 'Ngruki Network' in Indonesia*. Jakarta and Brussels: ICG, 2002.

International Crisis Group (ICG). *Indonesia Backgrounder: How the Jemaah Islamiyah Terrorist Network Operates*. Jakarta and Brussels: ICG, 2002.

International Institute of Islamic Thought (IIST). *Islamisation of Knowledge: General Principles and Work Plan*. Herndon, Virginia: IIST, 1987.

Ipgrave, Michael. *The Road Ahead: A Christian-Muslim Dialogue*. London: Church House Publishing, 2002.

Iqbal, Muzaffar. *The Making of Islamic Science*. Kuala Lumpur: Islamic Book Trust, 2009.

"'Islamic Indoctrination' Taken to Supreme Court," *WorldNewDaily*, June 9, 2006. Available at: http://www.worldnetdaily.com/news/article.asp?ARTICLE_ID=50562. (Accessed February 2, 2009).

Ismail, Noor Huda. "Schooled For Jihad." *The Washington Post*, June 26, 2005. Available at: http://www.washingtonpost.com/wpdyn/content/article/2005/06/25/AR2005062500083.html. (Accessed September 6, 2010).

Ismail, Noor Huda. *Ngruki: Is it a Terrorism School? The Jakarta Post*, March 14, 2005. Available at: http://www.thejakartapost.com/news/2005/03/14/part-1-2-ngruki-it-terrorism-school.html. (Accessed September 6, 2010).

Ismail, Noor Huda, and Carl Ungerer. "Jemaah Islamiyah: A Renewed Struggle?" *Policy Analysis* July 16 (2009): 1–6.

Jabali, Fuad, and Jamhari. *IAIN dan Modernisasi Islam di Indonesia* [State Islamic Institutes and the Modernisation of Islam in Indonesia]. Jakarta: UIN Jakarta Press, 2002.

Jaiz, Hartono Ahmad. *Ada pemurtadan di IAIN* [The IAIN Encourages Apostasy]. Jakarta: Pustaka Al-Kautsar, 2005.

Jamhari, and Jajang Jahroni, eds. *Gerakan Salafi Radikal di Indonesia* [Radical Salafiyyah movements in Indonesia]. Jakarta: Raja Grafindo Persada, 2004.

Janin, Hunt. *The Pursuit of Learning in the Islamic World 610–2003*. Jefferson: McFarland & Co, 2005.

Jasper, James M. *The Art of Moral Protest: Culture, Biography and Creativity in Social Movements*. Chicago: University of Chicago Press, 1997.

Jerome, Frank D. *Persuasion and Healing*. New York: Schocken Books, 1963.

Jones, Sidney. "Terrorism and 'Radical Islam' in Indonesia." In *Islamic Terrorism in Indonesia: Myths and Realities*, edited by Marika Vicziany and David Wright-Neville, 3–14. Victoria: Monash University Press, 2005.

Juergensmeyer, Mark. *Terror in the Mind of God: The Global Rise of Religious Violence*. Berkeley and Los Angeles: University of California Press, 2000.

Kadi, Wadad, and Victor Billeh, eds. *Islam and Education: Myths and Truths*. Chicago: University of Chicago Press, 2007.

Kelly, A.V. *The Curriculum: Theory and Practice*, 5th edition. London: Sage Publications, 2004.

Kenan, Seyfi. "Reconsidering Peace and Multicultural Education after 9/11: The Case of Educational Outreach for Muslim Sensitivity Curriculum in New York City." *Educational Sciences: Theory and Practice* 5/1 (2005): 172–80.

Khatab, Sayed, and Gary D. Bouma. *Democracy in Islam*. Oxon: Routledge, 2007.

Kilpatrick, William Heard. "Indoctrination and Respect for Persons." In *Concepts of Indoctrination: Philosophical Essays*, edited by I.A. Snook, 47–54. London and Boston: Routledge & Kegan Paul, 1972.

Kurzman, Charles, ed. *Liberal Islam: A Sourcebook.* Oxford: Oxford University Press, 1998.

Kurzman, Charles, ed. *Modernist Islam 1840–1940: A Sourcebook.* Oxford: Oxford University Press, 2002.

Laura, S. Ronald, and Michael Leahy. "Religious Upbringing and Rational Autonomy." *Journal of Philosophy of Education* 23/1 (1989): 253–65.

Leganger-Krogstad, Heid. "Dialogue among Young Citizens in Pluralistic Religious Education Classroom." In *International Perspectives on Citizenship, Education and Religious Diversity*, edited by Robert Jackson, 169–90. London: RoutledgeFalmer, 2003.

Levitt, Matthew. *Hamas: Politics, Charity, and Terrorism in the Service of Jihad.* New Haven: Yale University Press, 2006.

Li, Xueying, and Keith Lin. "Does God Get in the Way of Social Cohesion?" *The Straits Times*, October 21, 2006, S12.

Lia, Brynjar. "Doctrines for Jihadi Terrorist Training." *Terrorism and Political Violence* 20/4 (2008): 518–42.

Lifton, Robert Jay. *Thought Reform and the Psychology of Totalism: A Study of 'Brainwashing' in China.* Chapel Hill & London: The University of North Carolina Press, 1989.

Lukens-Bull, Ronald. "Between Text and Practice: Considerations in the Anthropological Study of Islam." In *Defining Islam: A Reader*, edited by Andrew Rippin, 37–57. London: Equinox Publishing Ltd., 2007.

Lukens-Bull, Ronald. *A Peaceful Jihad: Negotiating Identity and Modernity in Muslim Java.* New York: Palgrave Macmillan, 2005.

Macan-Markar, Marwann. "My Roommate, the Terrorist." *IPS News*, November 25, 2008. Available at: http://ipsnews.net/news.asp?idnews=44841. (Accessed May 26, 2010).

MacIntyre, Alasdair. *Whose Justice? Which Rationality?* Notre Dame: University of Notre Dame, 1988.

Madjid, Nurcholish. "The Necessity of Renewing Islamic Thought and Reinvigorating Religious Understanding." In *Liberal Islam: A Sourcebook*, edited by Charles Kurzman, 284–94. Oxford: Oxford University Press, 1998.

Magouirk, Justin. "Connecting a Thousand Points of Hatred." *Studies in Conflict & Terrorism* 31/4 (2008): 327–49.

Majelis Ulama Indonesia (MUI). *Keputusan Fatwa Majelis Utama Indonesia Nomor: 7/Munas VII/MUI/II/2005 Tentang Pluralisme, Liberalisme dan Sekularisme Agama, 2005* [The Decision of Indonesian Ulama No7/Munas VII/MUI/II/2005 on Pluralism, Liberalism and Secularism, 2005]. Available at: http://www.mui.or.id/. (Accessed February 2, 2009).

Majlis Ugama Islam Singapura (Muis). *Our Neighbourhood, Our World.* Islamic Social Studies. Primary level 2A. Singapore: Muis, 2003.

Majlis Ugama Islam Singapura (Muis). *Our Society, Our World.* Islamic Social Studies. Primary level 4B. Singapore: Muis, 2006.

Makdisi, George. *The Rise of Colleges: Institutions of Learning in Islam and the West.* Edinburgh: Edinburgh University Press, 1981.

Maksum. *Madrasah: Sejarah dan Perkembangannya* [Madrasah: History and Development]. Jakarta: Logos, 1999.

Mapes, Timothy. "Indonesian School Gives High Marks to Students Embracing Intolerance." *Asian Wall Street Journal*, September 2, 2003.

Martin, Richard C., and Mark R. Woodward with Dwi S. Atmaja. *Defenders of Reason in Islam: Mu'tazilism from Medieval School to Modern Symbol.* Oxford: Oneworld, 1997.

Martinez, Patricia. "Deconstructing Jihad: Southeast Asian Contexts." IDSS Working Paper, Institute of Defence and Strategic Studies, Nanyang Technological University, Singapore, 2003.

Maxcy, J. Spencer. "The Democratic 'Myth' and the Search for a Rational Concept of Education." *Educational Philosophy and Theory* 17/1 (1985): 22–37.

McCawley, Tom. "Indonesia Hotel Bomber: A Graduate of Jihad 'Ivy League." *Christian Science Monitor*, July 20, 2009. Available at: http://www.csmonitor.com/World/Asia-Pacific/2009/0720/p06s10-woap.htm. (Accessed June 12, 2010).

McLaughlin, Terence H. "Beyond the Reflective Teacher." *Educational Philosophy and Theory* 31/1 (1999): 9–25.

McLaughlin, Terence, H. "Parental Rights and the Religious Upbringing of Children." *Journal of Philosophy of Education* 18/1 (1984): 75–83.

Means, Gordon P. *Political Islam in Southeast Asia*. Petaling Jaya: Strategic Information and Research Development Centre, 2009.

Milton-Edwards, Beverly. *Islamic Fundamentalism Since 1945*. Oxon: Routledge, 2005.

Ministry of Home Affairs. "The Jemaah Islamiyah Arrests and the Threat of Terrorism." White Paper. Singapore: Ministry of Home Affairs, 2003.

Mohamed, Hj Ali Hj. "The Peaceful Message of Islam." In *Fighting Terrorism: The Singapore Perspective*, edited by Abdul Halim Bin Kader, 103–16. Singapore: Taman Bacaan Pemuda Pemudi Melayu Singapura, 2007.

Moosa, Ebrahim. "The Debts and Burdens of Critical Islam." In *Progressive Muslims: On Justice, Gender, and Pluralism*, edited by Omid Safi, 111–27. Oxford: Oneworld Publications, 2003.

Moten, Abdul Rashid. "Modernisation and the Process of Globalisation: The Muslim Experience and Responses." In *Islam in Southeast Asia: Political, Social and Strategic Challenges for the 21st Century*, edited by K. S. Nathan and Mohammad Hashim Kamali, 231–55. Singapore: Institute of Southeast Asian Studies, 2005.

Munjid, Achmad. "Building a Shared Home for Everyone—Interreligious Dialogue at the Grass Roots in Indonesia." *Journal of Ecumenical Studies* 43/2 (2008): 109–19.

Nasr, Seyyed Hossein. *Knowledge and the Sacred*. Albany: State Univerity of New York, 1989.

Najjar, Abd al Majid al. *The Vicegerency of Man: Between Revelation and Reason*. Translated by Aref T. Atari. Herndon, Virginia: International Institute of Islamic Thought, 2000.

National Commission on Terrorist Attacks. *The 9/11 Commission Report: The Final Report of the National Commission on Terrorist Attacks Upon the United States*. New York: W.W. Norton, 2004.

Noor, Farish A. "What is the Victory of Islam? Towards a Different Understanding of the Ummah and Political Success in the Contemporary World." In *Progressive Muslims: On Justice, Gender, and Pluralism*, edited by Omid Safi, 320–32. Oxford: Oneworld Publications, 2003.

Noor, Farish A., Yoginder Sikand, and Martin van Bruinessen. "Introduction." In *The Madrasa in Asia: Political Activism and Transnational Linkages*, edited by Farish A. Noor, Yoginder Sikand, and Martin van Bruinessen, 9–27. Amsterdam: Amsterdam University Press, 2008.

Noor, Huala. "Pride within Stigma: The Case of Indonesian Terrorists' Families." Master's dissertation, Syarif Hidayatullah State Islamic University, Jakarta, 2009.

Nord, Warren A. "Rethinking Indoctrination." *Education Week*, May 24 (1995): 44, 36. *Reprinted* as "Is Nothing Sacred?" *Teacher Magazine*, August (1995): 38–40.

Nord, Warren A. *Does God Make a Difference? Taking Religion Seriously in Our Schools and Universities*. New York: Oxford University Press, 2010.

Osman, Fathi. *Children of Adam: An Islamic Perspective on Pluralism*. Washington, DC: Georgetown University Press, 1996.

Osman, Fathi. "Islam and Human Rights: The Challenge to Muslims and the World." In *Rethinking Islam and Modernity: Essays in Honour of Fathi Osman*, edited by Abdelwahab El-Affendi, 27–65. London: The Islamic Foundation, 2001.

Osman, Salim. "Jakarta Arrests Rekindle Fears of Terrorism." *The Straits Times*, November 5, 2010. Available at: http://www.asianewsnet.net/news.php?id=11841&sec=1. (Accessed May 28, 2010).

Pape, Robert. *Dying to Win: The Strategic Logic of Suicide Terrorism*. New York, NY: Random House, 2005.

Pape, Robert. "The Strategic Logic of Suicide Terrorism." *American Political Science Review* 97/August (2003): 343–62.

Park, Jaddon, and Sarfaroz Niyozov. "Madrasa education in South Asia and Southeast Asia: Current Issues and Debates." *Asia Pacific Journal of Education* 28/4 (2008): 323–51.

Pavlova, Elena. "An Ideological Response to Islamist Terrorism: Theoretical and Operational Overview." In *Terrorism in the Asia-Pacific: Threat and Response*, edited by Rohan Gunaratna, 30–45. Singapore: Eastern Universities Press, 2003.

Pavlova, Elena. "From Counter-Society to Counter-State: Jemaah Islamiyah according to PUPJI." IDSS Working Paper, Institute of Defence and Strategic Studies, Nanyang Technological University, Singapore, 2006.

Pederson, Johannes. "Madrasa." In *Shorter Encyclopedia of Islam*, edited by H.A.R. Gibb and J.H. Kramers, 300–10. Leiden, Netherlands: E.J. Brill, 1953.

Peters, R.S. *Psychology and Ethical Development*. London: Allen & Unwin, 1974.

Pew Forum on Religion and Public Life. *Mapping the Global Muslim Population: A Report on the Size and Distribution of the World's Muslim Population*. Washington, DC: Pew Research Centre, 2009.

Pipes, Daniel. *Militant Islam Reaches America*. New York and London: W.W. Norton, 2003.

Plantinga, Alvin. "Reason and Belief in God." In *Faith and Rationality: Reason and Belief in God*, edited by Alvin Plantinga and Nicholas Wolterstorff, 16–93. Notre Dame: University of Notre Dame Press, 1983.

Plantinga, Alvin. *Warranted Christian Belief*. Oxford: Oxford University Press, 2000.

Platzdasch, Bernhard. *Islamism in Indonesia: Politics in the Emerging Democracy*. Singapore: Institute of Southeast Asian Studies Publications, 2009.

Pondok Pesantren Islam Al Mukmin. "Profile of Pesantren." Available at: http://almukmin-ngruki.com/index.php?option=com_content&view=article&id=46&Itemid=56. (Accessed August 23, 2010).

Popper, Karl. *The Open Society and its Enemies*. London: Routledge and Kegan Paul, 1945.

Pringle, Robert. *Understanding Islam in Indonesia: Politics and Diversity*. Singapore: Editions Didier Millet, 2010.

Puolimatka, Tapio. *Democracy and Education: The Critical Citizen as an Educational Aim*. Helsinki: The Finnish Academy of Science and Letters, 1995.

Pusat Pengkajian Islam dan Masyarakat (PPIM). *Sikap dan Perilaku Sosial-Keagamaan Guru-Guru Agama di Jawa: Temuan Survey* [Attitudes and Social Behaviour of Religious Teachers of Java: Survey Findings]. Jakarta: PPIM UIN Jakarta, 2008.

Quinn, Philip L., and Charles Taliaferro, eds. *A Companion to Philosophy of Religion*. Malden and Oxford: Blackwell Publishers, 1999.

Qutb, Syed. "A Muslim's Nationality and His Belief." Available at http://www.witness-pioneer.org/vil/Articles/politics/nationalism.htm. (accessed August 12, 2010).

Rahman, Fazlur. *Islam & Modernity: Transformation of an Intellectual Tradition*. Chicago: University of Chicago Press, 1982.

Ramadan, Tariq. *Radical Reform: Islamic Ethics and Liberation.* Oxford: Oxford University Press, 2009.

Ramadan, Tariq. *Western Muslims and the Future of Islam.* New York: Oxford University Press, 2004.

Ramakrishna, Kumar. "'Constructing' the Jemaah Islamiyah Terrorist: A Preliminary Inquiry." Working Paper, Institute of Defence and Strategic Studies, October 2004, Singapore.

Ramakrishna, Kumar, and See Seng Tan, eds. *After Bali: The Threat of Terrorism in Southeast Asia.* Singapore: Institute of Defence and Strategic Studies and World Scientific, 2003.

Rescher, Nicholas. *Pluralism: Against the Demand of Consensus.* Oxford: Clarendon Press, 1993.

Richardson, Michael. "Asians Take a Closer Look at Islamic Schools." *International Herald Tribune*, February 12, 2002. Available at: http://www.iht.com/articles/2002/02/12/rmalay_ed3_.php. (Accessed February 2, 2009).

Rifai, Nurlena. "The Emergence of Elite Islamic Schools in Contemporary Indonesia: A Case Study of Al Azhar Islamic School." PhD dissertation, McGill University, 2006.

Rosen, Ehud. "The Muslim Brotherhood's Concept of Education." *Current Trends in Islamist Ideology*, Vol. 5. Washington, DC: Hudson Institute, 2008.

Roth, Wolff-Michael. "'Enculturation': Acquisition of Conceptual Blind Spots and Epistemological Prejudices." *British Educational Research Journal* 27/1 (2001): 5–27.

Rougier, Bernard. *Everyday Jihad: The Rise of Militant Islam among Palestinians in Lebanon.* Cambridge: Harvard University Press, 2007.

Runzo, Joseph. "Worldviews and the Epistemic Foundations of Theism." *Religious Studies* 25 (1989): 31–51.

Sabarini, Prodita. "An Integrated Approach to Arrested Terror Suspects in Indonesia." *The Jakarta Post*, March 26, 2010. Available at: http://www.commongroundnews.org/article.php?id=27656&lan=en&sid=1&sp=0. (Accessed May 28, 2010).

Sachedina, Abdulaziz. *The Islamic Roots of Democratic Pluralism.* New York: Oxford University Press, 2001.

Saeed, Abdullah. "Towards Religious Tolerance through Reform in Islamic Education: The Case of the State Institute of Islamic Studies of Indonesia." *Indonesia and the Malay World* 27/79 (1999): 177–91.

Saeed, Abdullah. *Islamic Thought: An Introduction.* Oxford: Routledge, 2006.

Safi, Omid. "Teaching Islam Through and After September 11: Towards a Progressive Muslim Agenda." In *Religion, Terror and Violence: Religious Studies Perspectives*, edited by Bryan Rennie and Philip L. Tite, 201–20. New York: Routledge, 2008.

Sageman, Marc. *Understanding Terror Networks.* Philadelphia: University of Pennsylvania Press, 2004.

Samudra, Iman. *Aku Melawan Teroris* [I Fight Terrorists]. Indonesia: Solo Jazeera, 2004.

Schils, Edward A. "Authoritarianism 'Right' and 'Left'." In *Studies in the Scope and Method of Authoritarian Personality*, edited by Richard Christie and Marie Jajoda, 24–9. Glencoe, Illinois: The Free Press, 1954.

Schon, Donald. *Educating the Reflective Practitioner.* San Francisco: Jossey-Bass, 1987.

Shah-Kazemi, Reza. "Recollecting the Spirit of Jihad." In *Islam, Fundamentalism, and the Betrayal of Tradition: Essays by Western Muslim Scholars*, edited by Joseph E.B. Lumbard, 121–42. Bloomington: World Wisdom, 2004.

Shalaby, Ahmad. *History of Muslim Education.* Karachi: Indus Publications, 1979.

Shihab, Alwi. "Christian-Muslim Relations into the Twenty-first Century." In *Islam and Other Religions: Pathways to Dialogue*, edited by Irfan A. Omar, 53–65. Oxon: Routledge, 2006.

Sidel, John T. *Riots, Pogroms, Jihad: Religious Violence in Indonesia*. Ithaca: Cornell University Press, 2006.

Sidel, John T. *The Islamist Threat in Southeast Asia: A Reassessment*. Washington, DC: East-West Centre Washington, 2007.

Siegel, Harvey. *Educating Reason*. New York: Routledge, 1988.

Siegel, Harvey. "Indoctrination and Education." In *Freedom and Indoctrination in Education*, edited by Ben Spiecker and Roger Straughan, 30–41. London: Cassell Educational Ltd., 1991.

Siegel, Harvey. *Rationality Redeemed?* London: Routledge, 1997.

Singh, Bilveer. *The Talibanisation of Southeast Asia: Losing the War on Terror to Islamist Extremists*. Westport: Praeger Security International, 2007.

Smith, Jane Idleman. *Muslims, Christians, and the Challenge of Interfaith Dialogue*. Oxford: Oxford University Press, 2007.

Snook, I.A., ed. *Concepts of Indoctrination: Philosophical Essays*. London and Boston: Routledge & Kegan Paul, 1972.

Snook, I.A. *Indoctrination and Education*. London and Boston: Routledge & Kegan Paul, 1972.

Soeriaatmadja, Wahyudi. "Indonesia Arrests Cleric over Terror Ties." *The Straits Times*, August 10, 2010, A6.

Soeriaatmadja, Wahyudi. "Prison for Woman who Hid Terrorist." *The Straits Times*, July 30, 2010, B4.

Spencer, Robert. *Stealth Jihad: How Radical Islam is Subverting America without Guns or Bombs*. Washington, DC: Regnery Publishing, Inc., 2008.

Spiecker, Ben. "Indoctrination: The Suppression of Critical Dispositions." In *Freedom and Indoctrination in Education*, edited by Ben Spiecker and Roger Straughan, 16–29. London: Cassell Educational Ltd, 1991.

Spiecker Ben, and Roger Straughan, eds. *Freedom and Indoctrination in Education*. London: Cassell Educational Ltd., 1991.

Sprinzak, Ehud. "Rational Fanatics." *Foreign Policy* 120 (2000): 66–74.

Stern, Jessica. *Terror in the Name of God: Why Religious Militants Kill*. New York: ECC, HarperCollins Publishers, 2003.

Steutel, Jan. "Discipline, Internalisation and Freedom: A Conceptual Analysis." In *Freedom and Indoctrination in Education*, edited by Ben Spiecker and Roger Straughan, 58–69. London: Cassell Educational Ltd., 1991.

Stillwell, Cinnamon. "Islam in America's Public Schools: Education or Indoctrination?" *San Francisco Chronicle*, June 11, 2008. Available at: http://www.sfgate.com/cgi-bin/article.cgi?f=/g/a/2008/06/11/cstillwell.DTL. (Accessed February 2, 2009).

Stump, Eleonore, and Michael J. Murray, eds. *Philosophy of Religion: The Big Questions*. Malden and Oxford: Blackwell Publishers, 1990.

Swirko, Cindy. "New Dove World Outreach sign again takes aim at Islam." *The Gainesville Sun*, August 1, 2009. Available at: http://www.gainesville.com/article/20090708/ARTICLES/907081008. (Accessed September 14, 2010).

Synovitz, Ron. "Afghanistan: Would-Be Suicide Bomber Speaks of Indoctrination, Fear." *GlobalSecurity.org*, October 2, 2007. Available at: http://www.globalsecurity.org/security/library/news/2007/10/sec-071002-rferl02.htm. (Accessed February 2, 2010).

Talbani, Aziz. "Pedagogy, Power and Discourse: Transformation of Islamic Education." *Comparative Education Review* 44/1 (1996): 66–82.

Tan, Charlene. "Creating 'Good Citizens' and Maintaining Religious Harmony in Singapore." *British Journal of Religious Education* 30/2 (2008): 133–42.

Tan, Charlene. "Curriculum." In *Critical Perspectives on Education: An Introduction*, edited by Charlene Tan, Benjamin Wong, Jude Soo Meng Chua, and Trivina Kang, 96–111. Singapore: Prentice Hall, 2006.

Tan, Charlene. "Dialogical Education for Inter-Religious Engagement in a Plural Society." In *International Handbook of Inter-Religious Education*, edited by Kathleen Engebretson, Marian de Sousa, Gloria Durka, and Liam Gearon, 361–76. Dordrecht: Springer, 2010.

Tan, Charlene. "Improving Schools through Reflection for Teachers: Lessons from Singapore." *School Effectiveness and School Improvement* 19/2 (2008): 225–38.

Tan, Charlene. "Maximising the Overlapping Area: Multiculturalism and a Muslim Identity for Madrasahs in Singapore." *Journal of Beliefs and Values* 30/1 (2009): 41–8.

Tan, Charlene. "Taking Faith Seriously: Philosophical Thoughts on Religious Education." *Beliefs and Values* 1/2 (2009): 209–19.

Tan, Charlene. *Teaching without Indoctrination: Implications for Values Education*. Rotterdam: Sense Publishers, 2008.

Tan, Charlene. "The Reform Agenda for Madrasah Education in Singapore." *Diaspora, Indigenous, and Minority Education* 3/2 (2009): 67–80.

Tan, Charlene, and Diwi Binti Abbas. "The 'Teach Less, Learn More' Initiative in Singapore: New Pedagogies for Islamic Religious Schools?" *KEDI Journal of Education Policy* 6/1 (2009): 25–39.

Taylor, Kathleen. *Brainwashing: The Science of Thought Control*. Oxford: Oxford University Press, 2004.

Thiessen, Elmer John. *Teaching for Commitment: Liberal Education, Indoctrination and Christian Nurture*. Gracewing, Leominster: McGill-Queen's University Press, 1993.

Tholchah, Muchammad. "The Impact of Terrorism Issue on Parents' Trust (A Study of Ngruki Pesantren, Surakarta, Central Java)." Master's dissertation, Syarif Hidayatullah State Islamic University, Jakarta, 2007.

Tibi, Bassam. *Islam's Predicament with Modernity: Religious Reform and Cultural Change*. Oxon: Routledge, 2009.

Tibi, Bassam. "Islam and Cultural Modernity: In Pursuit of Democratic Pluralism in Asia." In *Islamic Legitimacy in a Plural Asia*, edited by Anthony Reid and Michael Gilsenan, 28–52. London and New York: Routledge, 2007.

Tim JSIT. *Sekolah Islam Terpadu, Konsep dan Aplikasinya* [Integrated Islamic School, Concept and Application]. Bandung: Syaamil Cipta Media, 2006.

"Times Square Bomber: I Plead Guilty 100 Times," *The Straits Times*, June 23, 2010, A10.

Toch, Hans. *The Social Psychology of Social Movements*. London: Methuen, 1966.

Tow, Timothy. *The Law of Moses & of Jesus*. Singapore: Christian Life Publishers, 1982.

van Bruinessen, Martin. "Traditionalist and Islamist Pesantrens in Contemporary Indonesia." In *The Madrasa in Asia: Political Activism and Transnational Linkages*, edited by Farish A. Noor, Yoginder Sikand, and Martin van Bruinessen, 217–45. Amsterdam: Amsterdam University Press, 2008.

van Bruinessen, Martin. "Divergent Paths from Gontor: Muslim Educational Reform and the Travails of Pluralism in Indonesia." Available at: http://www.let.uu.nl/~martin.vanbruinessen/personal/publications/Bruinessen_Divergent_paths_from_Gontor.pdf. (Accessed May 28, 2010).

van Bruinessen, Martin. "Genealogies of Islamic Radicalism in Post-Suharto Indonesia." In *Islam in Southeast Asia: Critical Concepts in Islamic Studies*, Vol. 4, edited by Joseph Chinyong Liow and Nadirsyah Hosen, 35–66. London and New York: Routledge, 2010.

van Bruinessen, Martin. "Muslim Fundamentalism: Something to be Understood or to be Explained Away?" *Islam and Muslim Christian Relations* 6/2 (1995): 157–71. Available at: http://www.let.uu.nl/~martin.vanbruinessen/personal/publications/muslim_fundamentalism.htm. (Accessed May 28, 2010).

van Bruinessen, Martin. "Pesantren and Kitab Kuning: Maintenance and Continuation of a Tradition of Religious Learning." In *Texts from the Islands: Oral and Written Traditions of Indonesia and the Malay World*, edited by Wolfgang Marschall, 121–45. Berne: University of Berne, 1994. Available at: http://www.let.uu.nl/~martin.vanbruinessen/personal/publications/pesantren_and_kitab_kuning.htm. (Accessed May 28, 2010).

van Bruinessen, Martin. "The Violent Fringes of Indonesia's Radical Islam." Available at: http://www.let.uu.nl/~martin.vanbruinessen/personal/publications/violent_fringe.htm. (accessed July 29, 2010).

von der Mehden, Fred R. "Islam in Indonesia in the Twenty-First Century." In *Asian Islam in the 21ˢᵗ Century*, edited by John L. Esposito, John O. Voll, and Osman Bakar, 11–30. Oxford: Oxford University Press, 2008.

Weinstein, Mark. "Reason and the Child." In *Philosophy of Education: Proceedings of the Forty-Sixth Annual Meeting of the Philosophy of Education Society in Normal, IL., 1990*, by the Philosophy of Education Society, 159–71.

White, John. "The Justification of Autonomy as an Educational Aim." In *Freedom and Indoctrination in Education*, edited by Ben Spiecker and Roger Straughan, 84–93. London: Cassell Educational Ltd., 1991.

Wiktqrqwicz, Quintan, and Karl Kaltenthaler. "The Rationality of Radical Islam." *Political Science Quarterly* 121/2 (2006): 295–319.

Wilson, John. "Religious (Moral, Political, etc.) Commitment, Education and Indoctrination." In *Freedom and Indoctrination in Education*, edited by Ben Spiecker and Roger Straughan, 42–50. London: Cassell Educational Ltd., 1991.

Winn, Denise. *The Manipulated Mind: Brainwashing, Conditioning and Indoctrination*. Cambridge, Massachusetts: Malor Books, 2000.

Wolterstorff, Nicholas. *Reason within the Bounds of Religion,* 2nd edition. Grand Rapids: Wm B. Eerdmans Publishing Co, 1984.

Yusof, Zalman Mohamed, and Mohammad Ishak, "Inside a JI School." *The New Paper*, January 4, 2004.

Zaini, Achmad. "Kyai Haji Abdul Wahid Hasyim: His Contribution to Muslim Educational Reform and to Indonesian Nationalism during the Twentieth Century." Master's dissertation, McGill University, 1998.

Zakaria, Rusydy. *Indonesian Islamic Education: A Social, Historical and Political Perspective*. Saarbrucken: VDM Verlag Dr. Muller, 2008.

Zaman, Muhammad Qasim. *The Ulama in Contemporary Islam*. Princeton: Princeton University Press, 2002.

Zia, Rukhsana. "Islamic Education: From Ancient to Modern Times." In *Globalisation, Modernisation and Education in Muslim Countries*, edited by Rukhsana Zia, 31–46. New York: Nova Science Publishers, 2006.

Zuhdi, Muhammad. "Political and Social Influences on Religious School: A Historical Perspective on Indonesian Islamic School Curricula." PhD dissertation, McGill University, 2006.

Index